SHAW 16

Fred D. Crawford   John R. Pfeiffer
General Editor   *Bibliographer*

UNPUBLISHED
SHAW

Edited by

Dan H. Laurence and Margot Peters

The Pennsylvania State University Press
University Park, Pennsylvania

Quotations from published Bernard Shaw writings are utilized in this volume with the permission of the Estate of Bernard Shaw. Shaw's hitherto unpublished writings © 1996 The Trustees of the British Museum, The Governors and Guardians of the National Gallery of Ireland, and the Royal Academy of Dramatic Art.

ISBN 0-271-01577-2   ISSN 0741-5842

bib # 35513

It is the policy of The Pennsylvania State University Press to use acid-free paper for the first printing of all clothbound books. Publications on uncoated stock satisfy the minimum requirements of American National Standard for Information Sciences—Permanence of Paper for Printed Library Materials. ANSI Z39.48–1992.

Note to contributors and subscribers. *SHAW*'s perspective is Bernard Shaw and his milieu—its personalities, works, relevance to his age and ours. As "his life, work, and friends"—the subtitle to a biography of G.B.S.—indicates, it is impossible to study the life, thought, and work of a major literary figure in a vacuum. Issues and people, economics, politics, religion, theater and literature and journalism—the entirety of the two half-centuries the life of G.B.S. spanned was his assumed province. *SHAW*, published annually, welcomes articles that either explicitly or implicitly add to or alter our understanding of Shaw and his milieu. Address all manuscript contributions (in 3 copies) to Fred D. Crawford, General Editor, *SHAW*, Penn State Press, Suite C, 820 North University Drive, University Park, PA 16802. Subscription correspondence should be addressed to *SHAW*, Penn State University Press, Suite C, 820 North University Drive, University Park, PA 16802. Unsolicited manuscripts are welcomed but will be returned only if return postage is provided. In matters of style *SHAW* recommends the *MLA Style Sheet* and advises referring to recent volumes of the *SHAW*.

Illustration opposite the title page: Bernard Shaw: self-portrait, 1882 (British Library: Add. Mss. 50721A, folio 87). By permission of the British Library.

CONTENTS

NOTICES

Request for Manuscripts: *SHAW* 19

SHAW 19, guest-edited by Gale K. Larson, will have as its theme "Shaw and History." The volume will include articles on various aspects of Shaw's concept of history (treated by J. L. Wisenthal in his 1988 publication *Shaw's Sense of History*) with special emphasis on the Shavianizing of history in the plays and other works by Shaw. Of particular interest are the uses that Shaw has made of history in delineating character while dramatizing historical events, often expressed as challenges to other artists/historians (one and the same for Shaw) with whose interpretation of people and events of history Shaw took issue. Articles that focus on specific historical/literary sources used throughout his writings and the manner in which they affected his own works will also be acceptable for *SHAW* 19.

Contributors should submit manuscripts in three copies by December 1997 to Fred D. Crawford, *SHAW* Editor, Penn State Press, Suite C, 820 North University Drive, University Park, PA 16802. Contributors should follow the MLA *Style Sheet* format (referring to recent *SHAW* volumes is advisable) and include postage for return of material.

35th Annual Season, Shaw Festival
Niagara-on-the-Lake

The 1996 playbill of the Shaw Festival (Artistic Director, Christopher Newton) will include three plays by Shaw: *The Devil's Disciple, The Simpleton of the Unexpected Isles,* and (as part of the Lunchtime Reading Series) two performances of *Farfetched Fables.* Other productions include *Rashomon* by Fay and Michael Kanin, *Hobson's Choice* by Harold Brighouse, *An Ideal Husband* by Oscar Wilde, *The Playboy of the Western World* by J. M. Synge, *Marsh Hay* by Merrill Denison, *The Hollow* by Agatha Christie, *Shall We Join the Ladies?* by J. M. Barrie, *The Conjuror* by Patrick Watson and David Ben, and the musical *Mr Cinders* (music by Vivian Ellis and Richard Myers, libretto and lyrics by Clifford Grey and Greatrex Newman, additional lyrics by Leo Robin and Vivian Ellis). The Lunchtime Reading Series includes, in addition to *Farfetched Fables,* one performance each of *Murder Pattern* by Herman Voaden and of *To Have and to Hold* by Jules Renard and two performances of *War of the Worlds* (Orson Welles's 1938 radio production) by Howard Koch.

For further information, write to Shaw Festival, Box 774, Niagara-on-the-Lake, Ontario, Canada L0S 1J0 or call (416) 468-2172. Toll-free from the United States, call (800) 724-2934. Toll-free from Canada, call (800) 267-4759. Direct from Toronto, call 361-1544.

Fifteenth Annual Milwaukee Shaw Festival
27 February–9 March 1997

The Milwaukee Shaw Festival (Artistic Director, Montgomery Davis) will feature performances of Shaw's 1929 "Political Extravaganza," *The Apple Cart,* and Jeffrey Hatcher's *Smash,* an adaptation of Shaw's 1884 novel, *An Unsocial Socialist.*

For ticket information, either call (414) 276-8842 or write to Milwaukee Chamber Theatre, Broadway Theatre Center, 158 N. Broadway, Milwaukee, WI 53202.

Dan H. Laurence and Margot Peters

GENERAL INTRODUCTION: UNPUBLISHED SHAW

Collected here for the first time are twenty-eight previously unpublished pieces by Bernard Shaw. The selections vary widely in length, from a brief pronouncement on the possibility of war in Abyssinia to a thirty-page fictional "reminiscence" of Hector Berlioz. Shaw's subject matter is even more diverse, ranging from oakum picking, boxing, orchestral conductors and borough elections to parent-child relationships and the future of marriage. Dates of composition span seventy-three years, from 1877 to 1950. Not surprisingly, however, the majority of pieces are very early Shaw: after G.B.S. became an established playwright, little of what he wrote—even his "scraps and shavings"—escaped print. Equally predictably, none of these previously unpublished pieces proves to be a lost masterpiece. Their worth lies rather in the biographical and artistic insights they offer scholars already familiar with Shaw's major works. In this respect, the surviving scenario of *Man and Superman* is in itself a treasure beyond value.

Many of these workshop pieces testify to Shaw's earliest literary activity in London. If he tried his hand at creative writing as a youth in Dublin—and it is impossible to believe he did not—his juvenilia have not survived.[1] Abandoning Ireland for England on 31 March 1876 at the age of nineteen, he carried with him only "several purses," three favorite volumes of Dickens, a few letters (subsequently burned), and a small notebook in which he had recorded, for example, the purchase of a new coat, waistcoat, and trousers in February and the draft of his letter of resignation from C. Uniacke Townshend's land agency.[2] Perhaps he destroyed his Dublin writing in the same fire in which, by pact, he burned the letters of his closest friend, Edward McNulty.

After visiting his sister Agnes's fresh grave on the Isle of Wight, Shaw joined his mother and sister Lucy in humble digs in London. Poverty could not keep him from the West End, however, where he saw Ernesto

Rossi as Lear, Tomasso Salvini's impressive Hamlet, and a performance of Offenbach's *Le Voyage de Lune*. Yet some employment was obviously necessary if he were to continue sampling London's rich menu of cultural offerings. Through the influence of his mother's mentor, the musician Vandeleur Lee, he began ghosting musical criticism for the satiric weekly *The Hornet*, getting his fill of concert halls and opera houses for nearly a year, but agonizing over his inability, without a real connection to the paper, to correct his proofs. The only non-musical essay produced by Shaw in this early period, an unsigned travel article, "Brighton Hotels," which appeared in *The Hornet* on 20 June 1877, was also written to order for Lee.

But anonymous criticism could hardly satisfy his creative urge. Late in 1877 he acquired a composition book; in it he penned an incomplete set of untitled narrative verses labeled "Fytte I" and "Fytte II," certainly among the first products of his adult pen. The poem looks back to Dublin, perhaps to the frustrated romance he would call "the Calypso infatuation," certainly *not* to the relationship with his employer's daughter, who, as he told McNulty, "would have been mine for the asking."[3] Significantly, the autobiographical hero of the "Fyttes" works not at a land office but at the Bank of Ireland, in which McNulty was employed—evidence of Shaw's taste for aesthetic distancing and passionate distaste for his clerking job.

Quickly discovering that poetry was not his forte, Shaw turned to prose, attempting four essays in 1878—"Oakum Picking," "Contemporary Art viewed from behind the Age," "Opera in Italian," and "Christian Names."[4] Payment for "Christian Names" obviously encouraged him, for in the following year he wrote far more prolifically. What were Shaw's subjects? Everything! Enormously stimulated by finding himself in the cultural center of the world, he submitted to editors his views on "Conductors and Organists," "Artists' Heroism," "England's Greatness Justified," "Old Husbands and Young Artists," "Unconscionable Abuses," "Thoughts on Conjugal and Parental Love," "On the True Signification of the term Gentleman," and "Journals of Society." Besides these essays, he also produced an amusing tribute to Mozart called "The St. James's Hall Mystery," a short story, "The Brand of Cain," and a "nonsensical narrative" titled "The Extinguished Lamp."[5]

The editors whose periodicals he bombarded with manuscripts remained stubbornly unimpressed. A novel outlined in his composition book in March 1879 and completed on 29 September shared the same fate: Hurst and Blackett refused *Immaturity* in November. Desperate for money, Shaw was forced to accept a position with the Edison Telephone Company soliciting permission from homeowners for the erection of telephone poles on their roofs. (In another half-hearted attempt at employment, he had crammed in 1876 for a Civil Service exam, for which he apparently never sat.) Instinctively certain he was not meant for ordinary commerce, he kept on writing.

After 1879 Shaw used the "opus book" only for outlining the five novels he produced at the rate of one a year, unsystematically penning essays and stories in black, blue, brown ink or pencil on whatever quires of paper came to hand. The young Shaw's method of composition was very much the method he retained all his life, just as his small, meticulous, well-spaced handwriting, slanting (like his views) slightly left, had been formed early. That is, he seldom completely rewrote a piece, or even produced a second or later draft. (The survival of two drafts, in the case of "The St. James's Hall Mystery," is a rarity.) Instead, he revised almost immediately on the original page in pen or pencil, chiefly excising, sometimes rewording, very seldom adding substantially to a manuscript. "[S]ome authors," Shaw wrote in 1928, "work at what they have to say completely in their heads before they take their pens up and simply copy the result (like Mozart) whilst others begin scrawling from the first, and correct and correct on paper until they rea[ch] the final expression of their argument with its verdict (like Beethoven) . . . My own practice is on the Beethoven side . . . I think that Shakespear deliberately abstained from revision on the ground that his time would be better spent in writing Macbeth than in revising Hamlet."[6] The holograph of "A Reminiscence of Hector Berlioz" is considerably scored over and revised, particularly the first four pages, after which Shaw seems to have better hit his stride—although revisions are still frequent. Surely in this case he must have made a clean draft before submitting the essay to *Cornhill Magazine* on 2 May 1890, only to have it returned a month later.

The answer is problematic. Shaw frequently submitted an essay to only one periodical, suggesting either that he slanted for that magazine or that he refused to keep flogging what were, after all, pieces of poor-paying ephemera. In 1882 he jotted in his opus book a list of pieces he had submitted to journals, titles he had either kept to that point or recalled. Of the seventeen, eight manuscripts are known to survive. Sometimes the publisher was careless: "Artists' Heroism," sent to *Figaro*, was "lost sight of"; *One and All* failed to return "The Extinguished Lamp." Yet even multiple copies did not guarantee preservation. Apparently Shaw actually drafted two copies of "The Brand of Cain," since submissions to *One and All* and *Cornhill* overlap with overtures to five other publications. We know of the manuscript, however, only from mention in the composition book: two copies apparently vanished. Considering that Shaw probably sent the original and only-extant copies of the "novels of his nonage" on the publishing rounds, his faith in the probity of editors—and the efficiency of the London mails—was as prodigious as his funds for copying were small.

"The qualities of style which I particularly aimed at at this period were exactness, modesty, and simplicity!!!" wrote Shaw in 1882.[7] Certainly in his early twenties his style was already formed: a style of challenge and argumentation; a style of clarity and logic, with meticulously placed commas, colons, and semi-colons belying the subversiveness of the author's text. Yet just as the heavily corrected drafts of these early productions give little sign of Shaw's eventual genius for striking the right note and running with it unerringly, so do the very early essays give only a hint of the sublime humor that would emerge in the plays. Shaw not only aimed at but achieved "the last thing in correctness,"[8] frequently at the expense of brevity and wit. The tone of "Exhausted Arts" and "On the True Significa- tion of the term Gentleman," for instance, is solemn, even didactic: this is a young man with opinions to lay down. Yet how easy to forgive a certain solemnity in the apprentice work of a writer who, not yet twenty-five, was trying to convince the mavens of London culture that an Irish upstart knew more about art, literature, and music than they.

With the exception of "Why Not Abolish the Soldier?"—inspired in 1899 by the specter of conscription and the Boer War—the later writings included here date from 1901, by which time Shaw was an established writer. They deal chiefly with politics and war, although they also include the extended outline for *Man and Superman,* the only play scenario known to survive besides a brief outline for *The Devil's Disciple.* The general tone of these pronunciamentos is vintage Shaw: confident and provocative; playful when humor will hone his point more sharply. If they reveal no startlingly new aspect of Shavian philosophy, they serve to remind us that the artist and political man were one.

In the nineteenth century Shaw wrote most of his manuscripts in long-hand (his typed musical and dramatic criticism, composed under a dead-line, is an exception) for the simple reason that unpaid amanuenses like his mother, sister Lucy, Kate Salt, and Charlotte Payne-Townshend could not read the shorthand Shaw found too laborious to transcribe himself.[9] In 1907, however, he solved that problem by sending his cousin Judy Gillmore to the Pitman school to learn shorthand. That year he finished his play *Getting Married* in shorthand, which Judy transliterated. Most of Shaw's shorthand drafts are amazingly clean, suggesting perhaps that the comparatively slower processes of typing and handwriting handicapped his flow of thought. In later years his secretaries Ann Elder and Blanche Patch typed everything he wrote in shorthand, including much of his correspondence. He reserved handwriting chiefly for very personal let-ters or correspondence answered while traveling—or for some spontane-ous response like his answers in 1920 to the *World of Trade* questionnaire.

The intent of the editors in this volume is to bring the reader as close to the original Shaw texts as possible without impeding comprehension or loading them down with editorial apparatus. We have retained Shaw's spelling, including inconsistencies and misspelled proper names (Hadyn for Haydn, Lizst for Liszt). We also retain his inconsistent italicization of foreign words and irregular punctuation, including placement of commas or full stops outside closing quotation marks, a practice he would for the most part later reverse. We have made a few silent revisions, principally editing out words Shaw accidentally duplicated or left in after a revision, deletion, or addition; once or twice we have matched the tense or agreement of a verb with a noun or pronoun that Shaw altered in revision. We have inserted into the text in square brackets significant omitted punctuation, conjectural missing words, or words carelessly written with letters missing. Bracketed question marks indicate that we are uncertain of a reading. And, finally, we have provided transliterations for shorthand notes Shaw occasionally inserted into manuscripts.

We wish to acknowledge our indebtedness and gratitude to the institutions, identified in the provenance notes preceding each Shaw text, who have made this volume possible by granting permission for first publication of manuscripts from their collections. Our warm thanks to Fred Crawford, the general editor of *SHAW: The Annual of Bernard Shaw Studies*, for patient and expert counsel; to Roma Woodnutt, estates manager of the Society of Authors, for personally blessing this project and recommending its publication to the Shaw Estate; and to John Wardrop and Barbara Smoker for their transliteration of Shaw's shorthand. At the British Library we are grateful for the cooperation of C. M. Hall, Higher Executive Officer, Department of Manuscripts; Dr. Anne Summers, Curator, Division of Manuscripts; Julian Conway, Superintendent of the Manuscripts Reading Room; Stewart Gillies, Reader Service Officer, Newspaper Library; and many helpful staffers throughout the Library whose names are unknown to us. Dr. James Tyler, former Shaw Curator of the Burgunder Collection, Cornell University Library, helped further this project, as did the late Dr. Lola L. Szladits, Curator, Henry W. and Albert A. Berg Collection, New York Public Library, Ron Abrahams, and Dr. Bernard F. Dukore.

Finally we heartily thank the ten cooperating editors of Team Sixteen for their efforts to make this unique Shaw project a success.

Notes

1. Shaw's first public production, signed "S," is a letter written 3 April 1875 to *Public Opinion* (27), "in which I sought to stem the force of the first great Moody & Sankey revival

by the announcement that I, personally, had renounced religion as a delusion" (*Shaw: An Autobiography, 1856–1898,* selected by Stanley Weintraub [New York: Weybright & Talley, 1969], p. 77). The letter is reprinted in Bernard Shaw, *Agitations: Letters to the Press, 1875–1950,* ed. Dan H. Laurence and James Rambeau (New York: Ungar, 1985), pp. 1–2.

2. The notebook, covering the years 1875–76, is in the Harry Ransom Humanities Research Center, the University of Texas at Austin. Entries indicate that Shaw's departure for London was planned and organized well in advance.

3. Shaw to McNulty, 3 June 1876, in *Collected Letters 1874–1897,* ed. Dan H. Laurence (New York: Dodd, Mead, 1965), p. 19. The genuineness of the letter, however, is questionable.

4. "Opera in Italian" was published in the *Saturday Musical Review* on 22 February 1879; "Christian Names" in *One and All* on 11 October 1879. The *Saturday Musical Review* did not pay for the unsigned article; when *One and All* accepted "Christian Names" on 18 September 1879 without enclosing a check, Shaw protested to the editor, G. R. Sims, that he was not an amateur. *One and All* replied that it paid ten shillings a column—"There are no amateurs on the staff"—but paid Shaw fifteen. It was his sole financial success of the year.

5. Most of these writings appear in a list drawn up by Shaw in brown ink in 1882 in his composition book. The book itself (British Library: Add. Mss. 50721A) has been disbound and its leaves individually mounted, making it impossible to ascertain whether the surviving pages are from a single notebook. "The St. James's Hall Mystery" (draft in the British Library, fair copy in the Berg Collection, New York Public Library) has been published in the New York Public Library's *Bulletin of Research in the Humanities* 81 (Autumn 1978): 270–96, edited by Jerald E. Bringle.

6. AMS, 1 p., 29 April 1928; written for unidentified petrologist of a department of geology, concerning literary discoveries that can be made from authors' proof sheets. Sotheby Parke-Bernet, New York, auction catalogue of Harry J. Sonneborn sale of autographs, 11 June 1974, lot 487.

7. Shorthand note of 2 November 1882 on the verso of leaf 8 of "Exhausted Arts," an essay written "in some haste" while Shaw was employed by the Edison Telephone Company, published in this volume.

8. *Shaw: An Autobiography, 1856–1898,* p. 84.

9. Shaw studied the Pitman method in 1880–81, testing his new skill by drafting *Cashel Byron's Profession* in shorthand, from 12 April 1882 to early February 1883. The earliest surviving shorthand draft of a critical essay appears to be "Music for the People" (British Library), dated 12 January 1883.

Richard Nickson

SHAW AS POETASTER: IN FYTTES AND STARTS

In 1876 nineteen-year-old Shaw moved to London, which he described nearly fifty years later in the preface to *Immaturity* as "the literary centre for the English language, and for such artistic culture as the realm of the English language (in which I proposed to be king) could afford."[1] But as a drop-out from school, country, and Christianity, he was certainly not then prepared for his coronation, except for the extraordinary virtuosity that had already grounded him in a sensitive understanding of many of the western world's finest creative works. One of the earliest known literary efforts that survive from the pen (or pencil, in this case) of the novice fresh from Dublin was begun in 1877 as an untitled narrative poem in (mostly) heroic couplets. Although soon abandoned, the fragment that survives offers glimpses, not only of an adept neophyte, but also of a provocative master aborning.

Shaw the steadfast Londoner yet suffered a fit, or fytte, of nostalgia as poet. For the scenes of his poem are all part of his native Dublin, and the narrative bears traces of autobiography. Speaking of his youth, Shaw confessed to Frank Harris: "I had no love affairs."[2] But as Larry Doyle, the Irishman turned Londoner in *John Bull's Other Island*, says, "an Irishman's heart is nothing but his imagination. . . . Oh, the dreaming! the dreaming! the torturing, heart-scalding, never satisfying dreaming, dreaming, dreaming, dreaming!"[3] And the nameless poet of the fantasizing poem has dreams of fair women. The first one is the aloof Elizabeth (the name of Shaw's mother), who "loves to play / With hearts awhile, then cast them smashed away," a resident of Clontarf, Dublin, on the coast of Dublin Bay. The love-lorn hero is next portrayed, in Fytte II, not as a clerk in a land agency, in the manner of Shaw himself, but as bent over a ledger in a Bank of Ireland office "In the dull citie's centre." Escaping from the office, he heads south from the Bank toward St. Stephen's Green and University College and across the Royal

Canal to Mount Pleasant Square in Ranelagh. Then, following close upon soaring and sobering daydreams of married life, he romanticizes over Emmeline, who—whether fact or fancy—soon departs. The poem breaks off with his accidental encounter with Elizabeth.

Each of the two surviving sections of the poem is listed as a fit, with the poet opting for the variant spelling "fytte" of a word already sufficiently archaic. No doubt he had recently read *The Hunting of the Snark*, Lewis Carroll's marvelous poem published in eight fits in March 1876. Shaw's first fytte decisively concludes with triplets, the final one an alexandrine. The second section leaves us without so much as a question mark for the lover's query, let alone the beloved's reply. Except for the variant lines and rhymes in Fytte II that introduce the false temptress, Shaw employs open iambic pentameter. Besides the alexandrine already remarked, only half a dozen other six-stress lines are used.

In his employment of these and other devices, Shaw—amid all the tomfoolery—performs effortlessly and proficiently as one who has read with care the English-language poets. The teenage Wordsworth wrote similar open iambic pentameter couplets in "An Evening Walk." Keats, a poet praised by Shaw, uses the same form in the narrative poem *Lamia*. Perhaps from Coleridge's unique narrative poem *Christabel* Shaw gleaned the temptress figure, the sportively rendered Emmeline. But by the time of writing his fyttes, he had read all of Shelley, the poet "sacred to me,"[4] who made him a socialist and a vegetarian, and about whom he has written more perceptively than anyone else. Shelleyan thought appears early in Fytte II, describing how "Different far / The things that in the homestead really are . . ." Unlike his contemporary A. E. Housman, however, who believed that Shelley "maintained a higher standard of excellence than all other English poets,"[5] Shaw was far more interested in Shelley's matter than his manner. The style of Shelley plays no part in Shaw's burlesque; his impassioned denunciation of injustice is writ large.

Many readers of Shaw's fledgling verses are more likely to be reminded of still earlier poets, notably Oliver Goldsmith of the popular *Deserted Village* (1770). Others will be put in mind of the Elizabethans, especially of the Bard never far from Shaw's own mind. The "gin" and "gins" for "begin" and "begins" bespeak poeticisms much earlier than those of Goldsmith, as does the exclamation "But soft!" The tone throughout presages something of the blank verse of the profane *Passion Play* (also abandoned) that Shaw began the following year "to give expression to the Shakspere in us."[6] And the arch lines about croquet ("The boxwood ball athwart the iron loop") herald "the primitive Elizabethan style" of the parodic *Admirable Bashville* of 1901.[7]

Throughout the narrative Shaw uses full rhyme, almost all of it masculine, as well as words traditionally accepted as rhyming in our rhyme-poor language, such as "home"—"come" and "striven"—"heaven." Numerous feminine rhymes appear in the shorter lines devoted to the fanciful Emmeline; elsewhere Shaw uses only three examples of feminine rhyme in describing Elizabeth (a.k.a. Eliza). One masculine rhyme might be deplored by purists: "glimpse"—"nymphs." And at least one of the pentameter lines is lacking a foot: "To seize, to play awhile, and destroy" in Fytte I. Do we also spot a pleonasm in "marshy fen" (Fytte II)? Are some of the inversions awkward, such as "naked all" to describe our mysterious hero in the sixth line, where we might expect "all naked"? Regrettably, the author of the ninth line did not create for us a poetic sequel, "Ballad of the Shuddering Toe."

The line sure to rivet the attention of readers is the ephemeral Emmeline's "Son of a gun", calculated to provoke exclamations like Robert Louis Stevenson's "I say, Archer, my God, what women!"[8] Emmeline arouses the proper hero's comedic reflection: "Thy slang assumed fastidious ears to vex. . . ." The playwright himself has owned, "I have unfortunately this desperate temptation that suddenly comes on me. . . . some absurd joke occurs and the anti-climax is irresistible."[9] As he once declared to the unreceptive Henry James, "Almost all my greatest ideas have occurred to me first as jokes."[10]

"There is a truly great poet in Shaw. . . ." Thus spake a non-native speaker of English, Luigi Pirandello, after attending a performance of *Saint Joan*.[11] Conversely, T. S. Eliot pontificated that "Shaw was a poet—until he was born, and the poet in Shaw was stillborn."[12] In between these extreme opinions, the voice of W. H. Auden should be heard in the land. "Shaw's writing," he has said, "has an effect nearer to that of music than the work of any of the so-called pure writers."[13]

Fytte I and what we have of Fytte II contain some pleasing lines, some amusing ones, and even a few interesting ones from the metaphorical left hand of a writer who used his right hand for creating memorable prose. The tyro as versifier quickly decided that verse of his making would be light verse, even doggerel—and strictly occasional.

[Narrative Verse, fragment, 1877]

[PROVENANCE: Unsigned holograph manuscript, lines 1–170 in pencil, lines 171–184 in ink (apparently copied from another draft), revised in ink, dated "1877" in ink at top right of each page. British Library: Add. Mss. 50721A, folios 2b, 3–4a, b, 5a. Small drawing on folio 4a.]

Fytte I

By that bleak shore whereon the eastern gale
Sweeps from the sea to Clontarf's bosky vale
A dwelling stands: its portals face the land.
Behold, a dreary boundary of sand
Repels the space where the lone sea bird flits
And naked all the shivering bather sits.
He views the cheerless foam with doubting eye
And casts his glance inquiring to the sky
Then cautiously his shuddering toe he dips,
Starts back, returns, crawls out until his hips
Are barely splashed, then ducks amid the foam,
Regains the shore and chattering turns to home.
Deserted now, the dreary beach appears
Stripped of the charm that such a scene endears
When on the deck the moon at midnight beams
Or where the orb of morning shoots gold gleams
To dance in dazzling radiance on each crest—
Or when the evening, beautifully drest
In robe of fiery purple, sheds soft rays
That stir remorseful thoughts of bygone days.

On deck the future in delusive sheen
For those too young to weep for that which might have been:
Such was the home and such the dismal place
That loved Elizabeth was born to grace[.]
No golden blossoms strike her tresses pale,
No lustrous roses o'er her cheeks prevail,
No toying zephyr on her brow to play,
No flowery pathway to adorn her way.
But in their stead the chilling orient blast
And rugged stones by restless billows cast,
Her wintry walks the briny drift attends,
Its saline whiteness in her gold hair blends;
Amid the waste she stands, a form divine,
The subtle contrasts all her charms refine.
She seems like one whom Nature's art had striven
To fashion forth exemplary of heaven,
Thrilling all gazers, making rivals sad,
Fools more voluptuous, and poets—mad.

Full well she knows her power, she loves to play
With hearts awhile, then cast them smashed away.

Whilst she insensible all art withstands,
Barren and shifty as the aimless sands,
Whereon her light foot rests, her dearest joy
To seize, to play awhile, and [then] destroy.
Even now a half-snared victim is her thought
Twice he already to her feet has brought
A store of lofty thought, a poet's wealth
Of delicate worship, soft he comes by stealth
Wandering with furtive steps about her bower
To ask his loftiest fancy to endow her.
With virtues worthy of her heavenly beauty
Such as might justify the toilsome duty
Of walking weary miles to catch a glimpse
Of the loved countenance that Diana's nymphs
Might put to shame, and often he returns
Unrecompensed, whilst in his breast love burns
With ardour tenfold multiplied. Meanwhile,
She sees it all with a triumphant smile
No visit lost on her, no midnight stroll
But she unseen, observes, whilst in her soul
Ambition and desire in envious conflict roll.

Fytte II

In the dull citie's centre stands the Bank
Girt by tall columns in majestic rank
Above, the sculptured pediment displays
Forms that reflect in bold relief the rays
Of the impartial sun, whose gleams enfold
Th' exterior pile with evanescent gold
More bright and glorious, tarnished less by sin
Than that which rusts in the dull vaults within,
But far more perishable. At a desk
Precise, mahogany, unpicturesque,
Eliza's lover sits; solid his form
And self-contained his look, no inward storm
Nor fretful fears nor any sordid strife
Mark the broad stream of intellectual life
Denoted by that brow o'ertopt by plumes
As black as those which ocean's god assumes
When forth enraged he rushes from his cave
And stirs to fury each unquiet wave.
On the broad ledger 'gins his head to nod

(I mean the lover and not ocean's god)
From out his nerveless grasp the pen escapes
Fade from his vision all the busy shapes
Of toiling clerks, his restless fancy roves
Far from the bank to dwell on her he loves
Imagination paints her darling face
Which, from his mind he strives { but ever fails to erase
                                { unceasingly

   Anon he stands in the broad street without
Uncertain to pursue the homeward route
Or yield again to love's enticing hand
That gently draws him to the northern strand
Awhile he vacillates, surveys the sky
Turns & returns again, then breathes one sigh
And slowly points his steadfast foot towards where
The vernal beauties of Mount Pleasant Square
Cheer the tired clerk who trudges from the town
Freed from his stern employer[']s awful frown
Freed from his pen, from toil by want enforced
From the green ledger for a night divorced
For his release; delusive smiles his home
His tender wife with outstretched arms to come
Greeting her lord, the glad and artless child
Lovingly owning his dominion mild
And suchlike phantoms which unmarried men
Like the dull peasant on the marshy fen
Chance to their own undoing. Different far
The things that in the homestead really are[:]
Reproachful slatterns and vicious slaves,
Too early versed in the apt lie that saves
From coarse invective or the tyrant birch
Brooding alike in home and school and church
On the injustice of domestic sway
Wielded by wretches who themselves obey
Only their nature's vilest prompts of evil
Glazed o'er with specious Scripture which the devil
Would blush to use. Such are the pleasant fruits
Of superstitious toil in making mankind brutes.

   Risen from the cheerful board, our lover strolls
Where the blithe schoolgirl with deft mallet rolls
The boxwood ball athwart the iron loop,
Ringing the bell suspended from the hoop—

But soft! What form crowned with supple ease
And delicate figure winds amongst those trees
Such charm ineffable Circe's pigs might find
In incarnation of the twilight wind.*
Such lithe unearthly symmetry the caves
Where mermaids dwell beneath the emerald waves
Alone contain, and even such waves themselves
Hide no such coral as her lips display;
Within her witching eyes two sapphire elves
Seem with men's hearts to gambol all the day
Oh, that these beings as fanciful and fair
Should be but samples of false Nature's care
To enshrine mere nothingness in temples past compare[.]

  'Daughter of the south wind
      Gentle and true
  If that thy heart be kind
      Let me not rue
  The hour I saw thee to my heart's undoing
  Grant me one kiss, tis time love's voice is suing.'

  'Son of a gun' she said
  'Stolid and black
  A German governess
  Is on my track
I'd fain consent, my wish with thine agreeing
Did I not fear that Teuton lady's seeing
  But on Sunday to church am I hieing
  When both pastor and master defying
  We may cast stolen glances unseen
  If thou art in earnest, determine
  To fly with me after the sermon,
  And clasp (as a wife) Emmeline.[']
She said and fled, nor backward glanced
To where her wooer stood entranced
Her words becloud his fainting brain
They echo in his ears again.
  Remorse and shame combined
Their mingled venom 'gin to dart
Painfully through his foolish heart
He feels in all his shrinking nerves
The punishment he well deserves

*Shaw added in the margin as an alternate line: 'Forsooth you know 'tis said / That pigs can see the wind.'

For conduct unrefined[.]
'Oh, base immodesty, accursed flirt
Thy spirit frivolous and mind inert
Thy slang assumed fastidious ears to vex
Unworthily befit thy graceful sex
Which here I utterly abjure, and swear
Never again for woman's smile to care[.]
Henceforth I leave them to their flesh and pelf
And hold my path sufficient to myself'—
Scarce had he finished speaking when a hand
His shoulder touched. No incandescent brand
More swiftly sets the gunpowder aflame
Than such a touch enthrills a manly frame[.]
Softly electric on his arm it lies
The landscape spins before his giddy eyes
He scarce can turn to greet the blushing fair
Nor to her dazzling eyelids does he dare
To lift his glance and learn Elizabeth is there.
At length he finds a voice for bland address
And fearful lest her doubts the cause assess
Of his soliloquy o'erheard, to love
And for another; lifts his eyes above
Her dainty boots, and boldly her glance meeting
Speaks thus (when finished the conventional greeting):
'Say, maid divine, if I may hope to know
To what benign god guardian do I owe
Within these rails the unaccustomed sight
Of thy fair locks aflame with heavenly light[?]
How does it come that thus I press thy hand
So far removed from thy native strand
Or why, no longer mirrored in the sea
Those eyes ineffable shine here on me' . . .

[*The text ends here*]

Notes

1. Preface, *Immaturity* (London: Constable, 1931), p. xxxiv.
2. 20 June 1930, in Bernard Shaw, *Collected Letters 1926–1950,* ed. Dan H. Laurence (London: Max Reinhardt, 1988), p. 189.

3. *Collected Plays with Their Prefaces* (London: Max Reinhardt, 1970–74), 2:907, 909.

4. Preface, *Immaturity*, p. xvii.

5. Richard Perceval Graves, *A. E. Housman: The Scholar Poet* (New York: Scribner's, 1980), p. 231.

6. "In Five Acts and Blank Verse," *Pall Mall Gazette* (14 July 1887); rptd. in *Bernard Shaw's Book Reviews in the Pall Mall Gazette*, ed. Brian Tyson (University Park: Penn State University Press, 1991), pp. 295–99.

7. "I poetasted The Admirable Bashville in the primitive Elizabethan style." Preface to *The Admirable Bashville*, in *Collected Plays*, 2:433.

8. Stevenson's parenthetical remark about *Cashel Byron's Profession* was made to Shaw's friend William Archer, who had sent him a copy of the novel. See Stanley Weintraub's introduction to *Cashel Byron's Profession* (Carbondale: Southern Illinois University Press, 1968), p. xiii.

9. Eric Bentley, *Bernard Shaw 1856–1950*, Amended Edition (New York: New Directions, 1957), p. xix.

10. 21 January 1909, in Bernard Shaw, *Collected Letters 1898–1910*, ed. Dan H. Laurence (New York: Dodd, Mead, 1972), p. 830.

11. "Pirandello Distills Shaw," *New York Times Magazine* (13 January 1924), pp. 1, 14. In this same article Pirandello states, "*Saint Joan* is a work of poetry from beginning to end." Rptd. in *Saint Joan: Fifty Years After*, ed. Stanley Weintraub (Baton Rouge: Louisiana State University Press, 1973), p. 27.

12. "A Dialogue on Dramatic Poetry," *Selected Essays* (London: Faber & Faber, 1932), p. 38.

13. "The Fabian Figaro," *George Bernard Shaw: A Critical Survey*, ed. Louis Kronenberger (New York: World, 1953), p. 156.

Dan H. Laurence

APPROACHING THE CHALLENGE

The back pages of Shaw's first opus book bristle with notations of apparent significance at the time they were indited. There are Biblical texts, memoranda for *Immaturity* labeled "Stray Notions—Plan N° 1"; musical citations; and autobiographic references ("18/8/77 Yolande—or *Disenchantment!*" and "Novr 7th 1877. Traum dolce. Blues! ! ! !").[1] Between the dated entries is an intriguing passage from Carlyle's *Sartor Resartus* reflecting the state of mind of the fledgling Shaw as he approached the challenge of literary creation: "Like a very young person, I imagined it was with work alone and not with Folly and Sin, in myself and others, that I had been appointed to struggle."[2]

B.C. (Before Carlyle), however, there was a far more inspiring, stimulating, captivating author, to whom Shaw gravitated in Dublin "when I was not much older than Pip was when the convict turned him upside down in the churchyard. . . ."[3] Between eight and thirteen Shaw read—most of them three times each—illustrated editions of all fourteen Charles Dickens novels, in addition to readings of the Boz sketches, the *Commercial Traveller* essays and sketches, the Christmas Books, and most of the volumes of *Household Words* and *All the Year Round*. When he set out for London near the end of his teens, it was necessary to part with nearly all of his precious library; but his carpet bag on the journey was weighted down with a trio of the Dickens novels, purchased from Carroll's.

He carried across the Channel too a concern for the social conditions besetting nineteenth-century Britain that Dickens had deprecated in his novels: poverty, bureaucracy, Victorian jobbery, snobbery, and hypocrisy, school abuse, factory exploitation of women and children, prison conditions, capital punishment—particularly in the late novels "with their mercifully faithful and penetrating exposures of English social, industrial, and political life."[4] Lecturing in Liverpool on Ruskin and Dickens at a book exhibition in November 1908, he informed his audience, "One of the reasons I am a revolutionist is that I read *Little Dorrit* when I was a very small boy."[5]

ON SHAW'S "CONTEMPORARY ART VIEWED FROM BEHIND THE AGE" (1878)

In his attempt to deal with the views he espoused or disparaged in this initial stab at polemical Grub-streeting for a livelihood, Shaw revealed coincidentally his ability to take an ironic stance and his inability to know what to do with it. A natural genius, intelligent, self-taught to an astonishing degree, with an impressive vocabulary and a precocity at twenty-one reflected in the bandying of "anacreontic votaries" and "metaphysical speculation," he yet could not dress—or address—his thoughts effectively. His inversions are here discursive, stilted, and forced. The impish humor displayed so abundantly in the surviving Dublin correspondence with his mother and sister is reduced here to adolescent self-consciousness and smugness. Handicapped by insecurity and earnestness, he lost the spontaneity, the buoyancy, the relaxed self that his schoolfellow Edward McNulty knew and so much admired. It is interesting that in "Contemporary Art" Shaw would draw on *Martin Chuzzlewit* for illustration, considering that a dozen years later he would single out this novel as displaying the "intellectual crudity" of its author's "first phase," the very weakness of which he himself in 1878 unknowingly was suffering.[6]

The article was sent to and rejected by an unidentified journal in April 1878 and by the *Saturday Review* a couple of months later. At the foot of the last leaf of the manuscript there is a note in Shaw's hand that appears to be a transcript of a criticism accompanying one or other of the rejections: "This article is very unskilfully phrased[;] the construction of the sentences is not sufficiently varied; and the subject matter is too feeble for the simplicity of statement affected throughout." The manuscript lay neglected until 1882, when, after a re-reading, Shaw emblazoned diagonally across the first pencilled page in heavy black ink: "All this is the most virulent trash that sarcastic ignorance can produce." Happily, he did not destroy the manuscript, thus enabling posterity to measure the extent of his growth as a craftsman when in 1880 A.D. (After Dickens) he re-worked the subject into the more mature "Exhausted Arts."

Contemporary Art viewed from behind the Age (1878)

[PROVENANCE: Unsigned holograph manuscript, in pencil, with ink revisions, dated "April 1878" at foot of folio 12, with note indicating the essay was submitted to an unidentified journal "about 30/4/78". British Library: Add. Mss. 50721A, folios 8–11a, b, 12a. At the foot of folio 12a Shaw added the text of an undated critical note following rejection of the article. Shaw's own criticism, dated 1882, was inscribed in black ink, diagonally, across the face of folio 8a.]

In a novel published in the early part of the present century, the experiences of a young Englishman in America are described very graphically, and with great earnestness and humour—literary qualities at that time looked for by the reading public, but since become happily obsolete, to the great facilitation of the art of authorship, and (consequently) to the general benefit of man. The hero of this novel, one Martin Chuzzlewit, is represented therein as being much struck by finding that each native whom he encounters is "one of the most remarkable men in the country". This conceit excited so much merriment amongst us at the expense of our transatlantic cousins when it appeared that to repudiate it as we have just done, would then have exposed us to contempt and ridicule, as trading[7] on a notoriously stale witticism. At present, when no man of taste and spirit can be expected to know anything more of the romances of the late Mr Dickens than the fact of their existence, or perhaps some childish recollections of their more frequently quoted characters, we may justifiably offer the above passage as a novelty, particularly as it serves conveniently for a text whereupon to base a short description of some features in the advanced culture represented by the artistic circles of London at the present time.

History sometimes revives old comedies and it is by no means improbable that an American writer may shortly visit us; return to his native land; and convulse his countrymen with an account of his successive introductions to our journalists, society poets, and novelists: each being the author of the cleverest thing ever done.[8] And whereas young Mr Chuzzlewit was somewhat at a stand to find that Webster and Franklin were held in no estimation by their compatriots, our hypothetical visitor may be equally amazed to find Shakspere and Shelley only mentioned among us with reference to the numerous modern geniuses who have equalled or surpassed them, and that a person professing to admire Oliver Goldsmith, Wm Cowper, or worse still, Thomas Moore, would be deemed no less extravagantly provincial than if he had visited the National Gallery, or incautiously betrayed a preference for the symphonies of Hadyn over the tone poems of Franz Lizst. Now it is obvious that whatever reason we may have to congratulate ourselves on this enlightened artistic condition, it is so little to be expected by outsiders that there is a danger in it that young and ambitious men, tempted from remote parts to the capital, may find themselves so uninstructed in those peculiar accomplishments which are in demand, as to run no small risk of starving before they have mastered them. For information of such, it may not be amiss to mention respectfully a few canons of the modern school, if so free souled a movement as the higher development of our day can be said to have any canons at all. Premising that the necessities of the case, and not any sentiments of vulgar formality, are alone responsible for such of our illustrations as may savour of the commonplace, we will address ourselves to the consideration of Poetry, giving it priority as the oldest, if not always the most respectable, of the arts.

In the lyricists of the present day we need not look for a celebration of the beauty of nature or anacreontic votaries of love, wine, and play. These materials are so readily exhausted that all distinguished poets have had to add to the possession of a correct taste[?] and fertile fancy, a knowledge of human nature only to be acquired by constant and sensitively intelligent observation of men and things, for which reason we find that such men commonly composed their works slowly and with great labour, and achieved thereby nothing but an elevation of mind which placed them above their contemporaries, and thus considerably diminished their profits and social popularity. A result so repugnant to the commercial spirit of our times, that poetry of this kind is no longer attempted save by a few obscure impracticables, and a new species of literary dish has been invented, the seasoners of which are known by the honorable title of Society Poets. They adopt for their lucubrations forms derived from the French—with which language they are frequently less indifferently acquainted than with their mother tongue—called rondeaus,[9] vilanelles, triolets, and so on, in which any line may be repeated some two or three times in each verse throughout the entire composition. The admirable economy of this arrangement is obvious and as neither the lines so repeated, or indeed any others, ever—save on rare and incidental occasions—convey any definite meaning whatsoever, they are equally appropriate for use at any juncture; the whole difficulty in poesy being thus reduced to rhyming. To lighten even this, many useful and ingenious jingling lexicons[10] are in daily use. The rhymes once found and arranged, and a female name or other heading selected, the requirements of all respectable readers are satisfied and the compiler is a Society Poet. In blank verse and deeply serious poetry, where these forms are discarded, and some little coherent matter is therefore desirable, the subjects most in vogue are the feelings of the writer, which are usually of a profound and entertaining description, illustrated with impossible similitudes drawn from the elements, the stews and the dust pit,[11] the whole being conceived in so grossly sensual a mood, as to place it within the sympathetic comprehension of the vilest of readers. The chief adornment of this manner is the liberal employment of alliteration, which serves to relieve the slight dulness inseparable from even the choicest verbosity.

The province of general literature is so vast, and the irresponsible toilers therein so extremely independent, that it would be manifest presumption on our part to attempt to cover the subject in less than twenty volumes. As, however, our remarks would be incomplete in the most important particular if we evaded it, we will endeavour to handle it as fully as may be. Of the art of novel writing, it is sufficient to say that its recent adoption by young ladies as an agreeable accomplishment, has tended greatly to the improvement of fiction by introducing a greater faithfulness to nature in the delineation of character, and a more unsophisticated manliness in the heroes, who, being conceived in the fresh and simple minds of our young authoresses, are free alike from the coarseness of the Tom Joneses of the old school, and from the pedantic virtue of the Waverlies & Copperfields of later times. It has also displayed the remarkable capacity of the female mind for metaphysical speculation in more abstract regions of human thought. Writers of the sterner sex only cultivate romance as a necessary ingredient in history, the which, thus leavened, is more acceptable to the taste of the age than the ponderous works of the late Dr. Robertson.[12] A slavish adherence to truth in works purporting to be narratives of fact, cannot be too strongly deprecated. Instead, the various events should be arranged with a view to dramatic contrast rather than chronology; hero worship should be the motive of the work; and incidents which are inconsistent with the theory of the writer should be suppressed, in order to preserve a general harmony of design. And here we may mention, once for all, that truth is a dangerous and unpalatable element in literary and artistic work of all descriptions, and cannot be too sedulously shunned by young writers who wish to advance themselves. Realism is, however, unobjectionable, provided it be morbid. The works of Macaulay may be studied in secret, as they contain much that may be advantageously retailed at second hand; but on no account must this author be referred to save as an example of meretricious brilliancy of style, a "book in breaches", or some similar stricture. His inaccuracy and partiality are notorious, and have been established by the unanimous verdict of public journalists, Irish patriots, Oxford undergraduates, and many other equally eminent and infallible authorities. His remark concerning speculation on the origin of evil & the first cause, to the effect that they are usually confined to intelligent schoolboys, would alone prove the narrowness of his intellect, inasmuch as these very subjects are the staple of a branch of literature of considerable magnitude which may be termed the word trade. Our dealers therein may challenge comparison with the choicest intellects of ancient Greece or modern Germany. They are proficients in epigram, and by their arguments in favor of "absolute negation" and other rhythmical phrases, have at one blow set at rest for ever the vexed question which has cost Dr. Darwin and other worthy but old fashioned workmen of the same stamp years of labour.

Passing over the drudgery of the daily paper as of no consequence in art, we come to the consideration of journalism in its exalted or sixpenny weekly aspect. The qualities demanded for its successful prosecution are not of a common order. The journalist of society must be communicative, yet mysterious; his gossip must range from the servants hall to the ministerial cabinet. He must be courageous enough to print what he dare not utter verbally, yet cowardly enough to insult women without remorse. He must be personal, and on occasion, obscene; and when not gossiping he must enlighten his readers by descriptions of scenes which are difficult of access to the respectable world. But lest he be misunderstood, he must preserve the most delicate feelings of honor, and the most exalted religious sensibility: losing no opportunity of assuring his readers that he is a gentleman—a fact which they might otherwise forget. Indeed, were he to neglect these particulars, the American visitor whom we have fancied might perhaps retort on us the first words heard by Martin Chuzzlewit on American ground[:] "Here's the New York Sewer, the Family Spy, the Private Listener, the Peeper, the Keyhole Reporter. Here's the Sewer, with a full account of the ball at Mrs. White's last night, where all the beauty and fashion of New York was assembled, with the Sewer[']s own particulars of the private lives of all the ladies that were there" &c &c &c.[13]

The art of Painting has of late years received such an impulse from enlightened public patronage, that chromatic tricks formerly practised only by facetious students in schools of design, are exhibited in our principal galleries and eagerly competed for by purchasers. A most remarkable development of taste is that for confessedly spurious old masters, whose mannerisms and weaknesses are faithfully reproduced by their modern imitators. These works are greatly relished by society poets and their admirers, who form, in merit and sentiment[,] a portion of the same sect. Many cherished canons of this school of Art, are derived from the criticisms of Mr. Ruskin, in whose works, however, we have wholly failed to find the views so freely attributed to him, insomuch that we have almost suspected him of being a misinterpreted author with a vulgar leaning towards common sense.

Of Music, it is difficult to treat without danger of being either diffuse or technical. The young critic will find it much easier to sneer at the modern school than to understand it, but practical aspirants will be encouraged by the extent to which composition has given place to mere orchestration, and the art of pleasing to the trick of startling. The melodies of the great masters of the past are preserved to us by the numerous tribe of song writers, whose elegant and scholarly effusions are replete with reminiscences.

We cannot but feel how inadequate is our brief treatment to the vastness of the matter in hand, which is nothing less than the effects of engrafting the fruit of latter day thought on the hollow conventionalism of the old forms of Art. But if we succeed in diverting some student from the contemplation of obsolete models, we do enough. Henceforth let no man suppose that an appreciation of Shelley, Scott, Addison, Raphael, or Mozart can give him claims as a man of culture. In their stead shines the glorious constellation of fleshliness, scandal, pre-Raphaelitism, and symphonic poetry. May they flourish as long as they deserve! Theirs is the homely recommendation of being "cheap, and within the reach of all".

ON SHAW'S "OAKUM PICKING" (1878)

Penal institutions loomed large in the novels of Dickens, a result of boyhood trauma when his father was incarcerated as a debtor in the old Marshalsea Prison in Southwark. Several of his novels contain graphic prison settings: the vivid, poignant scenes in the Marshalsea in *Little Dorrit* and the Fleet Prison in *Pickwick Papers,* limned from excruciating personal experience at the age of twelve enhanced by the faculty of imagination, are among his finest writings. It may be more than remarkable coincidence that the three Dickens novels Shaw carried with him from Dublin should have been *Little Dorrit, Pickwick Papers,* and, with its bold Goyaesque sequences in Newgate Prison, *Barnaby Rudge.*[14] All contain Shaw's signature "G. B. Shaw," with *Little Dorrit* dated by G.B.S. "1873" and the other two "1874."

Shaw had no opportunity to share Dickens's experience with the old-style prisons, except vicariously through the novels; but in his late teens he experienced a personal introduction to the new penitentiary system when a friend, who was clerk to a Crown Solicitor and had business there, escorted him into the confines of north Dublin's Mountjoy Male Prison (opened in 1847) with its clean rows of cells, silent and solitary, designed to allow for penance and meditation.[15] The cells of the penitentiaries were whitewashed cubicles about seven feet by thirteen, each with a high barred window (with sooty glass) opposite a black-painted door. "It is always twilight in one's cell," mourned Oscar Wilde, "as it is always midnight in one's heart."[16]

Shortly after Shaw's arrival in London, Parliament passed a new Prisons Act, calling for all local prisons to be brought under central governmental control, administered by a former military officer Sir Edmund Du Cane (1830–93), to be operated as a rigidly observed punitive system. As the London press reported extensively on the new Act, to take effect on 22 April 1878, Shaw learned enough about "innovations" of policy to make him a lifelong enemy of the penal "hard labour" enslavement that broke men—and women too—even for minor infractions of prison rules. To Shaw a system of imprisonment with little or no concern for reform was "a malicious injury . . . an act of diabolical cruelty";[17] and in an address in 1919 he inveighed against a system that "leaves every man who touches it worse than it found him."[18]

In the "enlightened" Victorian world of the 1870s, able-bodied prisoners (who could range in age from twelve to seventy) were assigned principally to one of three standard labors: the treadwheel, rock-breaking, or oakum picking. The treadwheel, used in some prisons for pumping water or grinding wheat, consisted of a series of steps on the circumference of a turning wheel, requiring ascent of about 57 steps a minute, each step being ten inches wide. The Prison Disciplinary Board recommended 12,000 feet of ascent daily, making it, for even the most able-bodied, a cruel and extreme punishment. It was not officially discontinued until 1898.[19] Rock-breaking, a task familiar to most Americans from prison sequences in films like *I Am a Fugitive from a Chain Gang* (1932), was performed within prison grounds, using granite blocks supplied by quarries in Dartmoor and Portland, under public works programs.

Oakum picking, physically the lightest of the labors, was for many the most demoralizing. As it required no equipment but an old ship's rope an inch or more in thickness, the hardest and firmest that could be obtained and freshly tarred to make the task more onerous, the work could be performed within the small cells at any hour of day or night. Prisoners were expected to pick at the tough ropes to separate the strands until the loose hemp fibers were fine enough to spin. A daily quota was set, usually of three pounds, which was more than most prisoners could accomplish, resulting in frequent punishments of reduced rations or cancelled privileges to a sufficient number to goad the others to work longer into the night.[20] Moreover, it was a singularly dirty task, one's hands, body, clothing, and quarters becoming rapidly stained with tar. A visitor to Oscar Wilde in 1895, just after his transfer to Wandsworth, "noted that his hands . . . were disfigured, their nails broken and bleeding," the effect of oakum picking.[21] And to what end? *The Times* on 20 December 1878 alleged that oakum contractors had stated at a meeting of the Holborn Guardians that "nothing would be paid for picking oakum . . . for which there was no sale."[22] It was solely a punitive measure, useless except to occupy time; yet it continued as a hateful chore into the second decade of the new century.

Shaw's indictment of oakum picking, his first recorded social polemic, was written with strong resolve and clearmindedness. The manuscript indicates a steady flow, with only one snag in the second paragraph and with fewer revisions than in any other surviving manuscript of the period. Whatever influence Dickens may have had in instilling in Shaw a loathing of imprisonment, he took a giant step forward, his conviction laying ground for the impassioned preface he would write in 1922 for the Webbs' *English Prisons under Local Government*, with its controversial but incontrovertible opening words: "Imprisonment as it exists today is a worse crime than any of those committed by its victims; for no single criminal can be as powerful for evil, or as unrestrained in its exercise, as an organized nation."[23]

Oakum Picking (1878)

[PROVENANCE: Unsigned holograph manuscript, in pencil, with ink revisions, dated "4/5/78" at foot of folio 17b. British Library: Add. Mss. 50721A, folios 16–17a,b.]

As we have encouraged the art of rope disintegration in our criminal prisons, workhouses, and other places of popular resort, until it has attained the prescriptive elevation of a National Institution, its merits cannot be deemed unworthy of examination by serious persons who consider that the work inaugurated by Howard still remains incomplete.[24]

In considering the nature of the penalties which society is entitled to inflict on those who disregard its interest, the question of how far torture is justifiable comes forward prominently. Torture is a word which jars on the sensibility of modern thought; but to speak of a term of penal servitude as a temporary inconvenience is mere euphuism. We have discarded the rack and the scavenger's daughter;[25] but we have adopted the solitary system, the treadmill, and the tarred rope; this last being, as we believe, the worst of the three. Isolation is terrible, but it is a refuge from vile associations, and a promoter of reflection. The wheel is at least free from false pretence. It is a torturing engine pure and simple, having professedly no other function than that of inflicting pain. Both of these punishments are deterrent, and neither disables the victim. Oakum picking, on the contrary, adds to the defect of uselessness, the sin of hypocrisy. The rope is wantonly twisted and tarred, that the felon may pick it to pieces by a slow, clumsy, and painful process, under the perfectly false pretence of making himself useful. If he be a scrivener, shirt maker or engraver, depending for subsistence on a cunning and sensitive right hand he is deprived of his means of living honestly. On such a felon we take, in effect, a lifelong vengeance; whereas the laws we have made may limit the extent of his duress to three months. But far more important practically is the fact that we hereby defeat our own end, which is the repression of crime. The great bulk of our criminal population have been convicted for theft or violence. The thief is at heart an envious idler: never a conscientious or artistic workman. The rough is usually a drunken loafer. One is essentially vulgar, the other essentially brutish. That we should degrade them when they fall within our grasp is inevitable; but, since we dare not exterminate them, we cannot for our own

sakes afford to brutalise or vulgarise them still further. And this is exactly what oakum picking does, more effectually even than the irresponsible tyranny of the gaol governer and his subordinates. It is not broad
handed repression, stern retribution, or terrible vengeance, which over-
awes or crushes. It is petty annoyance such as a small minded turnkey
might devise. It worries, irritates, and makes sullen the convict; leading
him insensibly to hate the law, and thereby acquire an additional induce-
ment to break it. The very injury it inflicts on the unsturdy few by
crippling, it inflicts so indirectly that it is useless as a deterrent. The most
imaginative oakum picker can not force a spark of interest into his occupation. The result is, that without gaining anything, we deliberately confirm in the felon, that very distaste for work which is the root of his
criminality. The moral sloth which we observe in those who have never
awakened to the pleasure of producing, which fills our prisons, and
stunts the mental development of our women, is the most powerful
enemy of reformatory civilization. Yet we incarcerate men in whom it is a
habit, and having intensified it into a principle, we let them loose; and
they testify to our success by speedily offending again.

In turning to the practice of employing casual paupers at the rope, we
may perhaps excite the attention of many who refuse to listen to any
suggestion concerning the treatment of criminals, and who, had they
lived in the last century, would probably have refused to spare Damiens
one turn of the rack, because they disapprove of "pampering."[26] The
cruelty of this system has been illustrated by the committal to prison of
refractory seamstresses, who, being driven to the casual ward, and aware
that their future freedom depended on the nimbleness of their fingers,
refused to ruin themselves permanently in return for a meal and a
night's shelter. Nothing is more to be deprecated than gratuitous relief to
healthy persons. But as they are relieved on the theory that everyone has
a right to live, they should be made to work as for a right, and not to do
penance as for an indulgence. What we have said of oakum picking as a
means of associating labour with the idea of an evil to be avoided and
resented, applies with double force in the case of workhouses. It is stupid
to confirm in the criminal the vicious mental attitude which led him to
crime; but it is barbarous to bring a pauper within the same influence. If
genuine work cannot be procured, it is better to let the iron law of nature
operate, and sweep away the remnant who cannot afford to support
themselves. Humanity, it is true, shrinks from the contemplation of a
fellow creature starving in the midst of plenty, and prefers to believe that
the conditions of existence are based on sentimentalism. But the fact
remains that the admitted necessity for making the workhouse only
more desirable as a refuge than the prison, leads with remorseless logic

to the abolition [of] pauperism as a recognised state. With this, however, we have at present nothing to do. Our object is to force oakum picking from the obscurity of a matter of course which is nobody's business. Hitherto its unpleasantness and meanness have enabled it to shun the light of discussion, whilst the terrors of the solitary cell and the grim treadwheel have evoked hosts of arguments in their favour; the chief being the advantage of isolation in the one; the formidable exertion compelled by the other; and the deterrent influence of both. We contend that oakum can boast none of these alleged effects. It has never been balanced and investigated after the cautious method of modern civiliza-tion, but has crept along, a petty but dangerous abuse, until it has come to be accepted like the stone wall, and the barred window, as a necessary adjunct of prison life. We think it is time to scrutinise its claims narrowly, and if it cannot render some more satisfactory account than appears on the surface, to dislodge it effectually and for ever.

ON SHAW'S "ASIDES" (1889)

The *Penny Illustrated Paper,* through its literary editor John Latey, Jr. (1842–1902), invited Shaw to provide a weekly social commentary, "Asides," amounting to a double column of 2,700 words, on whichever topics he chose to render "brilliant and sparkling."[27] Shaw opted for the initials "N. G." as a pseudonym, informing readers, with Dickensian zest and deviance, in the opening paragraph on 1 June: "My province is to say things that no gentleman would say. They are mere asides, it is true; but then it is a proof of my deficiency in gentlemanly instinct, that I always make my asides loud enough for everybody to hear them."

Casting his nets wide, Shaw dealt in the first column with the mobbing of the Prince and Princess of Wales on the Horse Guards' Parade, sump-tuary regulations at the opera, the Charringtons' production of *A Doll's House,* and radical political associations. A week later he wrote of "a nice little book" entitled *Deaths from Starvation, Metropolis,* Charles Booth's recently published *Life and Labour in East London,* the problem of lack of copyright in America, an alleged surplus of doctors, and Francis Galton's anthropometric laboratory. There was, however, nothing "sparkling," nothing "brilliant."

In the third week he suddenly hit his stride. After wading through a week's accumulation of lurid crime reporting in the *Star* as a springboard for the new column, Shaw was inspired to produce an incandescent, tongue-in-cheek dissertation on householders and housebreakers, deftly Swiftian in its ironic thrust, which conjures up a graphic cartoon image of the pseudo-burglar Billy Dunn in Act II of *Heartbreak House* angrily demanding of the Heartbreakers: "Is that justice? Is it right? Is it fair to me?"[28]

Shaw may have anticipated Dunn's complaint when Latey, a day after the submission, informed him: "I have read over your 'Asides,' and personally relish the wry humour and satire of your vindication of the poor burglar; but I fear the bulk of our readers are of opinion that 'the policeman's lot is not a happy one' when the burglar goes a-burgling, and that hence your 'Asides' would be caviare to the general. . . . I very much regret to have to return the article, which happens not to be in accord with the views of the paper; and I am sorrier to have to say we must fill the two columns from another source in the future."[29]

London was not yet ready for the Shavian technique of startling an audience to capture its attention, then deftly disarming it through laughter.

Asides (1889)

[PROVENANCE: Holograph manuscript, on blue paper, undated, with note at top right of first leaf indicating rejection on "10.6.89". Shaw's diary notes he had worked "all day" drafting the manuscript on 9 June. British Library: Add. Mss. 50693, folios 188–194, signed "N.G." on last folio, an abbreviation of the pseudonym "No Gentleman."]

The newspapers have been so pleasantly full of thrilling news. This column of mine is lost for lack of matter up to the level of the times in point of excitement. A tragedian of provincial celebrity is reported to have said once:- "I can draw a house against any living actor; but I cannot compete with a circus in which an elephant knits stockings."[30] I am no less handicapped in competing with news columns containing an inundation to the tune of 15000 lives—or rather deaths—and 8 millions' worth of property, with wreckers and robbers, lynchings and burnings, anecdotes and incidents innumerable.[31] Single handed as I am, I have enough to do to contend against the rivalry of such minor matters as "More Remains Found";[32] the committal of a lady of position on suspicion of arsenic;[33] the imprisonment of Mr Vizetelly for publishing Zola's novels;[34] the thunderstorms;[35] and the proceedings of a young gentleman who, for no adequate reason except a desire to *live* tragic poetry instead of reading it, shoots a lady in a railway carriage as a preliminary to throwing her out of window and killing himself.[36]

Even regarded purely as a week's entertainment for the breakfast table, this programme is overdone. The quantity of crime and catastrophe unnecessarily squandered during the past fortnight, would, if properly economised, have sufficed to keep every family in England happy for two months. I would earnestly press this point on the attention of persons who have romantic crimes in contemplation. Of course I know that the regular criminal cannot choose his time to suit the public. He is the breadwinner; and those who are dear to him must be fed all the year round. A burglar must live; and a [householder][37] must die occasionally if he interrupts the burglar at his work, an accident against which all burglars, to do them justice, take every precaution in their power. I do not see that they can be expected to do more.

* * *

It is only fair to add that a great deal of unjust prejudice enters into discussions of which burglars are the subject. Many persons would deny them the right to carry and use a pistol in self defence. Under the circumstances, such denial is monstrous. Here is a man industriously making his living in the sweat of his brow at a calling which demands not only a mechanical skill superior to that of the most eminent locksmiths and safe manufacturers, but nerve enough to exercise that skill with the utmost expedition under difficulties and anxieties from which lock-smiths are wholly exempt. The plant required is not extensive; but its cost is by no means insignificant; and the risk of having to abandon or throw it away is considerable. This risk is not great in one sense, since only a trifling percentage of burglaries are interrupted; but on the other hand, when interruption does take place the penalty is outrageous. For although the annual profits of the business are no greater than the average return to equal skill, capital, labor, risk, enterprise, courage and foresight in other occupations, yet the rich householder (usually a member of the class stigmatized as "drones" by the late eminent economist Professor Cairnes)[38] not only wrests from the burglar, if he catches him, these just profits, but inflicts on him in addition punishments so savage that no sophistry in the world can make them out to be less than a most horrible disgrace to a civilized nation. Twenty years penal servitude plus the lash are what the householder and the policemen bring in their hands. Is a man not to defend himself to the death against such vengeance as this? If not, against what, in the name of common sense, may he defend himself? If I were a burglar, and had a sufficiently comprehensive revolver, I would shoot the entire population of the United Kingdom, on principle, sooner than be captured. And if they asked me to shew mercy, I should reply:—"*Que messieurs les bourgeois commencent!*"[39]

* * *

Against these overwhelming arguments I have heard feeble folk urge that burglary is not socially useful. Perhaps not; but it is necessary to the subsistence of the burglar, and thus deserves the same toleration as a hundred other socially useless and even noxious callings which are recognized and protected by the law. Hundreds of flourishing industries are devoted to gratifying the luxury of the excessively rich and the vices of all classes. The slaughter of birds to ornament ladies' hats, the distillation of gin, the manufacture of roulette tables:—surely no self respecting burglar would soil his hands with such trades as these! As soon would he powder his head and stoop to wear a vulgar livery in a west end hall, or permit his wife to earn his money in ways more degrading. Then let us hear no more about the social uselessness of the burglar's profession. If it is no worse than useless, it ranks very high indeed among the crafts by which "honest" people get their living.

All this is a digression from my advice to romantic criminals not to bring their wares to a glutted market, but to wait until there is a real demand for some exciting topic. Most people who murder, or elope, or commit suicide nowadays do so because the reading of fiction has inspired them with a craving to figure dramatically before the public. Therefore they can put off their exploits to a suitable time by the exercise of a little patience. But I would also suggest to these romance lovers that their performances are of a very poor order. Anybody can commit murder & finish up by suicide. When the novelty wears off by repetition, as it soon will, the papers will cease to mention such cheap exploits. Then perhaps it will occur to amateurs that fiction contains a vast magazine of noble actions which are somewhat harder to imitate than the crimes, but which are undeniably effective when thoroughly executed. They are also less injurious to the individuals concerned.

On second thoughts it strikes me that this is a shallow suggestion, after all. To aspire to be a stage villain is a vile ambition; but to pose as a stage hero were worse by far. Better murder somebody at once and have done with it than go about knocking everybody down, uttering intolerable sentiments, getting lost and turning up again inconveniently when your wife has got used to her widow's weeds and your next of kin is comfortably installed on your property. And this suggests the grave question:— Are the novels in which these things occur—in which mere spite against unconventional conduct is held up as morality—in which the most serious problems of life and conduct are glozed or shirked—in which marriage is treated as the end of existence instead of the beginning of it— from which, nevertheless, nineteen out of twenty boys and girls of the reading classes now derive their ideas of the world upon whose threshold they stand: are these novels, I ask, more or less pernicious than the very coarsest book which their folly and insincerity have provoked M. Zola to write?

* * *

For my part, I answer, Certainly not less. I do not say, Decidedly more, because I am not sufficiently well read in Zola literature to feel sure that it may not on the whole fly as wide of the truth on one side as the conventional Mudie novel undoubtedly does on the other.[40] But the question at issue just now is not whether Zola hits the truth or misses it, but whether it is permissible to aim at the truth at all. The subject of the relations between men and women is not tabooed: it is the staple of all ordinary fiction: 999 out of every thousand books in Mr. Mudie's library are love stories. But for all that the subject has to be treated subject to a certain assumption, exactly as religion could only be treated subject to a certain assumption before the revolt of Voltaire. In the one case the assumption is the sacredness of marriage: in the other, it was the sacredness of the Scriptures as interpreted by the Church. And just as it was possible for hypocrites and fools to write the most grotesquely blasphemous books without trespassing against the Church, so it is possible at present for arrant sensualists to write very nasty novels indeed without transgressing the Mudie-Grundy regulations.[41]

Everybody now sees that Voltaire did a great service to religion by winning the right to criticise and question the authority of the Church as if it were no more sacred than any other human institution. Yet he did this service by shocking the world with lampoons upon the most sacred subjects—lampoons which were chaste in comparison to the rhapsodies in many books of devotion, but which, to the prejudices of his contemporaries, were beyond measure indecorous and scandalous. These lampoons did not, as shallow people feared, destroy religion and corrupt the world: nobody reads them now; but they secured the right of discussion which many great thinkers immediately availed themselves of to let light into dark places and fresh air into unwholesome sanctuaries.

Zola's books, like Voltaire's pamphlets, scandalize thoughtless people; and contain episodes which can have no further or higher effect than to scandalize them. But they are securing the right of way for thinkers who will bring light and fresh air into this sanctuary too, which needs it more than the other. The Vizetelly prosecution has been a mistake. When all the prisoner's stock has been confiscated and destroyed, his customers can still go to Mudie's and get books from which they can extract their fill of what is condemned in Zola without being forced into the salutary intellectual exercise of reflecting seriously on it. They can still go to the music hall and enjoy allusions and exhibitions from which M. Zola would turn away in cold disgust. They will, in short, get the poison without the antidote. It is therefore to be hoped that some publisher with motives high enough to inspire him to maintain the right which Mr. Vizetelly, conscience stricken, surrendered without a blow, may issue a complete edition of M. Zola's works in flat defiance of persecution. The very people who set this Vizetelly prosecution on foot ought to have been the last to believe that literature or society can be purified by a *police de mœurs*.[42]

N.G.

Notes

1. *Yolande* was a ballet at the Alhambra Theatre, whose leading ballerina, Erminia Pertoldi, became Shaw's dream lover.

2. British Library Add. Mss. 50721A, fols. 114–15. The Carlyle passage is in Book II, Chapter 4.

3. *The World,* 24 May 1893; rptd. in *Shaw's Music,* ed. Dan H. Laurence (London: Max Reinhardt, 1981), 2:891. Pip, at the time he was grabbed by Abel Magwitch, was about seven.

4. Introduction to *Hard Times* (London: Waverley, 1913); rptd. in *Shaw on Dickens,* eds. Dan H. Laurence and Martin Quinn (New York: Ungar, 1985), p. 30.

5. Published (untitled) in the *Liverpool Courier* (16 November 1908); extract rptd. (under the caption "Ruskin and Dickens") in *Shaw on Dickens,* p. 111.

6. "From Dickens to Ibsen" (unfinished manuscript, November 1889), first published in *Shaw on Dickens,* p. 12.

7. Inserted above "trading" in blue pencil is the noun "traders." Neither word is canceled.

8. Although Shaw later in the essay describes the American visitor as "fancied," it is possible he had Mark Twain in mind, for he had read *Innocents Abroad* (1869) in its first English edition, retitled *The New Pilgrim's Progress* (1872). His boyhood reading had also included *The Celebrated Jumping Frog of Calaveras County* (1867) and *Roughing It* (1872).

9. The rondeau, long unpopular in Britain, enjoyed a sudden vogue, principally in the verse of Swinburne, at whom Shaw appears to be taking a swipe, as he would continue to do for the next seven decades.

10. The reference to "lexicons" may be linked to a popular Victorian game called Lexicon (a proprietary name like Monopoly), played with cards marked by letters of the alphabet, from which "ingenious jingling" words might be created.

11. A "stews" was a brothel. A "dust pit" is a garbage dump.

12. William Robertson (1721–93), Scottish historian and principal of the University of Edinburgh, was the author of a *History of Scotland 1542–1603* (1759) and a *History of the Reign of Emperor Charles V* (1769). "I remember reading Robertson's Charles V. and his history of Scotland from end to end most laboriously," Shaw recalled in the preface to *Misalliance* (*Collected Plays with Their Prefaces* [London: Max Reinhardt, 1970–74], 4:71).

13. *Martin Chuzzlewit,* Chap. 16, condensed and slightly revised.

14. Examined by Dan H. Laurence in January 1959, in the library of Shaw's half-cousin Georgina (Judy) Musters, at Folkestone.

15. Preface (by Shaw) to Sidney and Beatrice Webb, *English Prisons under Local Government* (London: Longmans, Green, 1922); rptd. (as amended in 1925 and 1931) in *Complete Prefaces*, ed. Dan H. Laurence and Daniel J. Leary (London: Allen Lane, 1993–   ), 2: 437. The unfrocked priest Peter Keegan in Shaw's *John Bull's Other Island* (1904) identifies "our poetically named Mountjoy prison" as a "place of torment," although "the cleanest and most orderly place I know in Ireland" (*Complete Plays with Their Prefaces*, 2: 1015).

16. Philip Priestley, *Victorian Prison Lives: English Prison Biography 1830–1914* (London: Methuen, 1985), p. 27.

17. Preface to *Major Barbara*, in *Collected Plays with Their Prefaces*, 3:23.

18. "Never Have So Many Honest, Ultra Responsible People Been in Prison," *New York American* (15 June 1919), p. 2CE:3–4. A meeting of the Police and Public Vigilance Society, London, 8 May 1919.

19. Priestley, pp. 125–28.

20. Priestley, pp. 121–23.

21. Richard Ellmann, *Oscar Wilde* (London: Penguin, 1988), pp. 457–58.

22. "Oakum Picking," *The Times* (20 December 1878), p. 6:2.

23. "Imprisonment," *Complete Prefaces*, 2:440.

24. John Howard (1726–90), English philanthropist and prison reformer, was the author of *The State of the Prisons in England and Wales* (1777), a survey of prison conditions that proved to be a powerful instrument for much-needed reform. Howard was instrumental in the creation of the modern single-cell penitentiary.

25. A torture instrument devised in the reign of Henry VIII by Sir Leonard Skevington, Lieutenant of the Tower of London, that compressed the body until the head touched the knees, forcing blood from ears and nose.

26. Robert-François Damiens (1715–57), attempted assassin of Louis XV at Versailles on 5 January 1757, was put to torture before his execution.

27. John Latey, Jr., to Shaw: ALS, 17 May 1889. British Library Add. Mss. 50512, fols. 138b, 139a,b.

28. *Collected Plays with Their Prefaces*, 5:135.

29. John Latey, Jr., to Shaw: ALS, 10 June 1889. To soften the blow, Latey added, "If you will be good enough to drop me a line to say how many weeks' contributions you consider it right you should be remunerated for, I will hand the memorandum over to the cashier." British Library Add. Mss. 50512, fol. 145a,b.

30. Source unknown. A possible candidate, although he was not "a tragedian," is Charles Mathews the Elder (1776–1835), who informed his wife in a letter of 19 January 1815 that on the previous night in Liverpool "I finished with *eclat*," drawing a house of 721 (£72) despite the neighboring Circus's being "full every night" with "Horses against us . . ." (Mrs. [Anne] Mathews, *Memoirs of Charles Mathews, Comedian*, 1838).

31. On 1 June 1889, under the heading "A FEARFUL FLOOD," the *Star* reported on the now legendary Johnstown (Pa.) flood, with an estimated death toll of 2,200. All the news reports and headings enumerated in Shaw's first paragraph are drawn from the previous week's issues of the *Star*.

32. Portions of the trunk of a woman's body in the Thames, apparently following "an illegal operation," had been preceded by other body parts, as reported earlier in the week. 7 June (3:3).

33. "THE MAYBRICK MYSTERY." Mrs. Florence Maybrick, an American, was arrested on 11 May on a charge of the murder of her husband, a Liverpool cotton merchant. Inquest testimony was reported. 5 June (3:3). Subsequently Mrs. Maybrick was tried, found guilty, and sentenced to death. The sentence was later commuted. She

served fifteen years in English prisons, repeatedly proclaiming her innocence, before being released in 1905.

34. Zola's British publisher Henry Vizetelly (1820–94) was prosecuted in 1888 for publishing Zola's *Soil* (*La Terre*, 1876), which the crown termed "an obscene libel." Following the advice of his solicitor he later pleaded guilty and paid a fine of £100. 30 May (2:6). See also "That Realism is the Goal of Fiction," pages 111–18.

35. "A STORM AT HOME: Great Damage by Flood and Thunderstorm—Destructive Lightning." The storm hit hardest in Southport, Bolton, and Preston. 4 June (3:4). It also reached London, as evidenced by the heading on Shaw's unsigned music review of 7 June 1889 (2:4): "The Philharmonic. Thunder, Lightning, Madame Backer-Grondahl, Mr. Cliffe, and Beethoven."

36. "A RAILWAY TRAGEDY." A young teacher, [Augustus] Keeling, traveling from Bath in company with the recently appointed headmistress at the Devizes British school, Miss [Emily] Lister, shot the lady as the train neared Devizes, throwing her body out of the window. He then shot himself "with fatal effect." 8 June (3:3).

37. Apparently Shaw found no time for proofing his manuscript, for the word he thoughtlessly penned here was a careless repetition of "burglar."

38. John Elliott Cairnes (1823–75), Irish economist and professor of political economy, was the author of *Some Leading Principles of Political Economy* (1878). The reference to the idle rich as "drones in the hive, gorging at a feast to which they have contributed nothing" appears on p. 35.

39. Shaw is inverting an utterance of the French satirist Alphonse Karr (1808–90) who, in his journal *Les Guêpes* 6 (31 January 1840): 304, quipped: "If . . . it is desired to abolish the death penalty, in that case let the murderers begin." Shaw substituted householders (*les bourgeois*) for murderers (*les assassins*).

40. Charles Mudie (1818–90) founded Mudie's Select Library, in London, which rapidly grew into the leading subscription library in England.

41. Mrs. Grundy, an offstage character in Thomas Morton's comedy *Speed the Plough* (1798), became the emblem of Victorian social convention. There is another reference to her in "That Realism is the Goal of Fiction ': see page 117.

42. Vice squad.

J. L. Wisenthal

MUSIC: LAYING DOWN THE LAW

In these two pieces on music, the voice that is authoritatively laying down
the law for musicians and audiences, and chastising offenders with such
unhesitating assurance, belongs to a man in his early twenties. This is the
Shaw of 1879, the Shaw who had been in London for only three years
and who was just beginning his first novel. He started work on *Immaturity*
on 5 March, during the time he was trying to place the earlier of these
two essays, "Conductors and Organists"; and he completed the ill-fated
novel (which was to remain unpublished for over half a century) on 5
November, a month after he wrote the second of these essays, "Unconscionable Abuses."[1] The two essays have had to wait much longer than
even *Immaturity* to reach an audience: they were rejected by musical
journals at the time, and are only now being published, 117 years after
they were written by the unknown young Irishman who was trying,
without much success, to make his way in London.

It is, I think, altogether possible that Shaw would not have eagerly
welcomed the belated publication of these early essays. In 1894, writing
on "How To Become a Musical Critic," he was not particularly laudatory
about his earliest pieces of music criticism—the reviews that he had ghost-
written between late 1876 and September 1877 for *The Hornet*. He said
that to these articles "I owe all my knowledge of the characteristics of bad
criticism. I cannot here convey an adequate impression of their demerits
without overstepping the bounds of decorum."[2] One cannot be certain
that Shaw would have applied the same strictures to the unpublished 1879
pieces, but they too are part of this very early phase of his written work.
According to Dan H. Laurence, Shaw submitted "about a dozen essays to
numerous publications" during 1879, of which two were published (unsigned) at the time.[3] One of these, "Opera in Italian," was accepted by the
Saturday Musical Review, one of the periodicals to which Shaw sent "Conductors and Organists."[4] The two essays published here, then, represent
some of the very earliest professional writing that Shaw did, apart from
the reviews that were in effect ghost-written for Vandeleur Lee.

Although this work from the late 1870s betrays a stylistic stiffness that contrasts with the true Shavian flexibility and colloquial force that characterize such later prose as the music criticism of 1889–94, we can see at the outset of Shaw's writing career much that finds expression in his more mature phases. The very title of "Unconscionable Abuses," for example, points toward Shaw's critical stance on hundreds of issues over the many years of his combative, world-bettering (and world-battering) life as a writer. The title would do well for a very high proportion of Shaw's music criticism. The real business of the critic, Shaw writes in his music column in *The World* in 1892, "is to find fault; to ask for more; to knock his head against stone walls, in the full assurance that three or four good heads will batter down any wall that stands across the world's path" (*Shaw's Music* 2:666). In a review of a "recital-lecture" in the following year, he apologizes to the lecturer for the attention he has just devoted to the defects of her performance, but adds that "if the musical lecture is going to become an institution, it is my business to pounce on its weak points, with a view to its improvement, and, finally, to such perfection as it is capable of" (*Shaw's Music* 3:58). This critical habit of pouncing on weak points, of finding fault, is evident in both of the early unpublished pieces, and all through Shaw's music criticism in *The Star*, *The World*, and elsewhere—to say nothing of his drama criticism and other writing.

Sometimes Shaw makes his fault-finding sound like a personal matter between him and guilty musicians. "I *hate* performers who debase great works of art: I long for their annihilation: if my criticisms were flaming thunderbolts, no prudent Life or Fire Insurance Company would entertain a proposal from any singer within my range," he proclaims in 1894 (*Shaw's Music* 3:224); and in the previous year: "I am by nature vindictive, and find myself not always proof against the temptation to pay off old scores against hardened sinners" (*Shaw's Music* 2:827). But in spite of this self-dramatization, Shaw's thunderbolts are designed for a more public, improving purpose. The intended function of Shaw's music criticism is signalled in a phrase in the opening sentence of the first of the two pieces published here. "There is no class of musicians which has enjoyed greater opportunities of advancing musical culture . . . than the organists." "Advancing musical culture"—that is what Shaw himself sets out to do in these two articles, and that is his continuing purpose as a critic. Like Matthew Arnold, Shaw attaches great importance to the cultural function of criticism at the present time, and beginning in the late 1870s, during Arnold's lifetime, Shaw as a critic seeks to provoke the English musical world into realizing its best self.

One way to advance musical culture is to make audiences more critical, so that they will no longer be satisfied with the second and third rate.

Both of these articles assume that contemporary audiences are in great need of such improvement. "Unconscionable Abuses" alludes to "an ignorant and deluded public," while "Conductors and Organists" asserts that "Ninety nine persons out of every hundred cannot tell whether a performance has been an interpretation of the composer or not." Similarly, the *Hornet* pieces speak of "the extraordinary gullibility of the world in matters musical" and "the critical incapacity of the great body of music-hunters" (*Shaw's Music* 1:139, 156). The later Shaw does not always take such a dim view of the musical public, but he does always wish to raise audiences' demands to the highest possible level, and he tries to achieve this by flamboyantly exposing the defects of what is currently available. If the public can become real critics, people who are able to *judge* the quality of what they are hearing, then there will be pressure for improvement on the part of those who are responsible for musical performances. And to Shaw throughout his life, the quality of musical taste and musical performance was an important element in determining the level of a whole civilization.

In addition to this emphasis on defects, there are a number of specific issues that one notices in these two early pieces because they are matters that recur in Shaw's music criticism over the years. Both of these articles refer to Wagner, who more than any other single composer (even Mozart) dominates Shaw's music criticism as a whole. In 1879 Shaw discusses Wagner's limitations as a conductor ("Conductors and Organists"), and his position as "the greatest of living composers" ("Unconscionable Abuses"). Another, very different kind of issue that links these early articles to Shaw's subsequent music criticism is the unconscionable abuse of substituting the cornet for the trumpet in orchestral performances. This deplorable "musical fraud" (*Shaw's Music* 1:323) is one that Shaw frequently complains about over the years, as he does about the practice of charging for programs at concerts; he devotes a whole article to this in 1885 (*Shaw's Music* 1:410–15). Other subjects in these two 1879 pieces to be found elsewhere in Shaw's music criticism include audiences' unjust demands for encores, and the inadequacy of dull organists as conductors: "Every contingent [in the orchestra] trained by a mere organist, to whom the Messiah is but a part of the drudgery of his professional routine," Shaw writes in an 1891 review of the Handel Festival, "is simply a nuisance on the Handel orchestra" (*Shaw's Music* 2:385). Here we have a recapitulation of the theme of "Conductors and Organists" written twelve years earlier.

And then there are hints in this 1879 writing of themes, attitudes, and qualities that permeate Shaw's later work beyond the music criticism. One attitude in these articles that connects with Shaw's whole way of looking at the world is the emphasis on a conductor's *leadership*. "A conductor may be said to have done his worst when, through laziness or exhaustion, he permits his orchestra to conduct him," we read in "Unconscionable Abuses";[5] and "Conductors and Organists" draws attention to the importance of "initiative impulse." Here we can see a very early expression of the interest in leadership that runs right through to *Why She Would Not* in 1950. Another characteristic Shavian attitude is the link in "Unconscionable Abuses" between art and economics, as in the ways in which makers of pianos, and publishers of songs, intrude non-artistic criteria into the selection of pieces for the concert hall—an analysis of financial pressures that draws a line from this essay to *Mrs Warren's Profession* and *Major Barbara*. Or take the comment in "Conductors and Organists" that the positive musical qualities of a conductor "are no guarantee of taste or culture, and it is quite possible that the conductor of genius may be an egotistical charlatan." Here we have a very early anticipation of paradoxes in such works as *The Doctor's Dilemma* and *Heartbreak House* ("People dont have their virtues and vices in sets: they have them anyhow: all mixed," Hesione explains to Ellie).[6] In the work of the twenty-three-year-old novice, there are many signs of what was to come during the subsequent seventy-one years of his writing career.

Conductors and Organists (1879)

[PROVENANCE: Unsigned holograph manuscript, in pencil, with ink revisions, undated, with note on verso of final leaf indicating submission to the Musical Times *on "17/2/79". British Library: Add. Mss. 50721A, folios 23a,b, 24a,b (a slip, with text to be inserted in 25a), 25a,b, 26 (a slip, with brief text on 26b for insertion in 25b), 27–29a,b.]*

There is no class of musicians which has enjoyed greater opportunities of advancing musical culture, and which has made less use of them, than the organists. Outside our great cities, music is almost entirely in their hands. The public are willing to accept their official connection with the church as a guarantee for their social respectability and professional skill. Their emoluments are too small to relieve them of the most practical incentive to activity in the secular branches of their art. They are experienced in choral singing; and the majority of them know enough of the dogmas of composition to produce an anthem culminating in a harmless fugue.[7] The amateur who desires to join a society for the practice of concerted music and the body of amateurs, who, having formed such a society, need a conductor, naturally seek their assistance. Thus appealed to, the organist takes one of two courses. If he be timid, or sluggish, he discourages the scheme by enumerating those hackneyed difficulties which can be shewn so plainly to be in the way, and which are never met there, by a determined workman. He then continues his Sunday services and Thursday evening practices, eking out his income by giving a few lessons in organ playing, of which he knows something, a great many in pianoforte, of which he does not know so much, and perhaps some dozens in singing, of which he knows nothing at all. If, on the contrary, he be ambitious and energetic, he appoints the earliest date possible for a meeting. But whichever course he may pursue, and however deeply he may mistrust the efficiency of the amateurs, no doubt of his own capacity for the post of conductor ever crosses his mind. He can read a score. He can beat time. Therefore he can conduct. Nobody disputes the conclusion until the more musical members of the new society begin to complain that the works "don't go". They are promptly silenced by the reply that the conductor knows more than they do, and that his way must be the proper way. Now suppose a Cambridge professor of mathematics were to argue in the same spirit, thus. I am familiar with conic sections. I am versed in the conditions of trajectory and in the laws of gravitation. There is no part of a loaded rifle, from the composition of its charge to the order of lever to which the spring of its lock belongs, which I cannot explain. Therefore I will go to Wimbledon and carry off the Queen's prize. Such a conclusion would not in truth be more absurd than that of the organist. But its reception would be very different, and for this reason. Everyone can tell whether a bullet hits the target or misses it. Ninety nine persons out of every hundred cannot tell whether a performance has been an interpretation of the composer or not. No one will entertain the pretensions of the mathematician if he shoots wide. Everyone will sooner think himself an ignoramus, or classical music an incomprehensible bore, than suspect that the respectable stick waver, conscientiously working his way through a collection of notes written down some years before by George Frederick Handel, is no more competent to drag the fire and colossal depth of the *Messiah* out of the mass of commonplace individualities depending on him, than Maelzel's little pendulum[8] would be if it were put in his place. There are few popular conceptions so vague and comprehensive as that of a musician. It recognises no distinction between the various developments of the art, or between faculty for music and the acquirements incidental to its pursuit. It combines all in the image of a man who can play the pianoforte, who can sing, who can "put a second"[9] to an air otherwise than by ear, who can find a mysterious interest in bands which play for three quarters of an hour without any vocal relief, and who permits his hair to exceed the length at which ordinary men are expected to get theirs cut.

In anyone who answers to this description, the public are ready to place implicit faith. He may break their voices, cripple their fingers, and make them the butts or plagues of their social circle, yet they continue to believe in him. So long as he professes musical omniscience, they have no misgivings save as to their noncapacity for understanding his art. Only when a professor of harmony refuses to teach singing, or a pianist admits his ignorance of the French horn, they venture to conclude that the honest man knows but little of his business. The organist has yet to be found who entertains the slightest diffidence of his ability to give instruction in every practical branch of music and consequently organists enjoy the entire confidence of their parishioners, which follows them unquestioning when they mount the conductors desk. To those who gain their knowledge of the great masters by using their own brains and hands, the superstition may seem the outcome of want of musical perception. More probably it arises from the disappointment of the effort to perceive what—thanks to the conductor—is not forthcoming.

There are few people who read Shakspere. There are millions who go to see Hamlet. There are very few indeed who read Sebastian Bach. There are thousands who go to hear the Passion music. Thus, to most of us, art comes from the stage and concert-room. We learn of Shakspere only that which the actor shews us, and of Bach, not even that which the conductor feels, but only as much as he can find an attitude to express. What must a man who seeks in this manner an insight into the grandeur of the "Passion" think when he hears (for instance) those abrupt outbursts of the Jewish rabble,[10] so full of nervous vigour, delivered in a conventionally religious fashion? Yet this is what must happen when the conductor is no more than a bookish organist, confident in acquirements which can only enable him to pronounce whether the parts are accurately sung, and the *fortes* and *pianos* duly observed. This satisfies his mind because it occupies his attention; and occasionally a massive pedal,[11] which impresses by its own power without his assistance[,] assures him that the work is producing an effect. Thus he follows where he should lead, placing himself in an attitude of appreciative comment instead of initiative impulse. His choir derive no impetus from him, yield to his inertia, and content themselves with keeping their places. The orchestra, who know his weakness as instinctively as a horse knows a timid rider, despise him and play carelessly and without combination. Finally the audience leaves, thoroughly fatigued, and more than ever convinced of the dullness of the classics.

It is necessary to anticipate here some questions which the foregoing arbitrary association of a particular defect with a particular class of musicians, will suggest. Why should an organist conduct less efficiently than anyone else? If conducting is not a special gift, how is it to be acquired, and if it is, why do we blame those who are not endowed with it? We will consider the last questions first. Conducting in its rarest perfection may undoubtedly be called a gift, because it depends on peculiarities of natural temperament. The born conductor may be recognised by his first beat. Instead of waiting, as some of our young novices do, in a spread eagle posture, until the expectancy of the performers is so exhausted as to render a crisp start impossible, he intuitively seizes the opportune moment, and a simultaneous attack instantly responds. Thenceforth he never relaxes his grip of the orchestra. He inspires and commands it. The strings follow him as though he were their direct motive power. The brass, who are ordinarily taking breath when they ought to be entering, come in promptly on the first of the bar, and even the instruments of percussion yield to the magnetic influence, and abate their usual quaver's delay. The licenses which such a conductor can take are inexplicable, and are seldom credited by those who have not experienced them. It is in the emergencies which arise in opera, that his peculiar powers are most strikingly exhibited. If a nervous vocalist omits a bar, the band omit it too, pulled over the gap, they scarcely know how. To players forced to depend on their parts and their own counting, this feat would be impossible. To those who obey a chief who has excited their susceptibility to the utmost it is easy enough, and seldom produces a perceptible hitch. Unfortunately for the credit of this rare power, it is not always associated with the higher moral and intellectual qualities. Those who possess it are bold, sanguine, quick to conceive, choleric and of marked individuality. They have what is called natural facility in music. But these qualities are no guaranties of taste or culture, and it is quite possible that the conductor of genius may be an egotistical charlatan, delighting to startle the multitude with pistol shots and stage thunder, ready for the most shocking excisions and interpolations, and reckless of the composer's intentions when it becomes expedient to violate them. He may be ignorant of "theory". Personally he is self confident, ungovernable, and often actuated more by impulse than principle. In his profession he is feared by some, mistrusted by others, and hated by all. They ridicule his affectation, point out that he is "no musician", declaim against his bad taste, and console themselves with stories of the discomfitures to which his ignorance has exposed him; but they will not take to heart the lesson he teaches them, that pure conducting is an art to which that knowledge of music which can be acquired critically by the eye and reason, stands in the relation of a perfectly dispensable adjunct. They will not learn it even from sources to which they may without humiliation accord respect. Yet they have, in London at least, ample opportunity for doing so. Very recently we have seen Herr Wagner and Massenet wield the white wand.[12] The time has happily arrived when Herr Wagner may be described in English as the greatest of living composers, without exciting derision. No one, whatever their opinion of M. Massenet may be, will be likely to claim for him as high a place. But on the platform, their positions were reversed. The Frenchman dashed away with his subordinates as confidently as though they had been keys under his fingers. The German paralysed them, and they loudly demonstrated their relief, when Herr Richter took his place. There is not the slightest foundation for the common assumption that ability to organise and conduct performances bears any direct ratio to depth of musical learning.

With regard to the question whether the art of conducting can be acquired, we believe that any musician of respectable parts can by practice, and the exercise of tact and determination, make an orchestra convey his own conception of a composition. The worth of that conception will of course determine the value of the result. The best practice is to be obtained with new works and players. A picked London orchestra, engaged to play a familiar symphony by an incompetent conductor towards whom they are well disposed, will certainly not break down. An amateur orchestra under similar circumstances will not get successfully through 20 bars. Therefore a man who desires to know whether he can conduct or not, will do well to work with players who are entirely dependent on him. It is fortunate that poverty generally forces a beginner to this course. Without the experience derived from it, he might find himself at the mercy of a single unreliable performer. A comparison of the various conductors at present before the public in London, would be invaluable to the metropolitan student. He would find exemplified the power of perseverance, a well established mutual understanding, and artistic devotion, to overcome natural inaptitude for the bâton. He would see the perfect discipline and mechanical perfection which can be commanded by cold autocracy. He would see more satisfactory results achieved by an exact knowledge of what an orchestra can be made to do, acted on with a curious mixture of temerity and nervous care. Nor would he miss specimens of the organist conductor casting a plague of dull feebleness over the most inspired works.

This term "organist-conductor" reminds us of the other question. Why should an organist be specially inefficient as a conductor? We do not know why he should be; but we believe that he is so because of the narrowness of his musical training. In London, where organists are exposed so largely to the influence of secular music, there are brilliant instances of the contrary. But the average provincial and suburban organist is often the least enlightened musician in his parish. He stagnates in a corner of his art to the level of which and of himself he debases all music. In this corner, besides a vast heap of scholarly inanity, are some noble works; immortal choruses and fugues by Handel and Bach, and grand hymns of national growth stamped with no man's manner. But all masterpieces are produced by many sided men, and they can never be interpreted by a one sided agent. This onesidedness is the pride of the organist. He considers dramatic music as out of his province, and places himself in jealous antagonism to opera, which is the dictionary of music, and which alone develops the versatility which we have qualified as essential. He commonly believes that Donizetti wrote his choruses in consecutive fifths[13] and was ignorant of the correct resolution of the dominant seventh. He will admit that "Il Trovatore" is not after his fashion, and would not undertake to conduct it. But when the Messiah is mooted, he is ready to take the baton with perfect confidence. Yet it is certain that a man who cannot grapple with "Di quella pira", must necessarily be unable for "He trusted in God, that he would deliver him", which is more intensely dramatic, and demands more concentrated expression than anything which Italian opera contains.[14] Similarly, he repudiates dance music, but allows the claims of symphony, apparently thinking that a ballet by Meyerbeer is more recondite than a scherzo by Beethoven. His extreme concession to progress and the lyric drama is a tolerant admiration of "Tannhauser", wherein he finds good twelve part counterpoint, instead of the thirds and sixths which he despises. Executively, he has few resources. He has no need to conduct his choir. He "keeps them together" by the use of a powerful engine with which he can overwhelm them. They are usually lagging half a bar behind him. If they shew a disposition to sing with spirit, he quells it by following them at the same distance. His readiness in accommodating clerks who intone at a variable pitch, and whom he can scarcely hear from the organ loft, is worse than useless outside the church, as it confirms his habit of waiting and adapting himself instead of commanding. It is not to be wondered at, that when he essays to conduct, he proves a millstone on the necks of his forces. Something resembling an awkward service is the most he can achieve. His ideas of orchestral effect are based on the stop of his organ. The coarsest playing is as remote from what he is thinking of as the most refined, and the trombones and trumpets take advantage of this without mercy. Still he cannot be made to see where the radical fault lies.

That there is a new race of organists springing up through the country, we are glad to believe. But the danger yet exists, that these too may fancy that the power to conduct is acquired as a matter of course with the classification of chords and the doctrine of fugue. We need not say that we have no wish to discourage technical studies; but we are desirous to point out that proficiency in these has never made a conductor, however greatly it may [have] assisted those who were already made. We would also warn the beginner against that want of independence which often cloaks itself under the reverence due to a composer; and that weakness which fears to offend the vanity of individuals. A conductor who is not the master is the laughing stock. If he fears to obtrude himself into the music he will express neither himself nor the composer, like some artists of great technical skill who of a mistaken faithfulness have succeeded in concealing their own individuality with no better result than to make themselves and the music uninteresting. Above all, let him constantly remember the dignity of his position, as the most responsible of interpreters, and the one who of all others exercises the most direct influence in bringing home to the people the masterpieces of art.

Unconscionable Abuses (1879)

[PROVENANCE: Unsigned holograph manuscript, dated "3/10/79" on verso of final leaf. British Library: Add. Mss. 50693, folios 2–45.]

By unconscionable abuses is here meant all those sins of commission or omission which are common in musical performances in this country, and which are due to laxity of conscience on the part of the undertaker, the conductor, the artists, and the audience. An enumeration of them, though unfortunately not novel, may be useful to remind those who have through custom lost all resentment at traditional vices, how greatly our concerts and operas might be improved by a trifling exercise of vigilance and firmness.

The conductor is directly or indirectly responsible for every abuse which is practised by those under his command. However, as he cannot exercise upon all occasions the absolute authority which should appertain to him, no more will be charged on him than he can expediently answer for. He is, for instance, undeniably accountable for correctness in the details of the orchestra, especially in London, where, with a body of players to the number of seventy or more, there can be no excuse on the score of economy for putting upon one man the work that should properly be done by two.

There is an instrument, the cymbal, formerly little used except in what was called Turkish music, but very extensively employed of late in scores of the modern school of Berlioz and Wagner, the effect of which, when the brass plates of which it consists are made to impinge delicately on one another, is peculiar; and when they are clashed together, extraordinarily brilliant and exciting. A good instance of the latter method of using them may be found in the overture to Tannhauser, in which four successive clashes mark the climax. We will suppose that a musician, familiar with the work, is waiting breathlessly in an English concert room for this exultant clamour, satisfied with the execution so far, and almost wishing to have the cymbals in his own hands in order to secure the anticipated effect. When the beat arrives, the musician sympathetically snaps his teeth. Then he hears an execrable noise, as though the door of a pantry, the shelves of which were occupied by empty bottles, has been slammed. His disconcertment is as abrupt as that of the traveller on a dark staircase who lifts his foot for a step more than exists in the flight. The explanation is not recondite. One cymbal has been fastened on a military drum, and merely slapped by the drummer, whose right hand and half his attention is occupied by his drumstick. This arrangement spoils the performance, but it saves the conductor the trouble of insisting that the player shall detach his instrument, stand apart from his drum, and discharge his duty in the manner contemplated by the composer.[15]

Far less [in]tolerable than the cymbal abuse, but requiring firmness as well as attention to stamp out, is that of the substitution of the cornet a pistons for the trumpet. This practice has wrought the great evil of bringing the trumpet into disuse, and the minor one of bringing the cornet into disrepute with good musicians. The former is the result of the greater ease with which the cornet can be played, a consideration which would equally justify the substitution of euphoniums for horns, ocarinas for flutes, or English concertinas for clarinets. The disadvantage at which the cornet is placed by its usurpation depends on the fact that whereas its bright timbre in florid passages, and its soft tone (which popular performers rarely have the self denial and good sense to rely on) in sentimental melodies, are well worthy of employment in serious scores; in the fanfares and penetrating held notes written for the trumpet, it is wholly detestable. That it is a degree less odious in combination with the trombones may be grudgingly admitted; but even in this case it produces an effect different to that aimed at by the composers who have written for the trumpet. Yet this abuse has become so firmly rooted that many professors of the cornet, and even some musicians, regard a demand for trumpets as a proof of innocence in the practical working of the orchestra. Conductors profess to discourage the substitution as much as possible, but allege that trumpet players are very scarce. Thus it would appear that the slackness of conductors has rendered a mastery of the old instrument not worth the trouble it costs, so that they cannot procure its services now that they have awakened to the offensive inadequacy of its representative. But this is not really the case. It is true that if a conductor engage an orchestra in London, stipulating expressly that he shall have two trumpets, no difficulty is ever raised; but when the band assembles, there are the cornets. Few men care to push their authority so far as to insist on the withdrawal of the delinquents, and maim the rehearsal by the omission of their parts. Nothing short of this, however, will extirpate the abuse. Those conductors of whom it is known that they are neither indifferent on the point, nor to be trifled with with impunity, are never troubled by the improper appearance of a cornet, or the special pleading which begins with a bold assertion that the cornet is the proper instrument, and ends with the excuse that the part is too high for the trumpet at modern pitch. Those who are young at the *batôn*, or perhaps too nervously polite to combat the manifold evasions which bandsmen are prone to attempt, will find that firmness is the best policy in this matter. In one of Shakspere's histories a lame beggar is represented displaying perfect locomotive powers at sight of the beadle's whip.[16] In much the same fashion will an artist who has just superciliously informed an untried conductor that the cornet is "his instrument", sometimes develop into a competent trumpeter when he is made to understand that in no other capacity will his presence be tolerated. Let the demand be inexorable, and the supply will be forthcoming. However, here arises, according to some authorities, a further difficulty. They grant that the men can use the trumpet, but they prefer to dispense with it on the ground that the results are usually bad, and that good cornet playing is better than villainous trumpet playing. If this were true, it would only be so because the disuse of the instrument had prevented its efficient cultivation; and the evil would quickly remedy itself. But experience proves that it is not true. Care is a necessity in trumpet playing; and for this reason, even without calculating the natural superiority of the tone, it gives better results in the full proportion of the greater trouble. Again, we have good trumpeters; but good players of the cornet eschew orchestras, and become heroes of military or seaside bands, where solos in operatic selections, or that ingenious double-tonguing torture, the *staccato* polka, obtain enthusiastic recognition. Yet the school of orchestration crowned by Beethoven, which has for many years been the staple of all good instrumental concerts, has done little to deserve the gratitude of trumpet players. Whilst the horn and bassoon were brought into a beautiful and fanciful prominence, the trumpet lost the proud position accorded to it by Purcell, Bach, and Handel; and the parts written for it were scarcely worth playing for their own sakes until Meyerbeer came upon the scene; and with him the cornet a pistons, for which he wrote appreciatively. Nowadays a trumpet is like the player[']s best hat, only produced on solemn occasions, such as a performance of the ninth symphony, or the like. Modern composers write important trumpet parts with a zeal which consists in equal proportions of love for the instrument and hatred for its rival; and the services of Mr Harper[17] are as indispensable to a performance of a concerto by M. Saint Saens, as to the *Yorkshire Feast,* or "the trumpet shall sound".[18] Another abuse which occurs in the same ill regulated family is the desuetude of the bass slide trombone and the alto trombone, both of which are frequently supplanted by tenors; a proceeding quite comparable to relegating the viola and double bass parts to violoncellos, which, nevertheless, few conductors would care to attempt, except perhaps with a second rate English opera troupe in the provinces. Some composers, by writing for three tenor trombones (perhaps making a virtue of necessity) have seemed to undervalue the distinction between the three varieties; but the individuality of the alto is as marked as that of any other instrument in the orchestra; and nothing can supply the place of the bass trombone. With reference to the latter, a vulgar error, which even Berlioz has helped to spread, prevails amongst those who know no more of the conditions of wind instruments than the novelists who make merry over the anomaly of the smallest boy in a horde of itinerant musicians being entrusted with the bassoon. (It will of course be understood that in novelistic nomenclature any very large brass instrument, such as the contrabass helicon, or the bombardon, is a bassoon). The capacity of the tube is supposed to necessitate such an expenditure of breath on the part of the player, that a sustained performance is impossible. Berlioz[19] expressly warns the composer that notes of moderate duration only, and those separated by rests sufficient for breathing, must be written for the bass trombone, the player of which must, moreover, be a robust man. He seems to have supposed—and the same erroneous supposition is at the root of the inferiority of the hard brass, to the horn and other bands in our orchestras—that the player[']s function was to fill the tube with air from his lungs, instead of to set up and maintain vibration in the air already contained in it. There is scarcely a "German band" in our streets in which may not be found an *improvisatore*[20] of tonic and dominant roots, who plays the bass trombone or the bombardon for half an hour without resting, and who expends at least thrice as much breath on every note as would suffice a fine player for an entire bar. An amateur of this instrument, if he can induce a deaf friend to play dance tunes on the pianoforte, will accompany them in an uninterrupted series of rattling barks for several hours at a time. Nor need he be at all a robust man. The larger a brass instrument, the easier it is to play. Equally natural adaptation for "lipping" being granted in the performers, brass contrabasses of any family give the least trouble; trumpets the most. The cornet is easier than the trumpet; but the forgotten cornetto defies all ordinary lips. Hence the dictum of Berlioz cannot be accepted as an excuse for the absence of the bass trombone, and the conductor who dispenses with it may be fairly charged with a preventible abuse. Even that form of the instrument which is manipulated by valves, and which appears often at St James's Hall and elsewhere, ought to be strongly discouraged. Pistons have so made their way, and are undeniably so convenient, that the questionably superior open horn can no longer be reasonably insisted on; but in the trumpet and trombone, where the perfect principle of the slide is available, a stand should be made against the distorted wind ways of the valve mechanism. However, if conductors are particular in other respects, they may be pardoned for submitting to valves, or, in the case of the contrafagotto,[21] to the substitution of an ophicleide, or even a tuba.

Other abuses are those which are practised with transposed parts, by playing them upon instruments whose pitch is not that specified by the composer. Clarinets in various keys differ so markedly, that they are, in effect, distinct instruments. Unfortunately the limits assigned to them in the theorist's text books are so extended in the tradesman's catalogues, that almost any passage within their compass, short of an unbroken chromatic scale, can now be achieved in all keys, and thus the substitution of the clarinet in *A for that in C, producing an entirely different effect, is by no means impossible, and is often done to save the transport of an extra instrument or two. The conductor will need to be constantly on the alert to baffle the wiles of players who, by experience in the difficulties raised by the common practice of transposing vocal music for the convenience of singers, have become expert in every species of makeshift for achieving the unplayable.

Whilst checking the misdeeds of his subordinates, the conductor should not permit his own conscience to be too easily silenced. How often do conductors make any effort to secure basset horns, English horns, or bass clarinets; all exceptionally used instruments, but by no means obsolete, as ma[n]y text book compilers insist on calling them? Modern composers are slowly forcing them into use, but they are frequently treated as though they were as unattainable as the *viole d'amore*, in *Les Huguenots*. Nevertheless, the latter case is different, as players cannot be found; whereas, in the former, a little importunity will surely discover competent professors.

A conductor may be said to have done his worst when, through laziness or exhaustion, he permits his orchestra to conduct him. This is invariably occurring when there is no definite beat at the subordinate divisions of the bar. Many chiefs of undeniable ability consider themselves at liberty, as soon as they have started the quick movement of a symphony, to sit down, poise the *batôn* horizontally, and duck the point about an inch at *one*.[22] Doubtless they flatter themselves that they are leading by this method, and are satisfied with the consciousness that they can at any moment resume a more energetic sway. An informed listener will hear plainly enough that they are following, and will not be disposed to accept potential conducting in lieu of actual precision. It will be observed that all our conductors who are remarkable for thorough command of their orchestra, and who stamp the performances they direct with their own individuality[,] beat distinctly for every accent, and are not afraid of being deemed pedantic for giving, when the speed or construction of the movement renders it desirable, a separate beat for each count in a bar.

* ? of B♭ for A & C[.] [Marginal note by Shaw, with *his* asterisk inserted in text.]

We are only beginning to outlive the fertile crop of abuses sewn [sown] of the vanity, and manured by the ignorance of singers. The disfigurement of songs by interpolated passages of display is still so common, that even the most unpardonable instances escape critical reprobation, except they happen to be ill executed, which is quite a different question. In Mozart's exquisite air from the *Figaro*, "Deh vieni non tardar", most public singers introduce a florid cadenza bringing the voice up to B♭ (much easier to sing, be it observed, than the notes written by the composer), and for this barbarism no critic seems to have a word of reprehension. The same licence is taken with the sacred airs of Handel, and no doubt the songs of Beethoven would be similarly treated if the culprits had sufficient enterprise to make them known to the public. Fortunately, excitable concert goers, well acquainted with the original, occasionally receive the offence with a burst of indignant sibillation; and a custom instituted to catch applause, rapidly succumbs to the danger of provoking a hiss. Whether from this reason, or in consequence of the spread of culture amongst musicians, the practice has of late lost the countenance of the better class of artists. But offenders are still numerous, and it is much to be desired that they would confine themselves to "O luce di quest' anima"[23] and similar vehicles for the displays which constitute their stock in trade. In opera, abuses of a graver complexion exist. Attached to most Italian companies, is to be found a peculiar species of parasite, usually a broken singer or unsuccessful singing master, who officiates on emergencies as accompanyist, chorus grinder, prompter, or in any other capacity in which he can induce the minor artists to tolerate him. He is often an amiable and well intentioned man; but he is a propagandist of superstitions by which he will sometimes discredit in a week the principles which a good master has spent years in impressing on a pupil. For instance, all German music, according to him, is unsingable. *Don Giovanni* is one of the worst operas ever written; *Un Ballo in Maschera* by far the best.[24] A voice cannot be heard in a theatre unless it is produced with the utmost force on the syllable *i* (in English, *ee*) or some other hard and destructive sound. An opera voice is one which has survived five years['] teaching on this system. Contraltos must force their chest register to the top of their compass; must recognise no tone except brawling; and must transpose concerted light soprano passages, such as occur in the part of the page in *Les Huguenots*, a third, a sixth, or if possible an octave down. A singer who acquires the smallest technical knowledge, even so much as is required in order to read music, ceases to be an artist. A singer learns his or her business once and for all before going on the stage, and never practices subsequently. No great artist ever practises *solfeggi*[25] in private. No principal acquainted with the stage ever dreams of singing whilst their part coincides with one sung by the chorus. There is, literally, a voice in the head, immediately behind the frontal sinus; another in the throat; and a third beneath the breast bone. And so forth. The influence of such an authority—for his nationality so accredits him to many ill instructed persons—cannot fail to be most pernicious on young artists, newly come, as the fashion is nowadays, to learn their business on the stage. Lest they should be thought ignorant of theatrical usage, even the better informed among them too readily adopt the essentially unconscionable abuses recommended by him, and alter their music, omit their parts in the *ensembles,* and sacrifice all their own taste and their master's precepts to the insatiable appetite of their perverter for screaming and brawling. He has, by his own account, taught all the artists in the theatre, and his victims foolishly believe that so successful a teacher cannot err. They do not know that this species of misrepresentation is epidemic amongst all theatrical officials who are neither players nor manual labourers. Most people are acquainted with the typical retired manageress, who, honest on all other topics, yet cannot hear the celebrities of her profession mentioned without claiming for her instruction a share in the credit of their success.

Before quitting the subject of the Italian operatic parasite, the humiliating fact must be recorded, that not a few of his most senseless dogmas are often thoughtlessly repeated, and sometimes actually adopted, by men whose eminence gives authority to their lightest musical opinions.

Among the most honest and cultivated class of musical executants may be reckoned the pianists and violinists who expound the concertos and sonatas of the great masters from our concert platforms. As editors, some of them have taken liberties which may fairly be described as outrageous with venerable works; and in executing music before the public from memory, they occasionally vamp[26] a bar, or, more frequently, indulge in violations of *tempo* which are sometimes pushed so far as to affect the rhythm. Violinists too, have been guilty of intentionally playing a shade sharp in order to gain prominence in the *tuttis*[27] of a concerto. That the rank and file of the orchestra are addicted to evasions of their strict duty to the composer, has been already implied by the record of abuses due to the conductor's negligent supervision. But it should in fairness be stated that despite the characteristic perversity of orchestral players, and their proneness, when confronted with a new score, to declare at once that it cannot be executed, and to laugh disrespectfully at its novelties; the good humour and fertility of resource shown by them in the face of the most awkward transpositions and the most unexpected emergencies, render an orchestra the most amenable, as it is the grandest instrument which a master is privileged to play upon. However, they may with advantage be reminded that private conversations are out of place during rests in the performance; and that no matter how exhilarating may be the consciousness of having conquered some eccentric passage by Lizst, or come in at the death with the triplets in the bridal prelude to the third act of *Lohengrin,* it is not dignified to turn round to [a] neighbour and challenge his applause by a grin of self-congratulation.

So far, the backslidings of instrumentalists are not very serious. But they share with vocalists the blame of participation in abuses which, being lucrative, do not succumb without a pertinacious struggle to the advance of the public taste. All extraneous profits are injurious to professional and artistic integrity, and are the origin of some of the darkest blots on commercial morality. Unhappily, commissions are to be earned at every turn in the musical profession: commissions which come directly out of the pocket of the public in large sums when they purchase instruments, and indirectly in fractional amounts when they pay for admission to concerts. So monstrous are the charges made for grand pianofortes, that some makers can not only afford to give commissions on the sale of a single instrument amounting to upwards of a hundred guineas, but to divert the public patronage of eminent players from all rivals, however superior in merit, who cannot afford to outbid them either in direct retaining fees, or the many conveniences which their business enables them to offer to professional musicians. Hence the frequent appearance at concerts, of pianofortes which the players do not advance their reputations by condescending to use. The public, who have a right to expect that the finest instruments will be procured for their entertainment, are put off with an advertisement of the most generous maker; necessarily the maker who overcharges them most. It has been said, with some plausibility, that dealings in horses, pianofortes, and theatres, are not controlled by conscientious considerations. In some countries this would appear to be true. Stuttgart, for instance, is a town where materials for pianoforte manufacture are cheap. But the professional discount allowed is paltry, and sounds modest even if stated in shillings. Materials are dearer in America, where magnificent percentages are showered on successful agents. The public, however, pay to the Yankee maker four times as much as to the German, from whom they could obtain an instrument which would suit them quite as well as the more expensive one, and probably preserve its original quality of tone much longer. Good foreign makers will not trouble themself to enter into this undignified contest of percentages; and even the American makers for a long time held aloof, and professed themselves indifferent to the custom of a country where a few makers, considerably behind their time in technical excellence, contrived to maintain a policy of exclusion by engaging the patronage of every celebrated player, and securing in various ways a cold reception for enterprising rivals. The artist cannot be held blameless in this matter. No sophistry—and all that is advanced amounts merely to the plea that the practice is general—will justify an artist in making his art a cloak for advertisement, and receiving in return material gratification, whether pecuniary or otherwise, from tradesmen. Let him play the instrument he likes best; but let him not sell it; for this will end in his playing, not the pianoforte he likes best, but that which he makes most by selling. He is under quite enough obligation when he is supplied with instruments for public and private use, gratuitously.

That form of the advertisement abuse which audiences most readily feel and resent, is the crowding of programmes with songs which are sung, without regard to their merit as compositions or their interest as ballads, because the singer is paid a royalty of from threepence to sixpence on each copy sold. Amateurs for the most part, have not the slightest power of originating an interpretation of any piece of music. They must hear it played or sung before they can make anything of it. For this reason, any ballad, however worthless it may be, will be bought if it is heard in public; whilst without this advantage, a good song will not become known for a long time. Singers, song makers, and sellers know this, and finding it possible by combination to turn it to account in obtaining money for rubbish, they combine, and share the profits. The royalty system once established, composers and scrupulous artists are forced to adopt it, on pain of serious pecuniary loss, and the unpopularity which attends those who venture to be better than their neighbours. Singers in particular, though they may make a stand at first, soon find themselves forced by the dearth of good songs to sing flimsy ballads, and they naturally do not see any useful reason for refusing eagerly proffered payment for the unpleasant task. A market is made for pianoforte pieces in the same way; and the system, in its completeness, results in the annual issue in England of many tons of inane compilations which are purchased at about fifty times their intrinsic value (they have none other) by an ignorant and deluded public.

It must not be supposed that the public have no offences against honesty and good taste to account for. The theory that music has a depraving effect on morals has now been abandoned to the old women of both sexes. Yet people do things openly in a concert room that would consign them to the hands of the police if attempted elsewhere. There is certainly no sane and respectable man who would demand a second bun *gratis* from a confectioner, on the plea that the first was a very nice one. Yet hundreds of persons of unimpeachable character, having entered into a bargain that they shall hear so many songs in return for so much money, will, if the contractor supply the best artists, enforce by clamour a repetition of the entertainment without offering a farthing in return. That this way of regarding the encore system is not merely jocular, is proved by the fact that some of the greatest ballad singers calculate their terms by the number of times they sing, and stipulate expressly that encores shall be paid for as though they were mentioned in the programme. Encores are also inconvenient, in consequence of the length to which they prolong concerts; and they are aesthetically barbarous, because they destroy the balance of any extensive work of art, such as an opera or oratorio, when they cause a repetition not foreseen by the composer. If managers, instead of a feeble request that, owing to the length of the performance, redemands might be refrained from, would post up placards in prominent positions with the inscription Those who encore are thieves, fools, and Philistines, many worthy persons would feel hurt; but the nuisance would probably be checked. A similar plan might be employed to impress the many who walk into a theatre or concert room after the overture has begun; converse during all music that is not vocal; and leave before the performance is over; that their conduct causes extreme annoyance to every musician present, and is at once a distraction and an insult to the executants. It is painful to see a stall holder at the opera hissed by a shilling gallery, for behaving as though the entry of the statue in Don Giovanni, with the accompanying reduction of light, were a signal to rise, put on outer garments, and discuss the merits of the singers or the chances of getting a cab.

Since so much consideration is necessary on the part of the audience, it is proper that a certain amount should be extended to them in arranging the details of the auditorium. Unfortunately, their first necessity is taken advantage of for purposes of extortion, instead of being ministered to at a fair price. The use of a programme should be included in the charge for admission, as it is at some of the theatres. If it be charged for, no more than a penny should be demanded. Since there are a large class of amateurs who like "analytical" programmes, let some be provided for their instruction. But let the adept, to whom these volumes are an impertinence, and the uninitiated, to whom they are unintelligible, be enabled to obtain a simple list for an inconsiderable sum, and not be forced to pay fifty percent on the price of admission for a budget of information which they do not need. Some of our musical societies issue programmes at a shilling: the price of admission. This charge for a book which is but the ordinary sixpenny one extravagantly spaced, is excessive, but not more so than the eighteenpenny operatic *libretto*, which is eagerly offered for a shilling outside the theatre, and which should be obtainable in the stalls for twopence. If this were the case, the number sold would probably be multiplied sufficiently to make the reduction remunerative as well as honest; and few persons would take the trouble to preserve their *libretti*, or borrow them from friends, as they take care to do at present. Of late an attempt has been made to give the purchaser some additional value for his money by the insertion of transcriptions of the music for the pianoforte; but these, like the analytical programmes, are open to the objection that many persons do not desire them, and should therefore not be compelled to pay for them on pain of remaining unenlightened as to the plot of the opera. On the same principle, a charge of half a crown might be justified by the addition of excerpts from the full score, which few even of the musical amateurs present would be able to follow. Such a volume would at least look more respectable than the common "authorised version", for which in the case of the older operas there is no copyright, and which in some instances has not even the excuse of adaptation to the notes to extenuate its literary demerits.

Managers, it is to be feared, sometimes commit graver sins than the sanctioning of small extortions in the auditorium. It is evident that they sometimes accept payment for permitting a singer to perform; for houses are occasionally packed to welcome individuals whose appearance can be accounted for on no other hypothesis. This is the most directly immoral action of which a manager can be guilty. If the performance be a successful one, the singer is robbed. If it be a failure, the public are defrauded. In either case, whether from the point of view of the good faith of trade, or that of artistic propriety, the transaction is utterly and indefensibly corrupt.

When from the abuses which can be imputed to some special department in the organisation of musical entertainments, the attention is led to those of which the blame is common to all who omit to protest against them, including the public; a lamentably backward condition of taste becomes apparent. The drama in England has happily emerged from the period when *Coriolanus* was advertised as "a tragedy by David Garrick Esq.". The omission of the last act of *The Merchant of Venice* is no longer a matter of course; and a German actor is said to be in the habit of confounding stage managers by requests for the restoration of Fortinbras to the representation of *Hamlet*. Even Colley Cibber's Richard has suffered Shaksperian interpolation at the hands of ungrateful tragedians.[28] Effete conventionalisms are disappearing, not before carelessness, but before a broader culture. Plays are carefully cast throughout; completeness in detail is insisted on; and actors are not esteemed according to the effectiveness with which they make "points".

To walk from a theatre into an opera house is to step back fifty years of civilization. Here the musical Cibber is at work cutting, transposing, interpolating; and supplying the scores of Mozart and Beethoven with trombone parts. Conventions languish because they are troublesome to learn, but are not replaced by new methods. The chief beauties looked for in the *Zauberflöte*, are F in altissimo for the soprano, and E below the lines for the basso. Young amateurs listen with delight, not to Rossini, or *Otello*, but to Signor Soandso's *ut de poitrine*;[29] just as their fathers sat out a long play in order to hear Kean decree the doom of Buckingham.[30] The beautiful finale of *Don Giovanni* succeeds to the oblivion of the last act of the *Merchant of Venice,* in order that the curtain may descend, amidst the only page of operatic music that is awful without being grotesque, on coloured fires and an obscene crew of imps with masks borrowed from the pantomime. The last fragments of the concluding act of *Les Huguenots* have vanished; and there is little doubt that, had the *Messiah* been written for the theatre, it would now be the custom to finish with the Hallelujah chorus. The star system is in operation, to the detriment of the ensemble. Musical and scenic details are capriciously neglected. Bells properly tuned astonish by their rarity. Papageno's glockenspiel is commonly in a deplorable state of cracked tone and flat pitch. As Richard III once figured in the slashed trunks and doublet of an era which he never lived to see; his halberdiers now appear in the train of Queen Anne as she goes a hunting in Richmond Park with the Lady Henrietta.[31] Bands on the stage afford opportunities of judging, from direct comparison, between the French and Philharmonic diapasons.[32] There is a constant tendency to curtail, which leaves, after its first season, little in an opera except that which the public would detect and resent the excision of. The enterprise that might restore the discarded numbers of *Don Giovanni,* is perverted to mutilate *Faust* and *Carmen.*

The root of most of these sins of omission is laziness complying with custom. The excuse offered is, that the public do not know the fraud that is practised on them, and that therefore it would be a loss of labour to correct it. The many who sincerely entertain this belief, reason unsoundly. The more ignorant the public are, the more completely must they depend on the performance for their knowledge of a composition; and therefore the greater the necessity that no factor essential to the most perfect effect be omitted. To cite one of the cases on which we have dwelt, do five per cent of any miscellaneous audience know the difference between a trumpet and cornet; or between the fine round tone of a trombone which is played, and the coarse bark of that which is only blown into? No. And therefore they lay the bad effect, which they feel quite as keenly as the technical musician, to the charge of the composer and the art of music generally. They know music only as they hear it played, not as the composer intended it to be played; and for their sake especially ought the difference to be reduced to a minimum. When we smile pityingly on the young lady who thinks Wagner noisy, Beethoven heavy, and Rossini vulgar; we forget that, as these composers have been interpreted for her, her judgment may be perfectly correct. It can scarcely be too much insisted on that it is for the inadept mob that fine execution must be provided. Hamlet, badly acted, is the most intolerable of dramas. The heroic style in painting, in the hands of a mediocre artist,

is the least interesting of all styles. Alike in music, a symphony by Beethoven badly rendered, or one by Mozart not exceedingly well rendered, is a
dull and disappointing infliction, which destroys the credit of the great
masters with the many who have been in every age the true supporters of
genius. In vain do foolish enthusiasts for art clamour to the public that
music should be a superstition; and that the concert room should be full
when the name of Beethoven is in the programme. Though ten greater
names (if such existed) were there; yet, if the spirit of the master be
absent from the performance, the room will be empty. Most of the nonsense which has been written comparing the people to swine, and the
classics to pearls,[33] might have been spared had its authors conceived
that music is to the hearers as it is rendered, not as it was written. The
least intelligent man who is susceptible of a desire to enter a concert hall,
feels that a bad reading and a fine performance of a great work are not
the same thing; and testifies his preference by the heartiness of his
applause.

A considerable addition to this long, but far from complete chapter of
abuses, might be made by including musical criticism in its indictment.
Unhappily, such addition would be superfluous, for criticism as yet lags
in the rear of musical progress. When it takes its proper place in the van,
it will possibly be above reproach. At present it helps no reform, since,
either from ignorance, carelessness, or a false conception of dignity such
as Macaulay[34] ridiculed in our old fashioned histories, it omits all notice
of those neglected details which mar our public performances, and
which by incessantly harping on, it might make our audiences aware of.
This done, the remedy would follow, and the ordinary critique might
cease to exhibit the vapidity which its conventional uselessness entails.
Some of the most practical critiscism of the day comes from serio-comic
writers, who, though obviously ignorant of music, yet find facetious
material in such scraps of technical information as they can extract from
acquaintances in the orchestra; and by turning them to account, sometimes do good service in matters which are held beneath the notice of the
ponderous barrenness or flimsy platitude which passes for critiscism in
more respectable quarters.[35]

Notes

1. Bernard Shaw, *The Diaries 1885–1897*, ed. Stanley Weintraub (University Park: Penn State University Press, 1986), p. 30.

2. *Shaw's Music*, ed. Dan H. Laurence (London: Max Reinhardt, 1981), 3:343. Subsequent references to *Shaw's Music* are in the text.

3. *Collected Letters 1874–1897*, ed. Dan H. Laurence (New York: Dodd, Mead, 1965), p. 21.

4. Shaw's manuscripts record the names of periodicals to which he submitted the articles.

5. Cf. Shaw's praise in 1885 for Carl Rosa, who "conducted the performance instead of allowing the performance to conduct him" (*Shaw's Music*, 1:262).

6. *Collected Plays with Their Prefaces*, ed. Dan H. Laurence (London: Max Reinhardt, 1970–74), 5:85.

7. In the latter part of the nineteenth century, according to the *New Grove Dictionary of Music and Musicians*, many younger composers of anthems (choral settings of religious or moral texts in English, generally designed for liturgical performance) "fell too easily under the saccharine influence of Spohr, Gounod and Mendelssohn."

8. A metronome. The instrument was developed around 1815, its invention generally (although erroneously) ascribed to Johann Nepomuk Maelzel (1772–1838), who usurped the principle from a Dutch mechanician, Dietrich Winkel (1780–1826).

9. That is, put a second line to a melody.

10. In Bach's *St. Matthew Passion* and *St. John Passion*.

11. The imposing effect an organist can achieve by pressing the foot pedals, or "pedal point," the device of holding on a bass note through a passage including some chords of which it does not form a part (*Oxford Companion to Music*).

12. Richard Wagner and Hans Richter, his associate and a leading Wagnerian conductor, conducted eight concerts at the Albert Hall in London in May 1877. Shaw's review in *The Hornet* (*Shaw's Music*, 1:126) makes a similar observation about the relative merits of the two men as conductors. Jules Massenet, the French composer, conducted some of his own works at the Crystal Palace in Sydenham on 4 May 1878.

13. A consecutive interval is an interval that occurs between the same two parts in two consecutive chords; in "traditional harmonic teaching there are two 'forbidden' consecutive intervals, the fifth and the octave" (*Oxford Companion to Music*).

14. The first is in Verdi's *Il Trovatore*, the second in Handel's *Messiah*.

15. Jacques Barzun informs me that "this practice is excoriated in Berlioz's *Treatise on Instrumentation and Orchestration* (1843) and repeatedly in his reviews. But the drum to which the cymbal is fastened is the bass drum. The 'military drum' is properly the side drum (snare drum), which is too small to have a cymbal attached and which is carried by the drummer with its surface horizontal. The bass drum stands vertical on its side, to which the cymbal is fixed. Shaw had probably seen military *bands*, of which the bass drum forms part, sometimes being carried when on parade." See also footnote 8 to Dr. Barzun's introduction to "A Reminiscence of Hector Berlioz," page 85.

16. *Henry VI, Part II*.

17. Thomas Harper Jr. (1816–98) was a noted English trumpeter and teacher.

18. That is, contemporary music, by Camille Saint-Saëns (1835–1921), or music of the seventeenth and early eighteenth centuries: the *Yorkshire Feast* by Henry Purcell (1659–95) or Handel's *Messiah*.

19. In his *Treatise on Instrumentation*.

20. One who composes music extempore (Ital.).

21. Double bassoon (Ital.).

22. That is, they fail to conduct every beat vigorously. Instead, they dip the point of the *batôn* (slightly) at the first beat of each bar, thus signaling only the downbeat.

23. An aria in Donizetti's *Linda di Chamounix*.

24. Shaw's own view, expressed in his music criticism, is that German music such as

Wagner's is more singable than Italian music such as Verdi's; that Mozart's *Don Giovanni* is the best opera ever written; and that Verdi's *Un Ballo in Maschera* "consists mainly of a cloying succession of arias inadequately relieved by a very small proportion of concerted pieces" (1877 review, *Shaw's Music*, 1:124).

25. A type of vocal exercise (Ital. pl. of *solfeggio*).

26. Improvise an accompaniment.

27. Passages for the whole orchestra (Ital. *tutti*).

28. Although *Coriolanus* was produced for eight performances at Drury Lane, under Garrick's management, in the 1754–55 season, it was not in fact among the plays of Shakespeare that he adapted, nor did he appear in it. Cibber's adaptation of Shakespeare's *Richard III* appeared in 1700.

29. High C from the chest (Fr.).

30. In Shakespeare's *Richard III* (Cibber's adaptation).

31. In the German opera *Martha*, by Friedrich von Flotow (1812–83), set in the reign (1702–14) of Queen Anne.

32. In 1858 the French Academy fixed the concert pitch (diapason) of the note A as 435 vibrations per second; the English pitch was higher. The distinction between the two was a subject that Shaw took up a number of times in his music criticism; see e.g. *Shaw's Music*, 1:259–60, 277–80; 2:456–63. He favored the French pitch, but the point here is that orchestras incompetently mix the lower and the higher.

33. "Give not that which is holy unto the dogs, neither cast ye your pearls before swine" (Matthew 7:6).

34. In his essay on "History" (1828).

35. Dr. Wisenthal wishes to thank Dr. Vera Micznik, of the School of Music, University of British Columbia, for her kind assistance.

Margot Peters

SHAW'S TRUE GENTLEMAN

Shaw was twenty-three and three years a resident of London when in December 1879 he decided to define "the True Signification of the term Gentleman." He had reasons other than the usual pressing financial ones for tackling the subject. Having arrived in London "without the credentials of a peasant immigrant,"[1] he was intensely aware of his own precarious status with caste-bound Britishers, many of whom considered no Irishman a gentleman. He was conscious of a lack not only of rank but of education, seeking in these years to cultivate himself through the study of French, Italian, counterpoint, and harmony. Even a great writer like Dickens, Shaw believed, might have escaped the label "Philistine" had he had "something of the systematic philosophical, historical, economic, and above all, artistic training of Goethe."[2] In June 1879 he had felt his penury when he was forced to refuse an invitation to Chichester Bell's place in Surrey "from want of money."[3] In November he had gone for the first time to the salon of Lady Wilde in Park Street, where an encounter with the celebrated author Eliza Lynn Linton reminded him that he had not grasped even the bottom rung of the ladder. And he had decided social prejudices himself: ". . . I still bear traces of the Shaw snobbery which considers manual work contemptible, and on no account will I enter an office again."[4] Robert Smith, the young hero of his first novel, *Immaturity* (1879), considers clerking the most contemptible profession in the world.

At the same time, Shaw was a decided iconoclast. He would adopt "No Gentleman," a pen name consciously reflective of the Philistine Dickens, in protest against the arbitrariness of rank. "I need not introduce myself," he begins a column of 1 June 1889. "Since I am 'No Gentleman,' you do not desire my acquaintance."[5] Shaw, however, was never a leveler, like another favorite author, Shelley. His sympathies lay with the exceptional, whether gentleman or genius. Thus he does not object to that superlative creature, "a thorough English gentleman," or even to a man "every inch a gentleman." What he deplores is the current debasement of the term to mean a man who wears a hat and gloves and refrains from carrying gravy to his mouth on the blade of a knife. Such a gentleman delights in proclaiming himself no better than the next man; indeed he "cannot enter a polite mob without meeting at least six persons exactly resembling him in all external details," writes Shaw with some contempt. The young author's point, therefore, is that the current leveling of the term "gentleman" renders it meaningless.

Unsurprisingly, no editor snapped up "On the True Signification." Its style is freighted with the ponderous locutions of a youth eager to appear learned; and Shaw's example of the solicitor's clerk who turns away the profligate colonel but admits the honest plumber says less about the meaning of gentility than about the clerk's lack of concern for keeping a job. Furthermore the point of the essay is blurred: what finally *is* a true gentleman? In the first paragraph a gentleman is "generous, honest, and refined"; in paragraph four he "has excellent morals and is courteous to all his fellows." It follows that being termed a gentleman "is the privilege of no class or garb." Yet there are also "classes usually admitted to be genteel." Or is gentility rather a question of public service and seniority, since people are likely to apply the term "perfect gentleman" to "the Chancellor of the Exchequer or some respected acquaintance much their senior"? Then there is the literary gentleman, noble of heart and soul; he, at least, is a poetic rather than an actual creature. Finally nobody seems to be quite certain what actually constitutes a gentleman—including Shaw. Yet if the term is completely hollow, how is it that some men are obviously gentlemen and others obviously not? Shaw may claim that the honest stone mason is a perfect English gentleman; the majority still feels that the state of gentlemanhood is inextricably tied to social position, income, education, and manners.

Although "On the True Signification" was rejected, the thrifty Shaw was not one to waste words. "The substance of this article," he noted, "was subsequently written into 'The Irrational Knot.' See conversation in the eleventh chapter between Conolly and the Rev. George Lind."[6] Tied to characters and events, Shaw's argument that merit and ability outweigh social rank is now sharp and effective.

Edward Conolly, the protagonist of *The Irrational Knot,* is Shaw's new aristocrat: a self-made electrical engineer already dominant in his firm, a coolly ambitious rationalist who (irrationally) has fallen in love with Marian Lind, the gentle, well-bred heiress daughter of his superior. Because, like Frederick Wentworth in Jane Austen's *Persuasion,* Conolly has "nothing but himself to recommend him," Marian's father and brother violently oppose the marriage. For the Linds, rank determines a gentleman—and Conolly does not belong to theirs.

Naturally Shaw's self-made realist argues rings around the Linds' outmoded appeals to his sense of honor, principle, and duty. For Conolly "gentility alone is no guarantee of suitability." A gentleman may well be a drunkard, gambler, or libertine. He, on the other hand, is eminently suitable for Marian because he possesses high morals, good manners, experience and ability, sufficient culture to sympathize with her artistic tastes, instinctive appreciation of her refinements, and—most important—the physical appeal that has made her fall in love with him.

Obviously Conolly's qualities are Shaw's own, and therefore those of the true gentleman. Ironically, however, this true gentleman makes a disastrous husband for Marian Lind, just as the young Shaw would have made a disastrous husband for any woman who clung to romantic ideals. In this case Marian romantically believed that the hard-headed Conolly could make her happy. But her charm, sympathy, and pretty little talents dissolve in the cold light of his perfect rationalism, sense of justice, and self-sufficiency; eventually she runs off with a complete cad.

Ultimately, however, Shaw cares little for Conolly's suitability as a husband or even as a gentleman. "A man of genius is worth fifty men of rank," cries Marian's cousin, Elinor, defending him. Here is the crux of the argument. If the thorough English gentleman is "a choice variety of nature's nobs,"[7] how much more so is that far rarer species, the genius. At twenty-three Shaw had more than an inkling of his stature.

Yet precisely because society ranked the gentleman above the genius and despised the artist, gentility became a subject that haunted the impoverished Irish son of a "downstart" all his life. It is a theme of the novels, autobiographical writings, theater criticism, plays, prefaces, and political works—from *Immaturity* to *Everybody's Political What's What?* Often Shaw wields the term "gentleman" to club mediocrity, in a *Saturday Review* article of 13 March 1897, for example, dismissing the painter Frederick Leighton as a "mere gentleman draughtsman."[8] He consistently refused to apply the term to himself: "My own success has happened because I recognised as a young man that I could not afford to be a gentleman, and I decided to be a literary artist instead."[9] Yet the concept of a "gentle" rank or class underlies Shaw's thinking on crucial issues such as economic equality and eugenics. The human race cannot breed successfully under capitalism, he argues in *The Intelligent Woman's Guide to Socialism and Capitalism* and elsewhere, not only because inequality of income restricts the choice of a mate to one's own class, but because people with different manners and habits cannot live together. In other words, a duchess with plenty of money of her own might tolerate a dustman who earned £100 a year, but she could never tolerate a husband who was not a gentleman.

Because Shaw wrote comedy, his plays necessarily deal with social manners and mores—and questions of rank. Even the early "Unpleasant Plays" concern themselves very much with gentility: "In the name of common decency, Harry," says Cokane in the first act of *Widowers' Houses*, "will you remember that you are a Gentleman, and not a coster on Hampstead Heath on Bank Holiday?" It is clearly understood in most Shaw plays that the main characters are genteel and strictly bound by their gentility. Nobody expects the Waiter to propose to Mrs. Clandon, Lady Cicely to run off with Drinkwater, Nobby Price to fall in love witth Major Barbara, 'Enry Straker to pursue Ann Whitefield, Alfred Doolittle to marry Mrs. Higgins, or Hypatia to succumb to Gunner. Such misalliances would be unthinkable. In fact—although Shaw in 1879 professed to find the term virtually meaningless—a good many of his plays spend a good deal of time exploring questions of gentility. Hardly surprising since Shaw, despite his denials, was himself a gentleman who associated with ladies and gentlemen.

For contemporary audiences, American ones particularly, the question of gentility is the most dated aspect of Shavian comedy. Few people today care whether someone is a lady or gentleman—or would recognize the species if they stumbled over it. The terms, in fact, are moribund.

Thus in *Getting Married* Lesbia Grantham's "But if she is an English lady it is her right and her duty to stand out for honorable conditions" sounds as antique as Sir Howard's, "You insult me, sir. You are a rascal. You are a rascal," or Mrs. Gilbey's "Is she a lady, Juggins? You know what I mean." The fillip has gone out of Philip Clandon's "We're from Madeira, but perfectly respectable, so far"[10] just as the energy has vanished from Johnny's fight to prove to Bentley that Tarleton's Underwear is just as respectable as Lord Summerhays's title and K.C.B. We don't need John Tanner the M.I.R.C. to tell us that 'Enry Straker is the coming man; we know he has arrived. We also know that if Boss Mangan visited a country house today he would be the guest of honor, not the butt of snobbish jokes.

Yet even while peopling his plays with characters who are without question ladies and gentlemen, Shaw paradoxically remained faithful to his youthful "Claude Melnotte" definition of gentility. Vivie Warren, Bluntschli, and Marchbanks are prototypes of the vital genius he would develop more fully in the characters of Dick Dudgeon, Caesar, Ann Whitefield, Andrew Undershaft, Epifania Ognisanti di Parerga, and Saint Joan. Shaw's vital genius may be a person of rank, but rank is incidental to the stature conferred by the Life Force's gifts of energy and vision. As he instructed Ellen Terry, the whole point of the third act of *The Devil's Disciple* is that while General Burgoyne is a gentleman, his hero Dick Dudgeon is "superior to gentility."[11]

Shaw's comedy, then, relies heavily on the subversion or inversion of ideals of genteel respectability. Henry Higgins is only the most obvious example of a Shaw character whom the solicitor's clerk would have pitched out of the office as "no gentleman a 'tall," while Colonel Pickering would have gained admission not on the strength of birth, breeding, or rank but because he behaved with the lowly clerk as one gentleman to another. The situation of Eliza being turned into a lady by a boor is Shaw's best caste joke. Conversely, the founder of Tarleton's Underwear deserves the title gentleman because he behaves in a benign, frank, courteous, unpretentious way, unlike the aristocratic Bentley Summerhays, whose idea of good manners is acting like a spoiled brat. Hector Hushabye is a gentleman but a wimp. Ann Whitefield is heroic because she does not permit ladylike conventions to divert her singleminded pursuit of a mate; in fact she exploits them to fascinate John Tanner.[12] Epifania Ognisanti de Parerga, Shaw's hell-raising millionairess, is no lady at all. Saint Joan is a country girl.

Thus while he could not avoid rooting his comedies firmly in a class and caste system, ultimately Shaw saw himself as creating women and men rather than ladies and gentlemen. Creative evolution, after all, remained his life-long creed—and creative evolution ultimately does not concern itself with questions of gentility. Lilith's concluding "Best of all, they are still not satisfied" speech in *Back to Methuselah* reflects a Shavian metaphysic to which material and temporal questions of rank are irrelevant in the light of Man and Woman's eternal quest for redemption of the flesh in the attainment of pure spiritual intelligence.

On the True Signification of the term Gentleman (1879)

[PROVENANCE: Unsigned holograph manuscript; six leaves, the first of which is a title cover with Shaw's name and address, with the text leaves foliated by Shaw: 1 to 5. The verso of the final leaf is dated "11th December 1879", beneath which is a later added, undated shorthand note: "The substance of this article was subsequently written into 'The Irrational Knot'. See the conversation in the eleventh chapter between Conolly and the Reverend George Lind." (Chapter Eleven of the manuscript and serial texts became Chapter Ten in the revised text for book publication.) Bernard F. Burgunder Collection, Division of Rare and Manuscript Collections, Cornell University Library.]

It has of late become usual to employ the word "gentleman" to denote such a generous, honest, and refined character as could scarcely appear at a disadvantage in any trial to which human manners or morals could be subjected. It is offered as implying so much, that the compound and highly general adjectives, "large hearted", "high souled" &c, often prefixed to it, are interesting rather as proofs of the enthusiasm felt by the writer or speaker than as elucidations of his exact meaning.

There are, however, degrees in the completeness of gentility. Thus, a person may have the hands of a gentleman, with the head of a Shakspere (who was no great things, socially speaking), and the arms of a blacksmith. Consequently, when a perfect catholicity of virtue has to be attributed to an individual, he is said to be "every inch a gentleman". Yet, unreserved as this eulogy is, it is only the comparative mood of gentility; for there is a superlative behind.

This superlative, unknown in other countries, is "a thorough English gentleman": an appellation which is intended to mean much more of strength, rectitude, antagonism to humbug, and gentleness towards the weak, than any foreigner could reasonably be expected to possess, or even appreciate; for it is the Briton alone who feels the full force of the qualification. The thorough English gentleman is a choice variety of nature's nobs; and nature's nobs, as Montague Tigg was inspired to say, feel for nature's nobs all over the world.[13]

In short, gentleman is a name for the man who has excellent morals and is courteous to all his fellows. It is the privilege of no class or garb, and may be claimed by the honest mason who helps to build the clubhouse, with more success than by the insolvent gambler who dines there. That few persons could be found with so little modesty as to claim this most comprehensive word of praise would seem natural. Nevertheless the case is contrary. Elijah, standing where he had no part to play, declared that he was not better than his fathers. Men of our day, in a different spirit, proclaim that they are no better than other people, and contemn persons who endeavour to prove themselves so. But far from therefore abdicating the rank of gentlemen, they proffer this very similarity to their neighbours as their chief claim to it; and any member of the classes usually admitted to be genteel will resent its denial to him as implying, not that he falls short of being an extraordinarily refined and scrupulous man, for such he does not, in his own phrase, "set up" to be; but that he is deficient even in that scanty integrity and address which civilization has as yet to accept as the average. Hence it appears that the popular value of the word is considerably less transcendental than the poetic. For instance.

Suppose (without prejudice to the reputation of the legal profession for disinterestedness) a worldly solicitor interposes between himself and the litigious public a stripling of Claude Melnotte's[14] way of thinking, who toils in an outer office for eighteen shillings a week. Let there enter and demand audience of the solicitor, a journeyman plumber, privately known to the clerk as a man of spotless honour, but a stranger to the lawyer, whose first question is: "Is he a gentleman?" If the boy, relying on what is said to be the true meaning of the term, replies in the affirmative, he is presently discharged for confusing the perception of his employer.

Again, suppose that to the same office comes a colonel in Her Majesty's service concerning whom the youth knows that he has ruined many friends by dishonouring bills to which he had obtained their endorsement, that he has seduced the daughters of respectable families whose hospitality he had enjoyed, and that he is capable of putting a slight on a fellow man of commercial extraction. The solicitor[,] on a stranger being announced, propounds the usual question. The clerk, thinking of Claude Melnotte, emphatically replies in the negative. The solicitor disregards the visitor's convenience accordingly, and, subsequently finding himself the victim of a wrong impression, dismisses his junior with a sarcastic recommendation to enter the church.

It is clear, if the meaning of a word be the idea which, without adjective or explanation, it conveys, that "gentleman" does not mean that noble creature which, according to recent literary fashion, it suffices to describe. Actually, it means very little. It is a term which emotion never dictates. Contemptuous though "fellow" seems beside it, most of those who feelingly praise their friends find "good fellow", "decent fellow", "splendid fellow", "capital fellow" nearer to their lips than "perfect gentleman", which they rather award to the Chancellor of the Exchequer or some respected acquaintance much their senior. The hollowness of the term appears startlingly when we think of applying it to the founder of Christianity, who, if the fashionable definition be worth anything, was surely a thorough gentleman. Yet the profanity of the epithet here would revolt an atheist.

A gentleman, then, is one who does not appear in the streets of the metropolis without gloves and a cylindrical hat, nor sit covered in the presence of his hostess, nor carry gravy to his mouth on the blade of a knife, nor manifest unfeigned sensibility. He is one who so comports himself that he cannot enter a polite mob without meeting at least six persons exactly resembling him in all external details. Many readers, especially ladies, will reply, "That is not *my* idea of a gentleman". Irrespective, however, of the peculiar idea which their honorable sentimentalism may think worthy of attachment to this word, it is here defined according to its current signification; and those who use it otherwise and omit to explain the sense in which they do so, will find themselves as unintelligible as if they persisted in using the word "three" to describe the quantity usually called four, or "white" to denote the colour of a raven.

Notes

1. Shaw to Matthew Edward McNulty, 3 June 1876, in *Collected Letters 1874–1897,* ed. Dan H. Laurence (New York: Dodd, Mead, 1965), p. 19.

2. Shaw to Henry Arthur Jones, 2 December 1894, in *Collected Letters 1874–1897,* pp. 461–64.

3. Holograph note by Shaw on ALS from C. A. Bell, which Shaw dated 18 June 1879. British Library: Add. Mss. 50508, fol. 153.

4. Shaw to Matthew Edward McNulty, 3 June 1876.

5. In 1889 Shaw contributed three "Asides" columns signed "No Gentleman" to the *Penny Illustrated Paper.*

6. Written in shorthand on verso of page 5 of "On the True Signification of the term Gentleman." Shaw began *The Irrational Knot* in June 1880, completing it in December.

7. "On the True Signification of the term Gentleman," pp. 1–2.

8. "Madox Brown, Watts, and Ibsen," 13 March 1897, in *Our Theatres in the Nineties* (London: Constable, 1932), 3:70. Shaw's dismissal of Leighton (Baron Frederick Leighton Leighton, 1830–96) elicited a protest from Ellen Terry: " 'Madox Brown—A *man.* W.—Artist and Poet. L.—Only a Gentleman.' *'Gentleman!'* Oh that word! SOME DAY define the term, not for me privately, but for your general readers. To *me* 'Gentleman' has always meant the highest and best. I think it must mean differently to different people." 13 March 1897, *Ellen Terry and Bernard Shaw: A Correspondence* (New York: G. P. Putnam's Sons, 1932), p. 123. Shaw replied the same day, "Leighton's plan was to give an elegant air to life, to soften and beautify what could be softened and beautified by fine art and fine manners, to help the deserving but not quite successful subjects by a little pretence, and to ignore all the horrors" (p. 124).

9. "Mr. Shaw on Artists," *Daily Express* (1 December 1927), p. 9:1, a verbatim report of Shaw's remarks at the Tate Gallery on the occasion of Lord D'Abernon's unveiling of new frescoes by Rex Whistler.

10. "You insult me, sir": *Captain Brassbound's Conversion;* "Is she a lady": *Fanny's First Play;* "We're from Madeira": *You Never Can Tell.*

11. 13 March 1897, *Ellen Terry and Bernard Shaw: A Correspondence,* p. 124.

12. Shaw advised Frances Dillon, an actress playing Ann Whitefield on tour, to learn to act like a lady by reading Queen Victoria's letters. "You will notice that Queen Victoria, even when she was most infatuatedly in love with Prince Albert, always addressed him exactly as if he were a little boy of three and she his governess. That is the particular kind of English ladylikeness in which you are deplorably deficient." 21 November 1908, *Collected Letters 1898–1910,* ed. Dan H. Laurence (New York: Dodd, Mead, 1972), pp. 816–18.

13. Montague Tigg, a sharper and friend of that "noble gentleman" Chevy Slyme in *Martin Chuzzlewit.* Dickens describes Tigg as "shabby-genteel," a state with which Shaw could sympathize during these years.

14. Claude Melnotte, the peasant protagonist of Bulwer-Lytton's enormously successful play *The Lady of Lyons* (1838), a man "who owes his position to merit,—not birth." Henry Irving produced *The Lady of Lyons* at the Lyceum in 1879 with Ellen Terry as the heroine Pauline. Shaw saw this production: "I remember, years ago, when The Lady of Lyons was first produced at the Lyceum, being struck with two things about it: first, the fact that Henry Irving . . . had at last discovered the method of heroic acting; and, second, that in the scene where Claude brings Pauline home after their wedding, Miss Ellen Terry, by a number of delicate touches, slipped into the scene a play of subtle emotion quite foreign to its traditions . . ." "Two Plays," 8 June 1895, *Our Theatres in the Nineties.* Terry did not share Shaw's opinion of Bulwer-Lytton's hero: "How could any woman fall in love with a cad like Melnotte?" she writes in her memoir *The Story of My Life.*

Jacques Barzun

BERLIOZ AND SHAW: AN AFFINITY

The young G. B. Shaw, dismally employed by the Edison Telephone Company to get householders' consent to the erecting of poles on their roofs, was not the first caged genius to draw comfort and inspiration from the *Memoirs* of Berlioz. Many other artists have told how much encouragement they owed to the vivid account of the creator embattled against indifference and envy and especially against entrenched "official" art.

That Shaw had read those *Memoirs* when he wrote "A Reminiscence of Hector Berlioz," dated 29 February 1880, is clear: what is said about Chateaubriand, Cherubini, and Berlioz's mother is enough to point to the original source. And as it happens, there is a document to confirm the inference. Shaw kept a fragmentary diary between February and June 1880, the very time when he was getting acquainted with Berlioz through his writings; it gives the dates of some of his reading sessions in the great rotunda of the British Museum.[1]

These diary entries are terse, as of appointments noted down after the fact: *BM—Memoirs; BM—Voyage; BM—Instrumentation.* This last refers to Berlioz's *Treatise on Instrumentation and Orchestration,* which is much more than a textbook detailing the technical elements and best practice; it is at the same time a work of criticism and an aesthetics of music that must have given Shaw plenty to think about. As for *Voyage Musical . . .* (1844), it refers to Berlioz's first account, published in mid-career, of his musical studies and experiences in Italy and Germany.

Thus Shaw read the best and the most that could then be found on his chosen subject. Whether he planned from the outset to embody his findings in a fiction, there is no way of determining. And in that spell of research lurks another little mystery. The *Treatise on Instrumentation* of 1843 had been published in London by A. J. Novello in 1856, translated by Novello's sister, Mary Cowden Clarke, then editor of the *Musical*

Times, and later noted as a Shakespeare scholar. But the two-volume *Voyage,* although twice translated into German in the 1840s, did not and does not exist in English.[2] As for the *Memoirs,* they first came out in English in 1884. Therefore Shaw had to read the *Voyage* and the *Memoirs* in French. The latter were available in German since 1877, but it does not appear that in 1880 Shaw knew any German. His French he must have acquired by himself, for there is no trace in his scant schooling of any foreign language but Latin. Curiously, his correspondence mentions struggling with French only some time later. By middle life he had mastered the language well enough to write passable letters.

Other signs that he knew some French by 1880 occur in the text of his third novel, *Love among the Artists,* begun a year after the Berlioz tale. The hero, Owen Jack, is a musical genius with rough manners and a vitriolic tongue, whom Shaw later described as "a British Beethoven." That is true of Jack's behavior, but his musical views and professional attitudes are really closer to Berlioz's—and to his creator's as well.

Shaw's acquaintance with French when he wrote the novel appears in the second chapter of Part II, which is laid in Paris and where the French exclamations are not the hackneyed ones. Throughout the tale, Aurélie's unidiomatic English translates some French expressions (e.g. "It is a horror") and again, not the usual ones. Finally, Owen Jack is made to say *partition* for score and *repetition* for rehearsal, which are Gallicisms—transliterations of the French terms.

The "Reminiscence" was no *jeu d'esprit;* it leads straight to the conception of "Owen Jack" and contains the essence of Shaw's musical creed, not borrowed from Berlioz, but helped into being by the teachings derived from reading him. Shaw had found a congenial spirit.

This is not to say that the young woman who "reminisces" portrays Berlioz accurately. In his shorthand note on the manuscript, Shaw terms his fiction "historically absurd," and he cites the fact that Berlioz was not reared on the piano like most composers. But other facts are distorted too: he calls the young musician "a raw provincial" who "did not frequent salons" as the tale shows him doing. Although remote from Paris in the southeastern alpine region of Dauphiné, the Berlioz family was well connected; and as a pupil of LeSueur, who had been Napoleon's court composer, Berlioz in Paris was not isolated in his modest room. If he was poor, it was only because the family had cut off his allowance, the standard parental method of discouraging artistic vocations.

In the tale, the relation of the young genius to the famous writer and statesman Chateaubriand is a little off-line also. Berlioz, urged by an influential friend, did ask for a loan of 1,200 francs to make possible the performance of a Mass he had just finished composing—a work which, incidentally, was lost in the 1830s and found again in 1993. Chateaubriand's answer was not haughty or humiliating. It said he had not the money to spare: "If I had it, it would be yours," which probably was true, for the famous and highly placed Chateaubriand was almost always in financial straits.

Other deviations from fact mar the characterization. The self-confidence of genius and the easy courtesy are well drawn—they were no less true of the young Shaw—but the mood of self-pity suddenly turning cheerful and the outbursts of rudeness instantly eclipsed by effusive speech are neither lifelike nor apt. They miss the right contrasts: the tone of defiant contempt for philistines, the tone of common civility, and the tone of devotion to art and its masters. Likewise, in the story Cherubini is made into an ogre absolutely, whereas Berlioz respected him as a composer and defied him only in his role of professor and bureaucrat who would keep him out of the Conservatoire library.

What led Shaw to Berlioz is a tantalizing question. The man and his music had enjoyed high repute in London in the middle of the nineteenth century, as they have once again in our day; but by the date of the "Reminiscence," the memory of his works, his conducting, and his personality had faded, and Wagner was the new excitement. Did Shaw hear the name Berlioz from his musical mother and her teaching partner, Vandeleur Lee? Whatever the answer, Shaw on his own made himself into one of the best-informed and most perceptive critics of the music of Berlioz.

This is not surprising. The affinity between the two spirits goes deep. Quite apart from their common stance as artists at war with the solid phalanx that Berlioz called "the routineers, the academics, and the deaf," he and Shaw are kin in some leading traits of character and habits of expression. Both were natively shy men who schooled themselves to showmanship, that is, self-exhibition (or at least sporting a made-up self, so as to signalize their shocking works). Seasoning the act with their abundant wit and humor, they were confident that no alert observer would mistake their apparent egotism for vanity.

As critics, their dedication to art and artistic integrity saved them from the danger of playing favorites and thereby casting doubt on their professional verdicts. Both declared that if the career of some dear friend or relative depended on a favorable review, no love or loyalty could deflect their judgment; both proved that this was no empty boast when, in the reverse case, they praised the work of some fierce opponent.

As artists, their integrity appears in the painstaking way in which they not only composed but also directed their works. Just as Berlioz taught orchestras all over Europe how to rehearse and their leaders how to conduct, so Shaw taught actors and directors how to put on a play wherever he had access to the participants, in person or through the written word.

The two men were masters of language, alike pursuing Shaw's ideal goal of "exhaustive literary expression." That is the secret of their achieving each an unmistakable style without ever aiming at style itself. Their prose is not simply lucid: it is rapid, dazzling, often overwhelming like the writers themselves. The thought modulates briskly; it links remote ideas unexpectedly; it exaggerates at a nod from the comic spirit. And it makes of every subject a narrative instead of an exposition, for the two men were born storytellers. Read Berlioz's *Evenings with the Orchestra,* a collection of his essays fashioned into a coherent whole by means of animated dialogues among the players in the orchestra pit, and you find yourself thinking of the Shavian stage directions and "retortive backchat."[3]

Through most of his life Shaw maintained that music was drama— character and conflict in sound. Every bar of Berlioz's music answers to that definition as it carries forward what has been the prevailing musical tradition of the West. In the same vein Shaw, although a man of the Nineties, was sure that the great artists in music were those who were not afraid to let loose all the thunders at their command when thunder was appropriate. At one hearing of the Rákóczy March in Berlioz's *Damnation of Faust,* says Shaw, "I felt . . . I must charge out and capture Trafalgar Square singlehanded."[4] The soft-spoken miniaturists in music might charm, but they missed the heights and the depths.

This does not mean that either Shaw or Berlioz was scornful of nuance or incapable of the intimate mood. Their equal appreciation of Mozart when he was rather neglected is proof that their ultimate criterion of worth, in art as in life, was neither the grandiose nor the delicate exclusively, but the full range of expressiveness.

Ample as this inventory of parallels may seem, it should not give the impression that Shaw and Berlioz were identical twins. Their minds and temperaments diverged on as many points as they agreed. For one thing, they belonged to different national landscapes and traditions; for another, to different halves of the nineteenth century. Berlioz lived from 1803 to 1869: he grew up in the feverish atmosphere of the French Revolution and Napoleon; Shaw lived from 1856 to 1950: his mind took its impress during the heyday of the Victorian Compromise and the unsettling war between Darwinism and the creeds. The contrast is enough to suggest the differences of concern, emotion, and philosophy that must result.

Chronology has one more thing to tell us about the "Reminiscence" and its incidents. Their starting point is the mention of Berlioz's request for help from Chateaubriand. This occurred toward the very end of 1824: we have the great man's reply dated 31 December. Hence the rest of the fiction takes place in the forepart of 1825. The narrator is remembering and setting down the events in 1827. The Postscript then states that she saw Berlioz again several years later, but she supplies only a round number when she says that it "all happened over fifty years ago." The one exact statement is that she is as old as the century, like Macaulay—precisely eighty.

A Reminiscence of Hector Berlioz (1880)

[PROVENANCE: Unsigned holograph manuscript, dated "29th February 1880" on reverse of final leaf, beneath which is a shorthand note of a later, indeterminate date (possibly November 1882): "This story, though not a bad one of its kind, is historically absurd. The dates, as regards Cherubini and Chateaubriand, are impossible. Berlioz never learned to play the piano. He was at this time a rawboned provincial, with a shock of red hair, and not in the habit of frequenting salons. I wrote the tale under the influence of the mortifications [to] which my business in the Edison Telephone Company exposed me." British Library: Add. Mss. 50693, folios 47–61, 63–77, plus two cover leaves (folios 46 and 62). In a diary that Shaw kept intermittently from 26 February to 7 July 1880, he recorded six sessions of Berlioz research in the British Museum, two each on the Memoirs, Voyage, *and* Treatise on Instrumentation, *between 6 March and 16 April, which suggests that the manuscript date of 29 February could be wrong. As Shaw's habit of dating his manuscripts was, however, precise to the point of obsession, it would be more reasonable to assume that he commenced his reading of Berlioz prior to the start of the diary.]*

Readers are so apt to conclude that a writer who employs the first person (as I do for the sake of simplicity) must be a man, that I think it best to begin my narrative by saying that I am a woman. I am twentyeight years old, and am accustomed to interest myself in the sorrows of the poor and unfortunate. Unfortunately, the attraction of the society of many clever and good people who like me, and my great love of music and pictures, has always prevented me from doing my very best in charitable work.

One evening, two years ago, I was in Paris, visiting an old woman, formerly employed in the chorus at the opera, but now broken in health and almost destitute. I am used to make my way through cities at night with no other protection than a dress, resembling that of a sister of mercy; and though it was dark when I left the poor woman's garret, I was alone. I reached the floor beneath by a dark staircase, at the foot of which some light shone across the landing from a partially opened door. Here I was arrested by a groan from within so bitterly expressive of despair that I stood trembling, and held my breath. Then I heard the sombre voice of a man, saying,

"Accursed be this miserable world, the paradise of pedants: the hell of

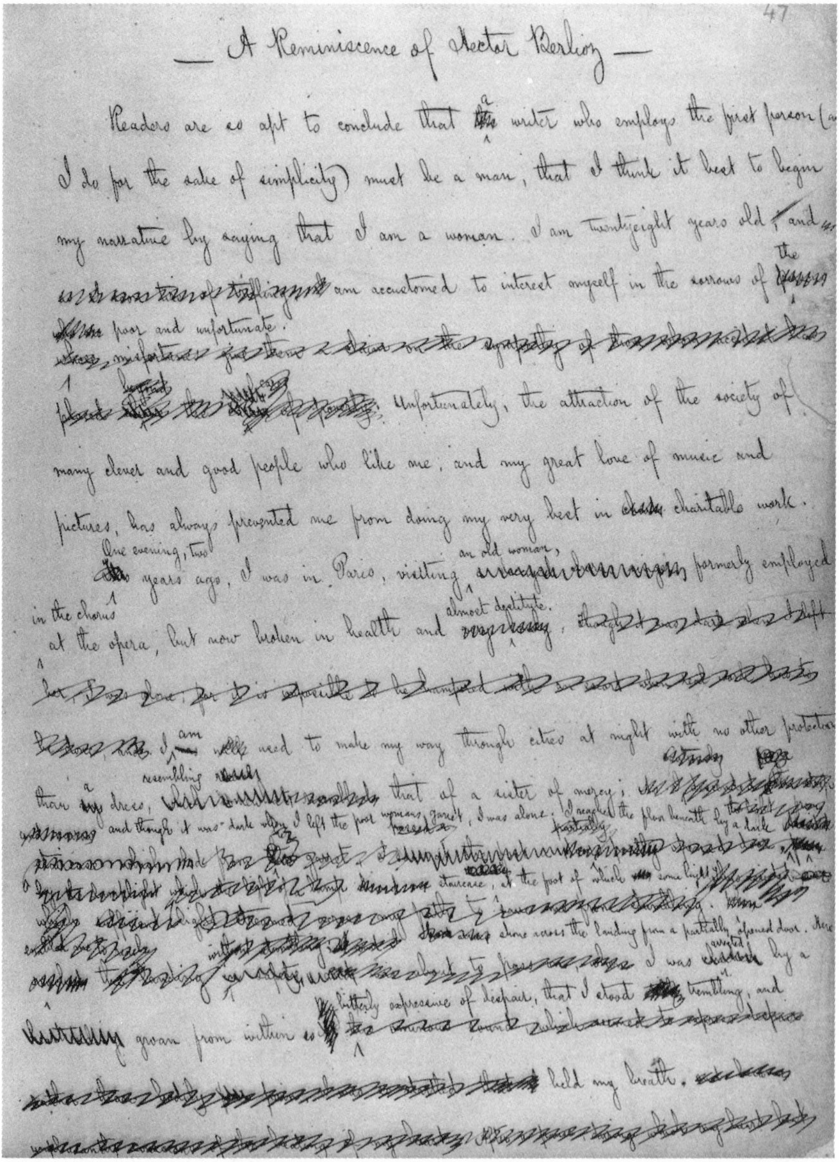

Fig. 1. Draft manuscript. British Library: Add. Mss. 50693, folio 47. By permission of the British Library.

genius. Let its own sordidness, like a cancer, consume it, that it may torture no more ardent hearts, and seal no more yearning lips. What tardy honour can compensate for a despised youth: what autumnal glory be to the hardened tree[:] what one ray of light would have been to the bud of spring? Oh for a smile, a kind word, a glimpse of a beautiful face, that I might no longer desire to die. Alas, I may more reasonably hope for another insult. And this man is a poet, had in his youth a soul like mine. Well, he is right, and I am a dreaming fool. Grant, oh implacable devil ruler of this lampless globe, that he may one day beg from me— that my bounty may revenge his polite caution. Yet, though I rave here till morning, I can not discredit his motives, nor dignify my own. Damn him. Damn him. A million million times damn him".

Silence ensued. I stole to the door and peeped into the room. There was a man sitting there dressed in a shabby black coat, which he had buttoned tightly about his slim figure, although the weather was not cold. His face and chest lay prone on the table, along which his arms were stretched. In assuming this position, he had scattered a quantity of scraps of music paper to the right and left, where they were heaped over a violin, an inkstand, and a common coffee service. I saw also an old flageolet and a French horn, lying on a ricketty square pianoforte which stood by the wall. I am never afraid of anyone who loves music; and when the man uttered a second groan, like that which had appalled me a few minutes before, I tapped gently on the panels, and drew back to await his answer without more nervousness than I was accustomed to feel in the presence of all strangers.

I heard him rise hastily, and he appeared before me on the threshold, cheerful and courteous, so that I could scarcely believe him to be the same man who, a minute earlier[,] had been lamenting over a miserable world. I had flattered myself that here I could play the part of consoler; but now I dared not assume such an attitude towards one whose bearing was so dignified, even had the pleasure which he politely evinced on seeing me betrayed anything for which I could excusably have offered him consolation. He seemed about twenty five years old, and had rich, curled hair, glittering eyes, and eager features.

"Monsieur"—, I began, and then hesitated and stammered.

"Madame"—he replied, with equal confusion.

At this, I so lost my presence of mind that I could not think of any excuse for having knocked; and I heartily repented of my inquisitiveness. Meanwhile his agitation surpassed mine; for he made two visible efforts to speak, moistening his lips before each, without succeeding in articulating a single word. In this distress, I fortunately gave way to an impulse of laughter. He immediately smiled, and said:

"I beg your pardon. I thought you knocked at my door".

"So I did", I replied, "but—". I paused, and he waited patiently. "—I mistook the room". No woman ever lied with a worse grace. He looked at me doubtfully, and then blushed, feeling that he was betraying incredulity. Suddenly he appeared to conceive some new idea. His colour deepened still more, and he moved uneasily, like one ashamed.

"I fear", he said, "that I alarmed you in some manner—led you, perhaps, to suppose that I was suffering".

"Truly", I replied, "I did think so; and as my calling at present is to console those who suffer, I ventured to knock. I confess that in my embarrassment on finding myself mistaken, I sought to cover my intrusion by a false excuse. Pray pardon me".

"Stop", he cried, as I made a movement in retreat; "you are not mistaken. I am indeed one of those who suffer". Here, checking his impetuous speech and gesture, he resumed in a subdued and courteous tone, "Do me the honour to enter my apartment for but a minute".

I was startled, but ashamed to hesitate, knowing that a question of propriety could be raised only by a display of uneasiness on my part. He handed me a chair, and seated himself at a little distance without speaking.

"I see you love music", I said, glancing at the pianoforte.

"I hate it", he replied gloomily. "It is the source of all my unhappiness".

"Then I fear I cannot assist you. Music is my ordinary prescription for all the evils that overtake those who are sensible of it". I looked anxiously at the door as I spoke; for I was beginning to doubt the wisdom of my visit.

"If music were your fate, as it is mine", he resumed, "you would rather warn all fragile souls to shun it. You are willing to listen to it, but I am forced to make it".

"Are you then compelled to gain a living by a pursuit which you hate[?]"

"Alas", he said, with a smile, "they will not give me the means of living by a pursuit which I love".

"I confess I do not understand you".

"Madame", he replied with simplicity, "I am a man of genius. My parents, who live at Côte-St-André, are resolved that I shall be a carpenter of live bodies; and my mother has rewarded my far different aspirations with her curse. I came to Paris to study medicine: I remain here to study music, which, if Beethoven have not strangled it, is the only art that survives. Look around my apartment, and you will see that I am poor. I will tell you something which will prove to you that I am a fool. Poverty and folly walk at either side of genius, until worldliness dislodges them. You know Châteaubriand?"

"What!" I exclaimed. "Are you Châteaubriand?"

"I", he cried, "Never. I am Châteaubriand's beggar. Listen to me, and judge whether Hector Berlioz—a name as yet unknown to you—be not a simpleton. I am a student at the Conservatoire, where Cherubini, the *gran' maestro,* the arch pedant, the Chinese puzzle monger of music, hates me, because I neither care nor pretend to care for fugues in five parts on the word Amen, much less write them.[5] In order to produce a work of mine, I needed money—only a few francs; but to my means, a million was as possible. I could not go to a Jew for the money; he would not have had faith in high art, or sympathy with honest effort. I wrote to Châteaubriand, thinking that the mind that conceived 'Atala' could comprehend me.[6] I have just received his reply. He is not surprised at my request; not disturbed by my stupidity, not moved by my desperation, to which my bitter position as a suppliant bore witness. He is amused, and has probably shewn my long letter, with the name of Hector Berlioz subscribed, to his friends, in order to make them merry. His reply is the perfection of good taste. It is polite; and his regrets that it is wholly impossible for him to place such a sum at my disposal, are expressed so as to conceal the abyss of contempt he must feel for the novice who thinks that the easiest way to get money is to ask for it. Easy! Easy to ask for money! Did he know me, my petition would have seemed written with my blood. But he does not know me, and he despises me. Ask as I will why I should care whether he despises me or not, his contumely rankles in me like a poisoned arrow, and wrings from my mouth peevish exclamations and vulgar curses, which only serve to increase my degradation".

"But if you earnestly desire such a sum—it is not a large one—can you not, by working hard and hoarding up for a short time, contrive to accumulate it?"

"You are right. I can rant better than I can labour, bringing forth many words and little print. Yet consider. How can I make money but by the production of my works. How can I produce my works without money".

"Surely some *entrepreneur*"—

"Some slave of the devil!" he screamed, interrupting me with sudden ferocity.

I rose and looked at him indignantly; for, accustomed as I was to the excitability of Frenchmen, I could not help feeling outraged by this explosion. He blushed, and, with an expression of confusion and remorse, moistened his lips with his tongue in a vain effort to speak, as I had seen him do before. He seemed to be capable of nothing between the extremes of fluency and absolute dumbness.

"Monsieur", I said, with as much dignity as I could assume, "it grows late, and I must ask you to excuse me. Good evening".

He made me a sorrowful bow, and let me go without a word. I had no choice but to depart, though his stricken aspect now filled me with such pity that I would willingly have forgiven his indiscretion, and endeavoured to fulfil my errand of consolation, instead of leaving him more wretched than before, as I knew I was doing.

When I arrived at home I had no time to think on my adventure, for I had engaged myself to go to the opera with Madame Le Jeune, and I had hardly changed my dress when her carriage was announced.

Our box was near the proscenium, and I sat facing the stage, with my back to the *parterre*, the occupants of which I did not trouble myself to scan. The performance failed to interest me. The orchestra was dull and noisy, and I believe I should have fallen asleep during the second act but for the appearance of M. Le Jeune, who entered the box accompanied by a precisely dressed old gentleman in whom I recognized the veteran Cherubini, of whom I was a little afraid, though, contrary to his usual cold fashion, he had made almost a pet of me during our frequent meetings in society. Once, indeed, in Madame Le Jeune's *salon*, he had honoured me by playing for me the accompaniment to "Un pauvre petit Savoyard".[7] He bowed solemnly to my hostess, and sat down beside me.

"Well, my child", he said, "have you come to form your taste for the new school—to learn modulation from Monsieur Meyerbeer, and counterpoint from Signor Rossini. As for me, I will soon know how to compose. I had a lesson the other day from worthy Herr Beethoven".

"Yes, I saw you at the concert, and tried to make out what you felt from your expression; but I could not. You know, master, that I like Beethoven".

"No doubt, no doubt", he replied. "Turkish dance music. An excellent fugue in the slow movement too". Here he gave a quiet chuckle.

This Beethoven was a Viennese composer whose music had lately been much discussed in Paris. Though very strange and boisterous, it seemed to me very grand also, and, whilst many of the most learned musicians declared that its popularity would be shortlived, and the very name of Beethoven forgotten whilst the memory of Mozart would be as fresh as spring, I ventured in secret to rebel against this condemnation, and to hope that it might be falsified by time, though I do not, of course, contend that this composer's music is as great as that of the old masters. Whether it was learned or not, I liked it for its own sake; and, knowing that Cherubini was bitterly opposed to the new school, and hurt by the indifference of the public to the pure style of his own operas, I was careful not to provoke a discussion with him.

"I do not know whether it is my indisposition or the orchestra that is at fault tonight", I said; "but everything sounds tedious and slovenly to my ears"—

A violent clash of cymbals interrupted me. Before I could resume, a general movement of surprise among the audience distracted my attention. Following the gaze of those about me, I looked into the *parterre*, and saw my acquaintance of that evening standing there on a seat, gesticulating violently.

"There never was, and never shall be a cymbal in that bar"[,] he shouted, with frantic vehemence.[8] "I denounce you, miserable *rataplaneur*,[9] to the French people. I denounce you also, unworthy chief of an unworthy band. Murderers of the beautiful, begone. Parricides"—

Here four *sergents de ville*[10] seized the speaker, and hurried him away. He suffered himself to be led out without either betraying the slightest consciousness of his captors or intermitting for an instant his denunciations of the orchestra, which were audible for some moments after he had disappeared.

"That is the second time this month that this has occurred", said Madame Le Jeune. "I wonder why they admit a known madman to the theatre. The audience took his part last time, and there was quite a disturbance".

"Perhaps he was right", I said.

"Bah!" replied Madame Le Jeune. "Is it likely that a young man whom nobody knows, is wiser than the conductor of the Paris opera?"

"Master", said I, turning to Cherubini, "who is this young enthusiast?"

"One of my pupils", replied the composer, "and, I am informed, a genius. Judging from his aversion to sound study, I can well believe it. I have no doubt that he consoles himself for failing in competition for the Roman prize,[11] by writing operas—perhaps symphonies. You will understand that he is only my pupil inasmuch as he is entered at the Conservatoire, to which he is not in any sense a credit".

"I feel quite an interest in this young man", I said, preparing to question Cherubini further. But the cold tone of his reply stopped me.

"*I* do not", he said.

Soon after this, he left the box. Then Madame Le Jeune yawned behind her fan, and I proposed that we should depart. She agreed willingly; and within twenty minutes I was seated by my own fireside.

"Well, Jeanne. Not yet in bed?"

"I never avail myself of madame's permission, save when madame is *very* late".

"Jeanne, I am lazy enough to wish that I could sit here all night".

Jeanne nodded.

"I wish I were in bed without having had the trouble of preparing for it", said I.

"If madame will but permit me to undress her this once?" said Jeanne, who greatly disapproved of my habit of doing those personal offices for myself which usually form part of the duties of a lady's maid. Whilst I hesitated, half disposed to comply, I chanced to look upon the table, and saw there a small handbag which I carried about with me when visiting the sick, and a letter. As I kept all such articles in an appointed place, I asked Jeanne how my bag had come there. At the same time I took up the letter, and read with astonishment the following address

Unto Miss—the beautifullest English
Homage of Hector Berlioz

"It was left after you went out by a strange gentleman. He explained to me that you had forgotten it at the house of Madame Dupin, where he resided. A gentleman of gracious manners, and very gallant". Here Jeanne blushed.

I now remembered that I had placed my bag on the musician's table; and as I had no recollection of taking it up again, I concluded that in the haste of my departure, I had forgotten it. I felt grateful to him for his delicacy in representing to Jeanne that I had left it with Madame Dupin; and yet I was a little annoyed that he should have thought such a precaution necessary.

"He was very inquisitive", resumed Jeanne, after waiting in vain to be questioned. "He wanted to know all about madame; asked if madame's husband was at home, just to see whether madame was married; and was quite sure that he was dealing with an infant or a fool".

"You should have told him everything, Jeanne. He would have given you five francs and a kiss, and I should not have minded at all".

"Madame jests", said Jeanne, blushing again.

I opened the letter, and read the contents, which the writer had been sensible enough to couch in his own language.

Calm visitor of Peace
I have seen you; and I love you. I have insulted you; and I hate you. I learn your address from the letters contained in the bag which you have forgotten here, and I seize the pretext of returning it to protest against the tortures which you have ruthlessly added to my former desolation.

I have confessed to insulting you; yet what have I said that a noble woman need take to heart? Why did you recommend Hector Berlioz to beg from slaves and hucksters? Alas! you did not know him. You heard him weep, and your mission was to the unhappy. You are an angel. You entered, and found no sick or lame wretch, but a devil in rebellion against providence. Yet you will one day acknowledge that the rebellion was that of genius against neglect. This letter, now tossed contemptuously aside, you will yet ransack your escritoire to find, because it is from the hand of Berlioz. Do not think me arrogant—intoxicated with self regard. Consider the ridicule I risk, and the burning faith I must have in my inward gift to brave it. Besides, how else can I recover your esteem, except by pleading that I am not one of those common men to whom alone a burst of heartfelt fury is never pardoned.[12]

When I read what I have written, I feel how desperate is my hope of being understood by you, and how ill adapted words are to convey those emotions which sway me when I think of you and of myself. I have been in a strange condition of exalted misery since you crossed my threshold in anger. I would fain have appeared at my best before you. An accident shewed me at my worst. Nevertheless, if you are indeed as I figure you to myself, you will visit neither the brutality of my speech, nor the folly of my writing too heavily upon me, should we meet again. If you can read the enclosed, you will understand what I feel. If not, so much the worse for me—I have no other vehicle for my emotions save music[.]

Hector Berlioz

"Cherubini is right", I said[.] "The same hand could hardly write that rubbish and a great symphony".

"Madame?"

"Nothing. I was speaking to myself". I then drew from the envelope a manuscript which had been enclosed with the letter, expecting to find a sentimental ballad. I was mistaken. I could not form the least idea of what the music was like. It was written on twenty separate staves, in full instrumental score, and over each stave was a minute direction as to how the notes were to be played. A perusal of these directions convinced me that their author must be crazy. The violins were to be played with the wooden part of the bow; the wind instruments were to be enveloped in baize sacks; and parts were written for several pairs of drums, to be beaten by a certain number of drummers with sticks of a peculiar material.[13] Many other particulars I forget.

This absurdity exhausted my patience. "Come, Jeanne", I said, "your gallant gentleman is very tiresome. You may undress me if you like. In any case, I am going straight to bed".

Four days later, Madame Le Jeune held an afternoon reception, to which I was invited. I went gladly enough, knowing that I would meet a few friends whose presence would compensate me for the loquacity and arrogance of many minor celebrities with whom, in default of men and women of real genius, Madame Le Jeune liked to adorn her *salon*. The chief drawback to my pleasure was the prospect of being asked to sing before this large assembly without the possibility of refusing, except I should be content to incur the reproach of affectation or ill nature.

When I arrived, the rooms were already crowded, and my acquaintance Annette Crespigny, who was fond of singing, but not of music, was going through "Voi che sapete"[14] very badly, to an accompaniment which seemed to express the impatience of the player rather than the tenderness of the melody, and discomposed even Annette, who was ordinarily impenetrable by musical impressions. When the song was over, the company intermitted their whispers to raise a hum of applause; and the vocalist came to resume her seat on the sofa which I occupied, with an ungracious expression which shewed how much she was annoyed by the treatment she had suffered from the pianist.

"So you have come at last", she said. "My God, what a player! Madame Le Jeune, if she expects one to sing for the amusement of her guests, should provide a respectable accompanyist".

"It is certainly very unjust to you, Annette", I said; "but happily the audience are none the wiser. A good performance would be wasted on them".

"That is all very well", she replied. "Still, when one can sing, it is not pleasant to be murdered by an unmannerly animal like that".

Here Madame Le Jeune approached, followed by an old gentleman, who looked at me with a smile of expectancy.

"Come", said my hostess with affected imperiousness. "We must have 'Kennst du das Land'[15] at once".

"Oh no", I exclaimed, terrified at the prospect of singing Beethoven's setting of these words, to an ill played accompaniment; "I cannot do justice to it. Indeed I would rather not".

I had been surprised into vehemence, and my protest caused several persons who stood near to turn round. To escape their curiosity, I was compelled to yield to Madame Le Jeune, who ridiculed my objection, and introduced her companion as a gentleman who had long desired to hear me sing this, his favorite song. I therefore rose reluctantly, and made my way to the piano, which had resounded with explosive preludes under the angry fingers of a young man, whom I now recognised with dismay as my crazy correspondent of the previous week.

"M. Berlioz", said Madame Le Jeune coldly, for the accompaniment to "Voi che sapete" had not been lost upon her, "you must be fatigued, and, if you please, I will play 'Kennst du das Land' "—

He rose abruptly, and, in the act of making way haughtily for Madame Le Jeune, caught sight of me with the music in my hand. I was too nervous to check an impulse to make him a slight bow. He returned it, drew back the chair which he had been about to offer to his hostess, and with a stern "Pardon me", sat down and led me through the first three bars of the song before I had made up my mind to begin. I had to go on. In the second verse, when I was calmer, I found that the accompaniment was all that I could desire. He supported me without attempting to domineer over my idea of the song; and he seemed able to anticipate every shade in my manner of singing it. He played so well, that my pleasure in singing to his accompaniment was mingled with a fear lest my performance should be unworthy of it. Only once—during the pause following the words "Kennst du es wohl?"—did he disturb me. Then, a lady behind us broke the silence by the whispered remark "Is it not superb?". He turned his head and looked menacingly at her for several seconds, causing an awkward moment of suspense. When the indiscreet chatterer was thoroughly quelled, he resumed his playing with more delicacy than before, but with a somewhat less complete surrender of his musical will to mine. At the conclusion, the company applauded noisily, influenced more, doubtless, by a desire to conceal the unpleasant effect of the interruption than by the tender seriousness of Beethoven and Goethe. I was a little bewildered, and deeply moved, not, I hope, by my own singing, but by the song; and this enabled me to thank my accompanyist in that tone which makes gratitude precious to an artist.

"Ah, mademoiselle", he replied, with emotion, "pardon my folly—my vulgarity. You will sing again, will you not? Not now, but before you go".

I made a hasty movement of my head, which might have meant anything, and retreated without answering. He made no attempt to detain or follow me, but turned humbly to the pianoforte, where he found "Kennst du das Land" replaced by a worthless Italian *aria*, imitated from the florid style of Rossini, about whose music all Paris was just then enthusiastic. Recoiling from the desk, he rose, and, with as little regard for politeness as he had shewn when Madame Le Jeune had attempted to supplant him, left the young lady who had just come forward, to get through her song as best she could without assistance. Perceiving the confusion of the poor girl, and not unwilling to rebuke the author of it, I returned to the piano, and volunteered to play the accompaniment myself. The offer was accepted, and I fulfilled it as well as my dislike of the trash I was playing permitted.

Hardly had I regained my seat when I heard the voice of the young musician close behind me.

"This time, mademoiselle, you are wrong. Good taste is but a title of courtesy for moral cowardice. You pitied this woman like an angel, as you pitied me. Nevertheless, in reading me such a lesson, you have publicly rebuked the cause of high art, from the temple of which frivolity will never be banished until those who move society cease to be polite to it. The profound effect made by your singing gave me a momentary hope even for a mob like this; but you have permitted another to obliterate the impression—nay, you have helped her with your own hands".

I am feminine enough to be very obstinate with men who place me at a disadvantage, and I retorted, I fear, spitefully, "I should have been more guarded, monsieur, had I known that my actions were supposed to have reference to a young gentleman self-appointed to take care of the interests of high art, which I nevertheless have always considered well qualified to take care of itself".

"Alas, mademoiselle", he said gravely, "you are no longer an angel, but only a woman. I long for the moment when you will spread your wings again, as you have faithfully promised me to do once more before we part today".

"You are pleased to be sarcastic, M. Berlioz", I replied.

He shook his head reprovingly, and walked abruptly away, leaving me annoyed with myself, and resolute to be revenged on him by singing the most meretricious song I knew to the worst accompanyist in the room.

Nevertheless, when Madame Le Jeune again appealed to me, I selected "Di tanti palpiti", which, though much hackneyed, and in a style far removed from that of Beethoven, was certainly not the worst song I knew.

"Annette", I said to Mdlle Crespigny, "come and play this for me".

"What", she replied, looking at the sheet of music which I had handed to her, "are *you* going to inflict the everlasting 'Oh patria'[16] on us?"

"I am".

"Then you had better get your latest victim to play for you. That odious Berlioz either spoiled my song out of sheer malice, or else you have charmed sensibility into his fingers".

"You are right, mademoiselle", said Berlioz, suddenly appearing beside her, and taking the song from her hands. "I will take your place". He went to the piano without another word, and seated himself there. Annette and I looked at one another. I felt half inclined to return to my chair. But my courage failed me, and I followed him to the instrument, secretly resolving to revenge myself by abusing to the utmost that fashion of altering and decorating the music which nobody at that time thought of disputing a singer's right to adopt. I failed to carry out this intention. Although I sang well, I retained my presence of mind with so much difficulty that I dared not depart from the printed notes before me; and, at the conclusion, a surly old gentleman near congratulated me in a harsh voice on being the first amateur he had met who had the grace to confess inability to improve Rossini's handiwork.

This time, my accompanyist rose and left the piano with a preoccupied air, and without taking the least notice of me. I am sure that no one will feel the least sympathy with me, but I felt inexpressibly hurt by this treatment. I could hardly force myself to smile in acknowledgment of the applause which greeted me as I returned to my seat; and when Annette addressed some rather bitter raillery to me on the subject of M. Berlioz, I almost lost my temper.

"Annette", I said, interrupting her rudely, "I must go home".

"Well, my dear", retorted Annette, raising her dark eyebrows in astonishment, "go home by all means. It is quite refreshing to hear a little explosion from you, you are such a Puritan. There is nothing the matter, is there?"

"Nothing, except that I am tired. I will slip away quietly, as I do not wish to be importuned to stay, or to be troubled with questions. Give me plenty of time to escape, and then make my excuses".

"What shall I say?"

"I don't care what you say", I replied, and left her. I went downstairs and entered a little room at the end of the hall, where I had left my bonnet and wraps. It was not used by the other guests; but I was a privileged friend of Madame Le Jeune's, and usually availed myself of it to escape the crushing which took place in the cloak room when the company broke up. I was therefore surprised to hear an unfamiliar footstep approach the door and hesitate on the threshold. I kept still, hoping that the intruder would pass on. Then the door was opened, and M. Berlioz, after closing it carefully behind him, advanced until he was close to me, and, without one preliminary word or gesture, threw himself on his knees at my feet. I have often thought since of dignified and considerate words by which I might have recalled his good sense, but at the time I lost all self possession, and said hastily,

"Get up at once, M. Berlioz, and do not be so excessively ridiculous. I insist on your letting me go—on your leaving the room. I am astonished at you, and annoyed—deeply annoyed, by your conduct".

"Mademoiselle", he replied ardently, "the spectacle of a young man bending his knee for the first time in loving worship, is not ridiculous, but rather sublime. A great man is never ridiculous, and I swear to you with the truest humility that with my hand in yours I will be the greatest man of this age, as you are the most angelic woman". In raising his hand toward mine as he spoke, he lost his balance, and, from being poised painfully on both knees, slipped over to a sitting posture on the floor. Immediately he scrambled to his feet, clutching my dress to assist him as he did so. This liberty enraged me so much that I turned to leave the room without trusting myself to speak. He prevented me by seizing my hand, which I angrily but vainly attempted to snatch away. Feeling that I must not condescend to struggle with him, I now yielded it to him without resistance, and, with the calm of despair, said:

"M. Berlioz, if you could understand the transport of humiliation with which I endure your violence, I think that even you would spare me".

Startled by the change in my manner, and moved by my tone, he released my hand, and looked at me with an expression of concern.

"Why will you not listen to me?" he said. "Is it a crime to express that which suffuses my heart and soul? Or does the impetuosity of a Frenchman offend your English ideas? How can I approach you formally? I may never see you alone again, unless"—

"I trust you never may, M. Berlioz".

"You treat me as though I were a common man, with twenty counterparts in every mob", he exclaimed bitterly.

"I expect exactly the same courtesy from you as I receive without question from other gentlemen", I replied.

"Well, mademoiselle", he said, subduing his vehemence, "you shall not force me to boast. I have told you, in a spirit which you seem to mistake for vulgar self-assertion, that I will one day be acknowledged a great man; but it does not become me to argue that point with you. Go now, if you will: I shall no longer importune you". As he spoke, he drew back, and waited for me to leave the room.

But I had now forgotten my anxiety to escape. His assured conceit enraged me. "Never", said I, indignantly. "You have neither good sense, good taste, nor good nature. You will *never* be great".

I went out, and—although it happened two years ago, I blush now to write it—I banged the door behind me.

I never saw him again.

Postscript

Poor Hector Berlioz! I hardly know whether to laugh or not at the concluding sentence of my old manuscript; for I saw him many times after it was written; and I well remember one evening in Paris, when he had been raving about "Ophelia Smithson",[17] as we called her, an English actress whom he subsequently married very unhappily, my husband shewed him my story, which he had found that morning in an old desk, and rallied him upon its contents. I intended, when I wrote it, to send it to some of the old annuals of the day, such as the Ladies Keepsake, and others that I forget the names of. It seems strange that I remember all about it so well, though it all happened more than fifty years ago. I was exactly the same age as Mr Macaulay and the century then, and now it is nearly twenty years since Lord Macaulay dropped out of the race, although the century keeps pace with me still.[18] Fancy, young ladies, being an old woman of eighty, and widow to two husbands, after beginning with such romantic ideas. There is no such singing now as there used to be, although the music, thank goodness, is there still. Not long ago, I was tempted to venture out to a concert, and I heard a piece of music there that made me cry. And what do you think it was? "Oh patria", which I shall never sing again. Think of how old a woman must be when Rossini's music is the most pathetic music in the world to her. I only met Rossini himself once, but I knew Meyerbeer very well, and I wish some of your modern men of genius, who take such pains to be rude, could have known him too, and learnt from him what kind manners are. My story was never published, because it had nothing exciting in it. Tom Hood[19] once read it, before I had put it by and forgotten it; and he told me that the young man who groaned in his lonely chamber was an imposter who looked like a murderer, and turned out to be good for nothing but making a fool of himself. Nobody cared about Berlioz then. However, "the whirligig of time brings its revenges",[20] and now that people are fond of hearing me talk about men and women who found little enough encouragement whilst they were alive to enjoy it, it has leaked out that I have my little experience of the author of "Benvenuto Cellini"[21] written down, and I have been asked to publish it. So, after having lain for fifty years declined with thanks, my story is to be printed at last. I wish they would bring out his opera instead of reading about his follies. I believe it failed here before; but it was good enough for Weimar, where I heard it, and, however you may flatter your foolish tastes, my countrymen, what was good enough for Weimar was too good for London. I suppose his turn will come yet. I used to think that Beethoven's music would never be known in England; and now Richard Wagner is popular.

I must stop my postscript now. I could tell a great many more interesting things that nobody alive knows except myself; but I have to take care of my eyes, and the little I have added has taken me twice as long to write as the story itself did long ago. I daresay if I were to go over it all carefully, I could improve its style, seeing how young I was when I wrote it. But I am afraid I could not face the labour of that, so I must curtsey to my readers, and ask them to excuse the infirmity of an old woman.

Notes

1. The diary is Blackwood's Desk Diary for 1880, inscribed "G. B. Shaw | 24th February 1880" on the front free endpaper, with brief entries of activities and accounts between 26 February and 7 July. Published in *Bernard Shaw, The Diaries 1885–1897*, ed. Stanley Weintraub (University Park: Penn State University Press, 1986), pp. 37–51.

2. A portion relating to Germany was indeed included in a translated collection of Berlioz articles and letters published in New York in 1879, but the British Museum had no copy of this book in the 1880s—or as late as 1951, when I looked for it there.

3. The work is still in print, in French and in English.

4. *The Star*, 9 July 1889; rptd. in *Shaw's Music*, ed. Dan H. Laurence (London: Max Reinhardt, 1981), 1:692.

5. Fugues on the word *Amen* were common in church music despite the absurdity of the endless repetition and the distorted accent "*men-a, men-a*," which the development brings about. Berlioz detested the practice and ridiculed it by writing such a fugue for the drunken revellers in *The Damnation of Faust.*

6. *Atala, or the Love of Two American Natives in the Desert* (1801) was the first part of a prose poem devoted to the glorification of primitive life on the new continent.

7. "Un pauvre petit Savoyard" is the opening air in Cherubini's opera *Les Deux Journées* (1800), which is also known as *The Water Carrier* and *Der Wasserträger.*

8. The young Berlioz was soon known at Paris concerts and operas as an on-the-spot critic of the "musical abuses," denouncing from his seat in the audience the misdeeds of "arrangers" of great works. Shaw in October 1879 wrote a long note on the same outrageous practices, echoing Berlioz on several points. (See pages 44–45.) It should be remembered that vocal criticism by audiences was usual until early in the twentieth century.

9. Colloquial for drummer, but used figuratively for "vulgar music-maker."

10. City policemen.

11. Roman Prize. Usually known as the *Prix de Rome,* an annual competition for composition students at the Paris Conservatoire. It carries a stipend and residence of three years at the French Academy in Rome. Berlioz won the prize in 1830 at his fourth try.

12. These half-dozen lines amount to a Shavian self-portrait and thereby confirm Shaw's identification of himself at that time with the young genius he found in the *Memoirs.*

\ 13. The violins to be played with the wooden part of the bow: this device, marked *col legno* in scoring, is used only for brief special effects and is not a Berliozian innovation. The rest of the description is correct, the "peculiar material" to be used on the tympani being sticks with sponge heads, again a common device. These details are to be found in the Berlioz *Treatise.*

14. An aria from Mozart's *Marriage of Figaro.*

15. Song by Beethoven, op. 75, no. 1 (1810). The words are by Goethe, for his wayward heroine Mignon in *Wilhelm Meister* (1796).

16. Aria from Rossini's opera *Tancredi* (1813).

17. The actress Harriet Smithson (1800–54), more Irish by her upbringing than English, is called Ophelia here because she captivated Paris (and Berlioz) particularly in that role during her Shakespearean appearances of 1827. The "barbaric" playwright was just beginning to be tolerated by the French, under the enthusiastic lead of the young Romantic artists.

18. This group of dates, beginning with Macaulay's (1800–59), places the "now" at 1879. The author then gives her age as eighty and the year also. To bridge the gap one may suppose the Postscript to have been written during the winter season that belongs to both years.

19. Tom Hood. This reference is ambiguous. Although Thomas Hood the poet (1799–1845) did do some assistant editing in his early years and could have been sent the "Reminiscence" if the author had known him before he himself became known, the figure universally called Tom Hood and known as the great editor of *Fun* and of many "annuals" was the son of Thomas, born in 1835, died in 1874. As the time when the fictional author tried to publish her story is left vague, the familiar name was probably thrown in for a similarly vague verisimilitude.

20. The line from *Twelfth Night*, spoken by the clown Feste (V.i.384–85), reads, "And thus the whirligig of time brings in his revenges."

21. This opera by Berlioz was downed by a cabal in Paris in 1838 but triumphantly revived by Liszt at Weimar in 1852. Again hissed in London in 1853, despite the presence of the Queen and Prince Consort, it has since found a place in the European repertory and been acknowledged as another Berlioz masterpiece.

Norma Jenckes

A SPRING-CLEANING FOR
THE ARTS

"Could you not send me some short middle article upon some social or other topic?" With this request on 2 June 1880, John Morley elicited for the *Pall Mall Gazette* the essay "Exhausted Arts" from Bernard Shaw, a novice who had been recommended to him by George Macmillan. Bernard Shaw was never an easy man; and the letters of his nonage reveal a sensitive nature stung by any encouragement or constructive criticism into a torrent of self-deprecation. Repeatedly in notes to well-meaning editors, he inveighed against his own work. In a letter to George Bentley on 5 March 1880, responding to his rejection of a story, "The Brand of Cain," Shaw escalated the criticism by insisting, "I shall not, however, abuse your kindness by asking you to read it again, because I think the failure of the story is more radical than you suppose." When Shaw was asked by Morley if he might be "willing occasionally to write for me on this paper," he submitted a review of a novel that the editor generously rejected: "I am not sure I can use your review, but I like the style of it."

When Shaw sent "Exhausted Arts," he also included a review of Irving's production of *The Merchant of Venice* with a note, "I should prefer writing on theatrical or musical events to manufacturing random articles, which is to me much the same thing as making bricks without straw." Shaw seems even at this early point in his career to have known his strengths, and Morley would have done well to have taken him at his own valuation. Instead he returned the material; not until five years later, under the editorship of W. T. Stead, would Shaw finally be published in the *Pall Mall Gazette*.

Shaw disparaged his essay, "Exhausted Arts," which, he warned Morley, "I am afraid you will find rather indigestible." In this mini-survey of the current state of the arts, Shaw mixed comments on major artists into a dense pastiche that cannot help but read like the under-argued lament of a newcomer to a field that he fears has been over-tilled.

In a kind of anxiety of belatedness, Shaw despaired that there was nothing left to write about. While he projected his own fears about exhaustion or lack of inspiration onto the arts, he also created a sense of hiatus, demarcating a ground zero from which something new might emerge.

Shaw labeled his essay "indigestible"; when the editor agreed, he pronounced himself "incorrigible." Self-deprecation concealed a strategy of self-protection that emerged early in his creative life. Hiding his injured pride, Shaw short-circuited any negative judgment by saying the worst things first and with greater force. After apologizing to Morley for baffling his attempt to befriend him, he signs off with a self-denigrating but amusingly mocking, "Should you ever require anything particularly disagreeable written about anybody, pray remember" G. B. Shaw.[1]

Not exactly "indigestible," the essay does need to be chewed over. What energy there is in it springs from the combative tone and the imagery of struggle that emanate from Shaw's conviction that the artists of the past forcibly block the would-be creators of the present. Giving proof of a theory of artistic development that Harold Bloom has popularized, Shaw evidences a vivid sense of "the anxiety of influence" that clearly held him in its grip.[2] The pervasive tropes of this essay convey blockage and sterility. Shaw sees active hostility between the artists of the present and the mighty dead. The artistic monuments of the past loom as obstacles that must not be imitated but disdained.

Much of Shaw's essay betrays the mixture of brashness and bewilderment of a young person of extraordinary promise. In an Herculean task of critical legerdemain Shaw makes all the areas of artistic activity disappear by dismissing them as devoid of interest. He tucked this essay in between the completion of his first novel, *Immaturity,* which would languish unpublished for fifty years, and the start on 1 December 1880 of his second novel, *The Irrational Knot.* Something happened to his authorial voice in that interval as he surveyed the fields of artistic achievement; he declared them barren, and so justified his own experiments in form and content. The great harvest that has been reaped has depleted the earth, and Shaw stands on fallow ground that he must cultivate in a new way.

Shaw constructs an imaginative double-bind for contemporary artists: the past blocks them and the future will outgrow them. Wondering what arts will exist to entertain posterity, he imagines a radically improved public that will have moved so beyond the moral and social dilemmas of the past that the art that expressed those concerns will only bemuse them. Shaw suppresses one of the assumptions of his argument to reach this conclusion, but it underlies everything that he predicts. The hidden figure in this carpet is the success of socialism. Never explicitly called for in the essay, Shaw's view of the future presupposes the existence of a majority of new men and new women forged in the struggle for a socialist society. What will such transformed audiences require in their arts?

Shaw responds to this question by examining the three literary genres. He finds that Shakespeare has so overshadowed the dramatic field that all successors from Betterton to Irving are adaptors and rewriters of the Bard's work. Here he digresses to include a thumbnail review of a recent revival of Colman's *Iron Chest*. In this small exploration of a current and particular dramatic work, what will become the characteristic Shavian critical voice gleams fleetingly.

As for poetry, Shaw declares that Shelley has confounded all followers. In a provocative description he conjures a line of blind poets groping to find their way either backward or forward from the point at which Shelley so prematurely left them. It is an odd and arresting image, and one that we wish he had glossed with some specific names and examples.

Perhaps it should come as no surprise that Shaw, an apprentice novelist, devotes the longest section to fiction, in which he argues that the novel's progress is "blocked by many hands." Praising George Eliot as its most advanced pioneer, Shaw lists Trollope, Thackeray, and Dickens as obstacles to change because they are imitated by "unreflective imaginations." When, a few weeks later, Shaw took up the task of writing his second novel, he had determined that it would be a non-Victorian work, reflecting his most advanced notions.

When Shaw turns his attention to music, he pronounces the exhaustion of "pure music" with great assurance, then discusses Bach, Haydn (whose name he misspelled), Beethoven, and Mozart. Already he has determined that Wagner is a genius "in a wilderness of clever men," and concludes by celebrating Mozart as the same monumental force in opera that Shakespeare is in drama.

Paradoxically, we begin to see that the ultimate praise for Shaw is his pronouncement that someone has completely blocked any further development in a field. No one need ever again attempt to write a Shakespearean play or a Mozart opera. Yet so compelling and powerful are their examples that lesser artists for centuries after are caught in a dream of imitation that comes close to parody.

Probably in inverse ratio to his knowledge of a field, Shaw sees greater hope in painting, for which he advances a curiously materialist analysis. The impermanence of canvas and the unique execution of each work prevent the masses from tiring of a painting. These factors make room for the contemporary painter; the fact that paintings perish "gives scope for activity." But even here he worries about the absence of new subject matter. He raises the question whose answer will come resoundingly from Paris in the next fifty years, "what new thing remains to be painted?"

In what may be one of the earlier expressions of *fin de siècle* malaise, Shaw asks in 1880, "what have we left for the twentieth century to do?" He clearly imagines himself active if not preeminent in that coming century. He anticipates "Homeric laughter" and a transformed world and audience for the arts. With high Utopian hopes, Shaw posits a culture wherein the arts will no longer serve a moral purpose; that purpose, being fully realized in society, need not be expressed in the arts. Optimistically, he prophesies a society that will meet all peoples' spiritual needs so that they will no longer yearn for them and recreate them in their artistic productions.

One of the most poignant aspects in reading the young Shaw is seeing how confident he was that the problems brought about by oppressive conditions would disappear with those conditions. Virile and aggressive, he took a kind of pugilistic delight in imagining the blocking hands of the dead masters and the feints and dodges of the new artists. He saw art as historically developing; he refused fixed aesthetic categories, theorizing a progression of taste in an ever-evolving society. In a way that current ideology and culture critics would endorse, Shaw denied universals; he expected old artistic forms to give way and be made obsolete by the new.

Shaw so envisioned radical change that he speculated that the very content and existence of his contemporary artists and their products would be a source of some puzzlement for the future. He wondered: "What motive will there be for psychological novels, compositions like the first movement of the ninth symphony, allegorical pictures of Pygmalion, and poems of baffled Fausts?"

What motive indeed? Shaw, already a consummate cultural relativist, recognized that society calls forth an art particular to its time and place. He pronounced the art of the nineteenth century insufficient for the needs of the twentieth. We can imagine him at the close of the essay rolling up his sleeves to pitch out the relics of the past and clear a space for his own work. In this mood he strode to his desk each day to complete the self-imposed discipline of the next thousand words of his second novel, *The Irrational Knot.*

In that next novel Shaw would begin to harness both aspects of his phenomenal mind, a mind that combined the polemical and the poetical in the same rare mixture that flowered in writers like Plato, Aristophanes, Dante, Goethe, and, in the twentieth century, Bertolt Brecht. In any of their efforts the poet or the polemicist might dominate, but in the greatest products of these minds, they are fused. In Shaw the balance would eventually find perfect expression in such masterpieces as *Man and Superman, Heartbreak House,* and *Saint Joan.* In the young Shaw struggling to write about exhausted arts, the two aspects of his mind conflicted and canceled each other. It is evidence of the immaturity of his imagination that he imposed a draconian division of labor on his own dualistic nature. That division produced the tone of uncanny emptiness and creative futility that defeated him in this essay. What he evokes as a polemical dead end for the arts, we can in hindsight see more clearly as a poetical "open sesame": the polemicist has cleared the cultural space in which the poet can create.

That new synthesis finds its first expression in *The Irrational Knot*. In this novel he used his powerful intellect to scrutinize the emotional life of his characters; under its brilliant light he exposed the conventional bromides of punishment for adultery or illegitimate pregnancy. He constructed a new basis for a true gentleman and gentlewoman to meet and mate. He himself recognized in the preface to the American edition of 1905 that he had broken new ground: "I seriously suggest that The Irrational Knot may be regarded as an early attempt on the part of the Life Force to write A Doll's House in English by the instrumentality of a very immature writer aged 24."[3] "Exhausted Arts" was the house-cleaning that same immature writer needed to finish in order to begin the task of expressing for the first time in his work a modern sensibility in fiction and later in drama.

In a rhapsodic conclusion Shaw prophesied the "artist of the future, no longer miserable in the proud function of educator." Unhappily, the future that Shaw evoked has not appeared; his own work could never "abandon the pulpit." Formed as he was in the Victorian era, he still shaped the modern one, and his writing will foster the moral education of his readers for as long as they need that education.

Exhausted Arts (1880)

[PROVENANCE: Unsigned holograph manuscript, eight unfoliated leaves, dated "13th June 1880" on verso of final leaf, beneath a small portrait drawing. On "2nd November 1882" Shaw added to this leaf a shorthand note: "The history of this article is as follows. John Morley, the editor of The Pall Mall Gazette, was asked by George Macmillan to give me something to do. Accordingly, he first got me to review a novel, and then requested me to write what he called 'a short middle article'. I sent him this! He immediately washed his hands of me. It was written when I was in the Telephone Company, in some haste. I was much worried at the time, but I have no reason to suppose that I could, under the most favourable circumstances, have done much better. The qualities of style which I particularly aimed at at this period were exactness, modesty, and simplicity!!!" Harry Ransom Humanities Research Center, The University of Texas at Austin.]

There are not so many paths in art for creative genius that we can look with complacency on the successive blocking of one after another of them by the hands of great artists in the past and present, or easily imagine how our posterity will entertain themselves when they are satiated with their great inheritance. That they will read magazine articles or speculative sub leaders is inconceivable; the better half of the world already yawns over such, and by judicious skipping, reduces its newspaper to an abstract and brief chronicle of the time. They will hold cynicism cheap as a dull trick, laugh at our Carlyle-inspired seriousness, pity our Dickens-derived facetiousness, and amaze each other by citing the commonplaces which were called principles and persecuted in the days when men were distinguished by such obsolete terms as positivist, materialist, agnostic, Comtist, critic, and gentleman. Nevertheless, they will have their literature, their music, their pictures, and their theatres, as we have. But what will they read? What will they listen to? What will they look at? Let us examine our own resources. In literature, there are three domains, drama, poetry, and novel. In all three, a mighty harvest has left the soil sterile. Every change of manners, it is true, brings forth a good comedy. But what credit as a measure of dramatic genius has the power of producing comedy enjoyed since the beginning of the seventeenth century? The standard of British drama is Shakspere, who strangled his successors, and left a line of Bettertons, Garricks, Youngs, Keans, Brookes,[4] Macreadys, Barry Sullivans, and Irvings, crying to his victims for new heroes to embody, and receiving in return a series of laughable travesties, of which the recently revived "Iron Chest" of Colman[5] may serve as an example. Poetry received at once its deathblow and its first justification as a rational pursuit from Shelley, who not only achieved the high intellectual feat of convincing the mob that he was incapable of reasoning, but imposed his unfulfilled promise on us as the consummation of his art. The few who started from the place where he fell, blindly set their faces toward the point from which he started, and, having passed that, are stumbling in the chaos in which he may have spent his silent period. Prose fiction is in like case, but its progress has been blocked by many hands instead of one, and now its most advanced pioneer,[6] confessedly in a difficulty as to her next step, stands between the forward impulse of her genius, and the clamour of an undiscerning rabble who would bait her back with a demand for another "Mill on the Floss". In another department, Mr. Trollope has left no room for a successor; hardly any for himself. He may long for new worlds to chronicle, but these will not come in his time. Even rebellion against the narrow line of noveldom has been exhausted. The funny reality of slatternly domesticity, and the humours of obstreperous hoydens have been made books of, and so, as far as future writers will be concerned, done with. A mixture of sterling comedy, farce, and harlequinade, with much intolerable sentimentality, has been tried; extravagantly and egotistically by Dickens, cautiously and garrulously by Thackeray; both of whom persuaded themselves that they were moralists, and consequently sacrificed naturalness as well as probability for the sake of effect. More easily imitable, and more attractive to unreflective imaginations than George Eliot or Mr. Trollope, they have popularised a style not less wearisome than the spurious Macaulayism of ordinary journalism, and have confused the boundaries of the track which (happily for the hours of our childhood spent with their books) they had not the far seeing self denial to confine themselves to.

In music, the path seems blocked too. When we talk of the music of the future, we think of the composition of the past. Pure music is confessedly exhausted. Each form of it has fallen into the toils of a giant. Sebastian Bach so dealt with scholastic counterpoint that he left not a fragment of it to be used by his successors. His son accepted the position frankly, and suggested a new vehicle, the symphony, which Hadyn developed into a form of perfect beauty and order, whereupon Beethoven convulsed it in the same spirit and at the same time as the French revolution convulsed Europe, and, having wrought it almost to the utterance of intelligible speech, proclaimed the end of its career by inaugurating the poem set to music. This in turn has had its due at the hands of Wagner, who still remains with us, one of a very few geniuses in a wilderness of clever men. In the meantime arose Mozart, the greatest of all artists, and wrote the symphony in G minor in a style which even Beethoven made no attempt to develop, and three typical operas which are as finally pre-eminent as the plays of Shakspere.

The prospects of painting are a degree more hopeful; for, though Michel Angelo long since left the art of design like a blown egg, and though branches of art which he never practised have each received sufficient exposition from greater hands—or hands which, more for the sake of defying his fascination than from conviction, we impartially call greater—yet pictures are perishable, and as, when we most applauded the old masters, we rubbed their works with porter in order to make them look venerable, our descendants will not be able to feast their eyes, as they will their ears and imaginations, with the labours of dead men. The painter, secure of an audience for his retold tale, and at ease in a profession of high historical and social interest is already the happiest of artists. Pictures are not regarded with familiarity like books, nor with solemn bewilderment like symphonies. Yet the difficulty is here too, for what new thing remains to be painted? The ground left bare by perished works may give scope for activity, but not material for creation.

Only four fine arts, and three exhausted, and fain to prop themselves by alliance with the instinct of romance, once despised in their academies! What have we left for the twentieth century to do? Only to burst into Homeric laughter at the spectacle of an age when the men who were rightly esteemed the very salt of the earth expressed their longing for a better civilization by the laborious plastering of canvas with imitations of human forms, the planning of sounds to be emitted from machines of brass, wood, and strings, and the making up of tales about passions the existence of which was incompatible with their social relations. The joke will not be in the existence of these practices, for they will doubtless survive, and attain to a variety and perfection in technical resources in comparison to which our meanly furnished palettes and our discordant equally tempered pianos will seem impracticable. But that, instead of being recognised as devices to gratify the senses, the fine arts are revered as vehicles of the highest moral aspirations of mankind, may well provoke amazement and laughter from a generation accustomed to give play to these in their lives instead of in their handiwork. The modern worship of art is only the worship of morality in disguise; for art is the only calling that can still boast of martyrs. Men who love truth, who hunger for austerity or loveliness of life, and who loathe fashionable conventions, must needs take up pen or brush, because society does not admit of the satisfaction of their radical propensities in the modes of intercourse which it permits. Besides, how can rigid morality preserve the geniality so essential to the completeness of its virtue, if it be perpetually in combat with neighbouring expediency? The same nobility which is so delightful in art, is intolerable in the artist, who is driven to reserve his yearnings for his craft, and blunt himself first to tolerance of, and finally to participation in[,] the dishonest complaisances of his fellow men. Shelley, Mill, Auguste Comte, and Wagner: would these have been comfortable companions for most of us? Yet [we] must believe that a day is approaching in which society will so completely satisfy all the spiritual needs of such men, that they will no more recognise them as needs than we feel the value of that degree of liberty for which an Egyptian slave schemes. In that day, what motive will there be for psychological novels, compositions like the first movement of the ninth symphony, allegorical pictures of Pygmalion, and poems of baffled Fausts? They will be referred to indigestion, and oppressive social conditions, and will be as impossible of reproduction as the legends of the Volsungs and Niblungs are nowadays.

There remains one sphere of art, as much despised as the art of dressing, as subject to the changes of fashion, and as immortal. This is the sphere of pure romance, of painting to excite admiration and pleasure, of composing to stir the blood or soothe the senses, and of writing to arouse interest, suspense, or mirth. An intellectual people will absolutely refuse to accept matter for reflection in lieu of emotional luxury. As soon as science shall make the world wiser than Hamlet, the abortive metaphysics of that prince will be deemed less meritorious than the laughable misunderstandings in the Comedy of Errors, or whatever newest farce may have supplanted it. The artist of the future, no longer miserable in the proud function of educator, will be happy as the entertainer and intellectual and moral equal of his companions, and will look back on that monstrous egotist, the artist of the nineteenth century, with a feeling of which it is fortunate for our vanity that we can form no presentiment. Works like the statues of Greece, impossible to the tormented sociologists of the Christian Era, will again be hewn by sculptors amidst the shapely republicans of Hygeia.[7] Art will abandon the pulpit, and, free from the diseased languor of modern æstheticism, flourish in perfect beauty and luxuriousness in the midst of a healthy Philistinism which will laugh— though not ungently—at the mystic pretensions of our workers in ink, plaster, and the sound loom of the orchestra.

Notes

1. John Morley to Shaw, 21 May and 2 June 1880; Shaw to George Bentley, 5 March 1880; Shaw to Morley, 13 and 15 June 1880, in Bernard Shaw, *Collected Letters 1874–1897,* ed. Dan H. Laurence (New York: Dodd, Mead, 1965), pp. 29–32, in which the first Morley letter is misdated 22 May.

2. Harold Bloom, *The Anxiety of Influence* (New York: Oxford University Press, 1973), pp. 30–32.

3. Bernard Shaw, *The Irrational Knot* (New York: Brentano, 1905), p. xxv.

4. Gustavus Vaughan Brooke (1818–66), Irish actor who performed in London, America, and Australia.

5. *The Iron Chest* (1796) by George Colman the Younger (1762–1836), a frequently revived adaptation of William Godwin's novel *Caleb Williams,* was performed by Henry Irving in London, 30 September 1879.

6. An asterisk in the original manuscript here draws attention to a tiny shorthand note subsequently inserted in the left margin: "*This refers to George Eliot, who died in 1881." Shaw was in error: Eliot died on 22 December 1880.

7. Goddess of health in Greek mythology, daughter of Aescalapius; by extension, a society dedicated to healthy living.

Brian Tyson

ENTER THE LITERARY CRITIC

Shaw finished his first novel *Immaturity* in 1879, submitting it to Hurst & Blackett, who rejected it on 13 November; next to Kegan Paul & Co., who rejected it twelve days later; and thirdly to Macmillan, who sent a more encouraging rejection on 31 January 1880. The novel was described as "the work of a humourist and a realist" by Macmillan's reader, whose report prompted Shaw to suggest in reply that he liberate his talent in "a series of magazine papers." John Morley, a reader for Macmillan, who, having been induced in May 1880 for a time to take command of the *Pall Mall Gazette* with a view to its "transformation into a genuinely liberal paper," wrote to Shaw on the 22nd of that month to say that he had heard from "a common friend" George Macmillan that Shaw "might perhaps be able & willing occasionally to write for me on this paper," and suggested a meeting. Shaw responded immediately in the affirmative and, following their meeting, submitted a specimen review of *George Vanbrugh's Mistake*, of which only a draft fragment survives. On 2 June 1880 Morley rejected the review, saying, "I am not sure I can use your review, but I like the style of it. Could you not send me some short middle article upon some social or other topic?" Shaw's diary reveals that he spent the sum of 2d on a copy of the *Gazette* on 3 June 1880, and almost immediately submitted further samples of his journalism to Morley, including an essay, "Exhausted Arts," and a review of *The Merchant of Venice*. These were returned before the middle of the month. Indeed, the sum total of Shaw's literary efforts at this time was Morley's discouraging advice that he would "do well to get out of journalism."[1]

[Review of H. B. Pritchard's George Vanbrugh's Mistake. *3 Vols. London: Sampson Low & Co., 1880.]*

[PROVENANCE: Unsigned holograph fragment (p. 3), undated. British Library: Add. Mss. 50699, folio 237. The review, written in May 1880, was

submitted to John Morley, editor of the Pall Mall Gazette, *who acknowledged its receipt on 2 June. The surviving text commences in mid-sentence.]*

. . . the colloquy with the herbalist which introduced him.

In so stretching a story as to imply that it was not worth the trouble of writing,[2] it is hardly possible to avoid exciting a sense of injustice in the author except by hitting his artistic conscience hard, and this, in the case of a writer of fiction, is difficult to effect; for the modern novelist, though admitting the bad effect of tautology, and the policy of writing words enough to fill three volumes, acts in every other respect as though bookmaking were a natural gift, born in a state of equal fertility and cultivation. The author[3] of "George Vanbrugh's Mistake", though an agreeable narrator and no novice, has apparently not yet deduced even a primer of fiction from the practice of the great English masters of the craft. Else, why is the geniality of the style so often confounded with the insolent familiarity of slang? When a polite writer describes an abashed person as "sat upon", and a heap of dusty bottles as being in "glorious" confusion, are we not entitled to ask coldly what these terms mean, without risking censure as hypercritical purists. If a work is confessedly ephemeral, it is not worth criticising. If it be written, like all good art work, as though it . . .

ON SHAW'S REVIEW OF *THE FUTURE OF MARRIAGE* (1885)

For Shaw's generation of Socialists, social inequities were perhaps most painfully expressed in sex relationships, at the storm center of which were the laws respecting marriage and divorce. In the winter of 1884–85 Shaw edited Laurence Gronlund's *Co-Operative Commonwealth,* which states bluntly that "In law the wife is nothing but the husband's property." Another book published in the same year, with which Shaw was familiar (he used it when writing *Mrs Warren's Profession* in 1893), was *Woman in the Past, Present and Future,* by the German Social Democrat August Bebel, who posed the contemporary Socialist question about marriage precisely:

> But we must ascertain which form of marriage is the more moral or, in other words, the more likely to conduce to the advantage of humanity in all its phases, a marriage founded on the bourgeois idea of property and therefore compulsory, with its many attendant evils and mostly imperfect realisation of its objects, a social institution beyond the reach of millions, or a marriage founded on the free untrammeled choice of love, such as is only possible in a Socialistic society.[4]

The "free untrammeled choice of love," however, although Shaw was later to reiterate its necessity in order that the "Life Force" have free rein, was being narrowly interpreted by some of Shaw's own acquaintances, who practiced various forms of free union. Charles Bradlaugh and Annie Besant, for example, both scarred by conventional marriages, were so linked in the public mind. Also living together were Edward Aveling and Eleanor Marx. She, in this same year of 1885, had encouraged Shaw to play Krogstad to her Nora in a reading of Ibsen's *Doll's House*, a play whose theme of the emancipation of women had brought the whole marriage question to public discussion. Among the books on the "marriage question" that Shaw reviewed for the *Pall Mall Gazette* were Ouida's *Othmar* (1885), which contains a Court of Love, a sort of symposium of views on love and marriage, and Richter's *Melita* (1886), which depicts the harem (in which Turkish women are "caged up birds") as the edifice of man's distrust and jealousy, and woman's subjection and degradation. Thus, the Eirenikon, which simply means a proposal tending to reconcile differences, was a most timely publication, and Shaw's initial disclaimer in his review that Socialism had anything to do with marriage was perhaps a reflection of his desire to separate Socialism from the hedonistic "self-culture" of the "New Life" movement, from which the Fabians had recently split, with its growing interest in sexual radicalism, rather than the practical problems of creating educational opportunities and better careers for women.

[The Future of Marriage, 1885]

[Review of The Future of Marriage: An Eirenikon for a Question of Today. By a Respectable Woman. *London: The Modern Press, 1885.]*

[PROVENANCE: Untitled holograph manuscript, on blue paper, undated, signed "George Bernard Shaw" on final leaf. Shaw's diary indicates it was written on 9 March 1885 for The Commonweal. *British Library: Add. Mss. 50693, folios 118–22. Critical comments in an unidentified hand in the margins.]*

As the question of the relation of the sexes is one with which Socialists, as Socialists, have nothing to do, and one which is likely to discredit them unnecessarily if they meddle with it, it was not to be expected—human perversity being taken into account—that they would long be discreet enough to let it alone. The subject, neither a delicate nor a dangerous one if reasonably treated, can be made offensive beyond any other that needs discussion, by the least shamefacedness in confronting it. An apology will only make matters worse: the only tolerable attitude towards it is purely rational. But even a purely rational discussion of the subject will often, by merely reminding readers of their sexual impulses, make those impulses importunate. Such importunity is resented by many persons as an indignity which they desire to be subjected to as seldom as possible. Hence the prevailing objection to be so reminded even by a purely rational discussion, unless the discussion compensates them by a sufficiently valuable contribution to their knowledge either of the facts or of the duties of the sexual relation. Two conditions are therefore imposed on debaters. First: that if they suffer themselves to be biassed by their own sexual impulses for an instant, they will be expelled from the arena for indecency. Second: that if they have nothing new to say, they had better hold their tongues.

The author of the pamphlet which has suggested these remarks very unnecessarily begs the question of her own respectability by announcing herself on the cover as A Respectable Woman. As the only classes in English society who are in the habit of loudly proclaiming themselves Respectable Women are ladies who let furnished apartments, and ladies who sometimes take them, I venture to condemn this title-page because it violates the first condition of the debate in anticipating by denial the irrational supposition that a woman that writes about marriage cannot be respectable.[5] The author should not have betrayed her consciousness by thus braving a feeling that exists only in the minds of people not sufficiently evolved to be trusted with any books except those written for grown-up children. Such superstitions should not be braved: they should be disregarded. The second edition of the pamphlet may better be issued as by Jane Smith or Harriet Jones, or simply as by a woman; though the feminine authorship is sufficiently evident without express statement. The book itself extends to thirty pages; but nothing comes out clearly except the writer's deep concern at the concurrent carnival and fast, each supported by and yet hostile to the other, presented by prostitution and marriage in modern societies. "A true human serviceable polyandry", says the author, "should be, according to analogy, the sole cure for the hideous and degrading polyandry that now runs riot in our streets". This is almost as irritating as the paragraph of their Manifesto in which the Socialist League, without the slightest provocation, announces "Our modern bourgeois property-marriage, maintained as it is by its necessary complement, universal venal prostitution, would" (under Socialism) "give place to kindly and human relations between the sexes". This is the language of emotion, not of science.[6] What is a true human serviceable polyandry? What are kindly and human relations between the sexes? Why this insistence on the qualification "human" for a relation which is not distinctively human at all, common as it is to beasts and plants? It may be urged that prostitution and the "bourgeois property-marriage" are distinctly human institutions to which plants and beasts have not yet attained; but these human institutions are precisely those to which the Socialist League and the Respectable Woman deny humanity. Until the terms have been defined, such declarations can add nothing to the controversy; and so, by our second condition, they had better remain unuttered. We are all agreed that, in modern society, the sexual function, though indispensable to the race, is a nuisance to the individual. No heralds of discontent are needed: we are discontented already. Ladies and gentlemen, respectable or otherwise, have only to state their remedies definitely to ensure attention, consideration, and, if practicable, adoption. They may call the remedy human and kindly if they please; but they must state what the remedy is. Human and kindly promiscuity, with human and kindly—though always precisely defined—provision for the custody of the children, is a discussable proposition. "Kindly and human relation between the sexes" is not, because the point at issue is precisely what relation is human and kindly. Even the "bourgeois property-marriage" founds its claims to recognition on the ordered kindliness and humanity which it claims to have substituted for the savagery which its supporters believe to be the only alternative.

The "bourgeois-property-marriage" [,] however, is not now enforced by law. Unmarried couples cohabit without incurring any legal penalty. More than that, the woman's legal standing is better every way than that of a wife; and the man, whilst he escapes heavy responsibilities, forfeits nothing but his control over his children: a disability which, judging from the average solicitude of men for their illegitimate children, he can endure with considerable fortitude. It is true that the pair are boycotted by many of their acquaintances; but this is not the fault of the law; and no change except a change in the opinions of the boycotters could secure recognition for the transgressors of custom. Women, ruthless boycotters on such occasions, are perfectly justified in being so. For them Free Love would prove just such another delusion as Free Contract for the labourer. It could benefit her only when her love happened to be a commodity in the market, and a very scarce one: that is, when there were much fewer women than men in the country. Her freedom, like that of the labourers, would only be to change her master: to take the highest wage offered: to compete for that wage at forty with rivals of twentyfive: to household without fixity of tenure: to drudge towards old age without even such chance of a legally secured maintenance in old age as a custom-shrunk procuress may now hope from a marriage with some provident pimp. Women may profit by the experience of Men to the extent of feeling assured that whilst she remains virtually a slave she had better be a chattel slave, as wives are now, than a wage-slave, as the "free labourer" is now. It may be hard on many a dutiful wife and mother at present to know that her husband keeps another woman for his pleasure in a suburban villa; but if marriage were abolished he would simply keep her at home in the drawingroom whilst the wife, when she grew old, would be sent to the kitchen or nursery, unless indeed she was not wanted in either place, in which case she would not improbably be driven into the streets. If there be any optimist mad enough to question whether men would so basely abuse their power, I would ask him what abuse of power have men ever foregone. Wedlock is a heavy chain for a man to rivet upon herself [himself]; but the woman is born with the chain on: to her, wedlock only means riveting the other end of it upon a man. Abolish wedlock, and the man is free; but the woman is left to bear the whole weight of her servitude alone. When Socialism is realized, men, in spite of their professions, will probably try to exclude women, directly or indirectly, from perfect equality with their former masters. If they succeed, their success will be the failure of Socialism. If they fail, or abstain in justice from the attempt, every woman will be able, should she wish it, to die a virgin after a life of comfortable independence.[7] Then the matter may safely be left to settle itself as it has already done in the case of the few women who are, by monopoly of genius and peculiarity of position, independent both pecuniarily and socially. But until such settlement be general, I would counsel every woman to connect herself with a man by no slighter link than the very heaviest fetter the law can forge. Some time ago a large firm of contractors gave orders for the discharge of all hands over fortyfive years of age. This was the fruit of Free Contract. A similar order on the part of husbands would not improbably be one of the first fruits of Free Love.

ON SHAW'S "SOCIALIST'S NOTION OF A NOVEL" (1887)

By 1887 Shaw had been a book reviewer for the *Pall Mall Gazette* for two years. According to his *Diary*, he received *Landon Deecroft* on 11 November 1886, read it on 5 and 6 January 1887, dispatched the review on 9 January, and had it returned on the 14th. Its rejection undoubtedly was due to the fact that his procrastination necessitated assigning another reviewer to the job, an unsigned review appearing on 14 January 1887.

A Socialist's Notion of a Novel (1887)

[Review of Laon Ramsey's Landon Deecroft. *London: William Reeves, 1886.]*

[PROVENANCE: Unsigned holograph manuscript, on blue paper, undated; Shaw's diary indicates it was drafted on 6 and 7 January 1887. British Library: Add. Mss. 50693, folios 140–43.]

"Laon Ramsey"[8] offers this book to the public as "a socialistic novel containing an Exposition and a Defence of the Principles of Socialism". Now if he had labelled it merely "a novel containing an exposition and defence of Socialism", one might fall back on individualistic definitions of the word novel to shew that "Landon Deecroft" is not a novel at all. Dr. Johnson says that a novel is "a small tale, generally of love";[9] and Landon Deecroft is certainly not that. Mr. Robert Hunter,[10] a lexicographer of the present hour, and so well abreast of his time as to insist on the difference between a novel and a romance, defines the former as a work of fiction in which the passions, especially that of love, are exhibited in a state of great activity. That, again, Landon Deecroft certainly is not. It is, as "Laon Ramsey" says, "a socialistic novel"; and the difference is so alarming, that in view of the inevitable dawn of a great Hyndmanic epoch,[11] lovers of the old school of Fielding, Scott & Dickens should lose no time in vehemently protesting against the term. A new edition of "Daniel Deronda", with Gwendolen, Grandcourt, and Daniel himself expunged, would, as a joy at Mudie's,[12] compete successfully with "Landon Deecroft". This opinion is not the outcome of prejudice against Laon Ramsey's views: the present writer has been entrusted with the duty of reviewing the book expressly on the principle of setting a socialist to catch a socialist. But mistakes in the classification of books must be set right in spite of the claims of fraternity; and the truth is that the so-called "novel" is nothing but a report of an imaginary discussion on socialism; and that light minded persons who may buy it on the usual understanding, to solace a railway journey, will find themselves grossly imposed on.

The exposition of the principles of Socialism will help inquirers into difficulties, but not out of them—will convince them that we are all wrong, but not that we are likely to come all right. The author does not seem to have kept pace with the development of socialism during the present century from the Utopias of Owen and Fourier[13] to the scientific systems of the disciples of Marx. For there are Utopian socialists and scientific socialists. The Utopian literary style is sentimental, humanitarian, prophetic, optimistic, and hi-falutin. The Marxist style is crisply dogmatic, and implacably and abusively contemptuous of all the idols of respectability. Socialist ladies, philanthropists, and clergymen lean backwards to Utopianism: pessimists, skilled thinkers, and the constitutionally hard-headed prefer Marx. Landon Deecroft is a belated Utopian who repeats the experiment made on the Vandeleur estate at Ralahine half a century ago by Mr. Craig.[14] The narrative ends before the exhaustion of the temporary and partial success which always attends such experiments when there is a competent despot on the premises.

In the meantime sundry visitors turn up and attempt to pose Landon

with the hackneyed objections which socialists answer with such triumphant ease, but which also a really skilled critic would never dream of
raising. There is the inevitable man who thinks that the State has no right
to interfere, who wants to know whether we are to be made a nation of
mediocrities, who is flustered by the prospect of having his individual
freedom curtailed by "a gigantic system of slavery", who does not believe
that people can be made virtuous by act of parliament, who is afraid that
the whole thing is a plot to defeat [the] survival of the fittest, who is not
going to be ordered about by an army of officials, and who points out that
as some will always be lazy and improvident, and others industrious and
thrifty, matters will always come round again to their present state. Landon Deecroft of course easily smashes, pulverises, and destroys these
commonplaces of amateur discussion; but in doing so he makes slips of
which an expert opponent would not fail to take advantage. He defines
exchange-value as "something over and above, or independent of labour-
value", and denounces the theory of market value of the current political
economy as "immoral". Now ever since the Ricardian theory of value was
brought into question by Jevons,[15] it has been impossible to say what
theory of value is entitled to call itself the current one; but in terms of the
view which prevailed from Ricardo to Cairnes,[16] it may be confidently said
that the labourers' present grievance as to market value is that it is something under and below labour value, and that normal exchange value is
exactly labour value. And if it is fair to call an economic theory of value
immoral, it is no less fair to call the germ theory of fever infectious.
Landon Deecroft's attempt to justify the expropriation of the instruments
of production will certainly not convert the Liberty & Property Defence
League.[17] "As man cannot manufacture land", he says, "so individual man
cannot manufacture the complicated instruments and machines which
are necessary to our present system of production: they are the results of
the labour of the great body of the people, and to the people they rightfully belong". But according to Landon Deecroft's own theory, the most
complicated machine may rightfully belong to any individual who pays
labour value for it to the makers, and rent to the whole people for the raw
material, a transaction which socialism proposes to render possible, and
indeed to leave without alternative. Again, on page 98, Deecroft demands
"What is the use of telling a mechanic who is out of employment that he is
at liberty to work at whatever occupation he may choose, when he has been
trained in one particular department of production, and is therefore
unable to perform any other kind of labour". The individualist objector
asks how socialism would help that mechanic, to which Deecroft on the
very next page replies that "the State or the community, having the means
of production under its own control, would be able to provide other kinds
of employment". Obviously, the individualist might meet this with

Deecroft[']s own previous question. The pages dealing with interest are useless, partly because interest can no more be abolished by a demonstration of its unfairness than toothache can be abolished by a demonstration of its hurtfulness; and partly because Landon is unacquainted with the economic theory of interest, and only deals with the sort of excuses for it that unreflective stockholders are wont to make. On page 125 he admits a common individualistic blunder—the confusion of inequality of ability with dissimilarity of talent: one of those rash concessions which sometimes make socialists pray to be saved from their friends, and individualists hope that their enemies will continue to write books. In blaming co-operators and others for buying in the cheapest market, he seems to forget that high prices are not at present a guarantee that the seller is not a sweater who prefers big profits and slow returns, and whose workpeople are no better off than those of sweaters of the opposite persuasion. His idea of a peaceful "transition" to socialism, is 1. Nationalization of Land, and 2. Communalization of the instruments of production and exchange: a programme which suggests that his idea of a gradual change of level would perhaps be realized by an invalid coming down the Monument stairs in two jumps.[18] But it is likely enough that the municipalization of land in towns, and the transfer of our vast centralized joint stock enterprises to the State, will be the actual steps in the transition—if it is to be a transition, and not "a header".

For the rest, the book is an earnest, sincere, and disinterested performance, and will doubtless set many readers thinking for the first time upon the extent to which our industrial civilization has outgrown our institutions.

ON SHAW'S "FOUND AT LAST—A NEW POET" (1887)

Edith Nesbit (1858–1924), English novelist, poet, and writer of books for children, began to write seriously in 1876, her first published piece, the poem "Dawn," appearing in the *Sunday Magazine* that year. She married Hubert Bland (1856–1914) in 1880. Like her husband, she was an active Socialist and one of the founders in 1883 of the Fellowship of the New Life, out of which grew the Fabian Society in 1884. Mrs. Bland haunted the British Museum, where Shaw habitually worked, throughout the 1880s. On 26 June 1886, Shaw discovered that she had become "passionately attached" to him (*Diary*, 34) and spent some time dodging her amorous advances. On 10 November that year, Edith showed Shaw her new book of poems *Lays and Legends* (1886), about which Shaw wrote the following review on 6 July 1887 for the *Pall Mall Gazette*, which did not accept it. Notwithstanding Shaw's asseveration that Edith Nesbit wrote poetry because "there is nothing else she can do so well," posterity has disagreed, settling instead on her incomparable children's fiction as her lasting contribution to letters. Shaw reviewed a later book of her poems, *Leaves of Life*, in *The Star* on 18 December 1888, saying "Miss Nesbit (Mrs. Bland) has already established her right to be called a poetess. She is not without her debt to sisters and brothers of her art, possibly to Mrs. Browning for spirit, and less markedly to Mr. Swinburne for form. But she has a line of her own, and no one who has followed her contributions to fugitive literature will have failed to note in her a real touch of original inspiration." It was not until the following year (1889) that "E. Nesbit," as she habitually called herself as author, published *The Story of the Treasure Seekers*, and established herself as a children's author of great merit. In this and subsequent children's books, notably *The Railway Children* (1906), she presented children as realistic beings behaving naturally, and her steadiness of character-drawing and excellence of style place her in the top rank of writers of children's fiction.

Found at Last—A New Poet (1887)

[Review of Edith Nesbit, Lays and Legends. *London: Longmans, 1886.]*

[PROVENANCE: Holograph manuscript, two leaves foliated by Shaw: 1–2, on blue paper, undated; Shaw's diary indicates it was written on 6 July 1887 for the Pall Mall Gazette. *Unsigned; but a holograph note on reverse of second leaf reads: "Proof to G.B. Shaw. . . ." William D. Chase Collection, Ellen Clarke Bertrand Library, Bucknell University, Lewisburg, Pa.]*

A sufficient authority lately declared that ambition to discover new poets, and to do for them what Mr. Ruskin did for Turner,[19] is a common form of critical mania. It is certain that a season seldom passes without an announcement, in some quarter, of the dawn of a true lyric genius, which the critic hauls above the horizon for a moment until his endurance is exhausted, when he lets go, and down it drops plumb into the blind cave of eternal night.[20] But the critics who have been "discovering" the author of these Lays and Legends seem this time to have found what they were looking for. Edith Nesbit succeeds Elizabeth Barrett Browning in English letters as a woman-poet by imperative gift and temperament. Hers is no case of a woman of letters learning how to write good verses because she loves poetry and desires to be a poetess: to write poems is her fate, because there is nothing else she can do so well, and because her strong, passionate, unerringly aimed utterance will take no other form. You do not pause to admire the verse, weigh the lines, or search for the meaning: the book is eloquent and talks to you, sometimes like an angry and unreasonable wife, sometimes like a restless and too sensitive girl, often like a noblehearted and intelligent woman; but always as a living voice and urgent song, never as the collected samples of a clever lady's acquired expertness in producing faultless verses about which you will have something nice to say presently.

The faults of the poems are so directly and intimately the faults of the woman that mere literary criticism cannot touch them effectively. She can sing almost without thinking; and is occasionally so unconscientious as to do it. When she does think, she does not always think enough, or pay much heed to the quality of her thought. And there is too much of the luxury of unreal grief, of getting into the vein by imagining church-yards and jiltings and the like, as people will do in spite of the remon-strances of people who have "come to forty year" and know better. But in poetry the strength of the chain is that of the strongest link, and the best of these Lays and Legends plainly owe their quick vitality either to the sting of personal experience, or the keen interest of a sympathetic and highly intelligent observation, lightened by an occasional inimitable dash of humorous shrewishness. Edith Nesbit will do well to look carefully to her next volume; for it will not escape exacting criticism.

ON SHAW'S LECTURE, "THAT REALISM IS THE GOAL OF FICTION" (1888)

Just as the reaction of the Romantics to the empiricism of Newton and Locke led to their insistence that the creative imagination illuminate reality, rather than passively reflect it, so Realism in the nineteenth cen-tury began in the wake of such influences as Comte, who argued that the key to understanding the world was careful observation and experimen-tation to reveal causes and effects behind events, and Darwin, whose *Origin of Species by Means of Natural Selection* appeared in 1859. In the same year George Eliot's *Adam Bede* was published, whose seventeenth chapter is taken by many to be a manifesto of fictional Realism. "False-hood is so easy. Truth so difficult," she asserts. "The pencil is conscious of a delightful facility in drawing a griffin—the longer the claws, and the bigger the wings, the better; but that marvellous facility which we mis-took for genius is apt to forsake us when we want to draw a real unexag-gerated lion." This warning against the excesses of Romanticism was one that Shaw, the young novelist and admirer of George Eliot, took seri-ously. His own novels had certainly attempted to be "realistic." Macmillan & Co., describing the first of them as "not common," went on to say, "It is the work of a humourist and a realist, crossed, however, by veins of merely literary discussion." Shaw's reply to them confirmed his intention "to write a novel scrupulously true to nature, with no incident in it to which everyday experience might not afford a parallel."

His interest in Realism continued and intensified throughout Shaw's tenure as book critic for the *Pall Mall Gazette,* 1885–88. With refreshing regularity and great good humor, Shaw lambasts the formulaic novels of Mrs. Braddon, attacks authors such as Fayr Madoc for the improbability of their plots, and others, like Henry Keenan, for the falseness of their dialogue. In his articles he seizes eagerly on any writer who exhibits signs of realism; a fact that leads him to praise Ouida (see below)—although he acknowledges her ignorance of some of the things she writes about— claiming: "She is true to herself and the facts as she sees them. Though her share of the optimistic illusions of humanity tempts her from within, and Mrs. Grundy threatens her from without, she insists on the naked truth."

Late in the year 1886, and early in 1887, Realism formed a talking point between Shaw and William Archer (see *Diary,* 14 August 1886 and 17 April 1887); and in the autumn of 1887, Shaw's views on the subject appeared in his review "Realism, Real and Unreal," 29 September, in the *Pall Mall Gazette.* The importance of this article lies less in the distinction it draws between Realists who present only the unsavory facts (with an eye to the profits of sensationalism), and those like Trollope and W. E. Norris who present the truth impartially, good as well as bad, than in the underlying assumption upon which the entire article is based, namely that Realism is the only desirable mode. Moreover, when Shaw presented Archer with the transcript of their collaborative effort, the play *Rheingold* (later to be called *Widowers' Houses*) less than a week after his *PMG* review, the covering letter insisted on the Realism of the piece. The idea occurs three times: Shaw complains that the "long-lost old woman," if introduced, will destroy the *realism* of the thing; he claims that his genius has brought Archer's romantic notion into contact with *real* life; and asserts that the title of the play *Rheingold* should be dispensed with on the ground that it is romantic, whereas Shaw's play is *realism.*

Unsurprisingly, when Shaw addressed the Blackheath Essay and Debating Society three months later on 18 January 1888, he moved that Realism is the Goal of Fiction. The caution with which his *Pall Mall Gazette* article began is, however, here intensified. The problem with Realism is that it depends upon individual perception. Shaw in this speech posits a spectrum of Realism. At one end is the unreal Romance; next come the novels of Trollope and Payn, which are true to the actual experiences of the writers *and a desire to use their art as a means of making that experience instructive and helpful*—that is, didactic. George Eliot, who occupies the next rung on the realistic ladder, is, according to Shaw, "purely didactic," because she teaches us about life; while the summit of didactic (and therefore, according to Shaw, Realistic) fiction is occupied by John Bunyan, Dante, and Goethe, whose Realism is an attempt "to get at the realities underlying even naturalism." Zola, who espoused "scientific" methods, was, to Shaw, a "naturalist," simply filling the void created by the omission of sexual discussion in English literature for a century and a half.

That Realism is the Goal of Fiction (lecture, 1888)

[PROVENANCE: Unsigned holograph manuscript in paper-covered composition book, title on inner front cover, in ink with a few pencil revisions, foliated by Shaw: 1–13, dated at top left of first leaf "13/1/88" and at end of text "14th January 1888." Stephen Winsten Collection, Harry Ransom Humanities Research Center, The University of Texas at Austin.]

The Resolution which I have to move this evening—that Realism is the Goal of Fiction—is one over which I am sorry to say—since this is a Debating Society—it is not easy to differ, because it means a great deal or means nothing, means one thing or means the opposite, according to the sense in which its terms are taken. I am not even sure that I could disturb the harmony of the meeting by defining my terms; for the definitions of ultimate terms like Realism are quite as equivocal as the terms themselves. A Philosopher and a Matter-of-Fact Man might cordially agree upon half a dozen verbal propositions concerning the Real, whilst interpreting them in different and diametrically opposed senses. A Philosopher opposes the reality of a thing to its mere appearance; but to the Matter-of-Fact Man the appearance *is* the reality, and things that have no appearance are less real to him than tangible, ponderable, visible things. There is something convincing to him in a brick, which he misses in, for instance, a number. He speaks of "hard cash", "nothing like leather", "solid British oak" with a sense of security which altogether fails him when the conversation turns upon value, gravity, cohesion, or patriotism. The mention of a differential coefficient makes him very uneasy indeed; and discussions as to the in-itselfness or for-itselfness of the idea he classes among the relaxations of lunatics. All that to him is metaphysics; and his short method of dealing with that science of the sciences is to kick a stone like Dr. Johnson,[21] and so annihilate the whole race of metaphysical pretenders, from Plato to Hegel.

To such a man Fiction must appear a more or less entertaining variety of Gammon[22]—one of his few admissible abstractions; but he would probably vote for my resolution under the impression that Realism in Fiction means the confining of its subject matter to descriptions of concrete objects, to the legal and conventional forms of human relations, to the commonest views of the commonest incidents, and to such simple abstract ideas as number in connection with shillings or silver forks, and time as connected with watches and clocks.

I think I had better not undertake an explanation of what the Philosopher, on the other hand, would understand by the term realism. Suffice it to say that he would strive to arrive at the Real by carefully abstracting all the realities of the Matter of Fact Man, and leaving only the subject matter of pure Reason. His realities would be to the Matter-of-Fact Man an unaccountable sort of sublimated Bosh: the Matter of Fact Man's realities would be to him a vulgar mass of misinterpreted sense impressions. Between these two extremes there are countless grades of capacity for thinking abstractly. Probably no two persons in this room are exactly alike in this respect. A concept which may be with you so intensely real in its intimate connection with the life of man and of societies as to remain an abiding conviction influencing all your thoughts, may be to me a knotty point which I can only hold most precariously whilst I strive to unravel it. To another it may be as meaningless as a page of Hegel is to an agricultural labourer. To yet another it may be merely a plausible fallacy seen through without effort at a glance. To some of us who are sound Evangelicals there is nothing more real than heaven and hell; to others who are evolutionists the God of the Evangelicals is an absurdity, and personal immortality a flattering dream. The ordinary citizen looks on the existing social order, founded on property as respectable, and practically eternal: the socialist wonders how much longer such a stupid and murderous tyranny will be tolerated. Some, again, ask what is the good of bothering one's head about such things: let us eat and drink; for tomorrow we die.

From the merry philosophers of this last section comes to me sometimes the question: what have you, a writer of fiction and therefore an artist, to do with philosophy and religion and sociology and such stuff? The business of the artist, whether poet, painter, musician, actor, architect or novelist, is *to please*. I reply "To please whom?" The same fiction cannot please the Matter of Fact Man and the Philosopher, the student and the foxhunter, the Tory and the Radical, General Booth and Mr. Bradlaugh.[23] Even were the fiction confined to certain matters such as love affairs, to which Matter of Fact Men, Philosophers, students, foxhunters, Tories, Radicals, General Booth and Mr. Bradlaugh are all susceptible, the same treatment will not please all these people. There are love affairs in Captain Hawley Smart's novels:[24] so there are in George Eliot's; but I suspect that the admirers of Captain Hawley Smart find George Eliot rather heavy. And I believe that "rather heavy" means to them "comparatively unreal". The things of which Captain Hawley

Smart writes, seen as he describes them, are vivid and interesting—
pleasant parts of *his* readers' daily life and thought. On the other hand,
the admirers of George Eliot do not see these things as Captain Hawley
Smart sees them, and take no interest in the excitements and gaieties
incidental to them. For example, one cannot imagine a disciple of
George Eliot reading the sporting column of the newspaper, or sympa-
thizing with the good luck of a hero who is saved from ruin by winning a
fortune at the expense of the other gamblers on a racecourse. Nor can
we imagine a disciple of Captain Hawley Smart subscribing to "Mind",[25]
or recognizing any sense or importance in the scruples of the man who
refuses to bet. Both disciples may find common ground in a purely
fantastic novel like Pickwick; but [without bringing in the large class to
which the reading of any novel would seem a mere waste of time,][26]
there are many lovers of fiction who are pained and repelled by the
shallow unreality of Pickwick, and the flippancy of the street boy humour which yet makes them laugh in spite of themselves. To them a man
is something to be taken seriously even if he happens to be stout, have a
red nose, and drive a stage coach. I remember once being present at a
debate on the works of George Eliot. One gentleman quoted with approval Mr. Ruskin's description of her characters as "the sweepings of a
Pentonville omnibus".[27] "Sir", said the lecturer sternly: "the people who
ride in Pentonville omnibuses have Mothers". "So had Hamlet", retorted
the objector, meaning, as I took it, that the possession of a mother was
not an excuse for dulness, since Hamlet was entertaining in spite of his
mother. But the lecturer was in earnest in his contention that every man
has what Mr. Browning calls his "soul's tragedy",[28] however shabby or
ludicrous his concrete circumstances may be; and an artist who cannot
see the tragedy through the circumstances is an Unrealist, however amusing he may be to other Unrealists, or even to Realists with a strong sense
of the ridiculous. Dickens was an Unrealist when he, in the most literal
sense, made fun of Tony Weller instead of making a man of him. We find
him later on, when he had become one of the greatest of the Realists,
taking his characters with tragic seriousness. The fun of Mr. Weller is the
poorest of chaff in comparison with the subtle ironies and rich absurdities of Mr. Dorrit, or of Pip in "Great Expectations": yet we are not
always sure which side of the mouth to laugh at them with; for they are
taken seriously, and are very real. Yet there are people who believe that
Pickwick is the best book Dickens ever wrote, and that his four last
books—his great works—are dull. These same people prefer Thackeray's "Book of Snobs" to "The Newcomes";[29] prefer the "Merchant of
Venice" to the "Tempest"; the caricatures of Cruikshank's[30] younger
days to those of Gavarni[31] and du Maurier;[32] Beethoven's Septet to the
Choral Symphony;[33] and so on. In every case they prefer what seems

more real, more lively, more interesting to them; and those who find their pet works false, fragmentary, and superficial, they suspect of folly, conceit, or lack of artistic sensibility. Here you have the secret of provoking dissension in literary circles like ours. Instead of moving a resolution in general terms like mine, of which every man will agree to his own private interpretation, suppose I were to move that Thackeray is the greatest English novelist of the 19th century. Imagine the rush of the Dickensites to storm that position. Or suppose I take up the cudgels for a reviewer who recently declared that Thackeray's knowledge of London was confined to Bryanston Square, Pall Mall, Fleet St., and the art academies in Newman St, adding on my own account that the true moral of "The Newcomes" is that the most dangerous of social pests is the fool with good intentions, and that Thackeray had not the penetration to see the lesson of his own story. Fancy the effect of that on the Thackerayites! Or how if I were to move that there is nothing to be learned from George Eliot except the base fatalism which is the fit creed for a class that has compromised with the advancing power of Science by surrendering its faith in God on condition that its property is not to be interfered with? What a lively debate we should have on that! However, I am not going to move any of these propositions. I shall stick to my platitude.

Still, I shall not leave the matter to discussion at a stage in which we have arrived at nothing except that realities appear visionary nonsense to those whose capacity they transcend, and that consequently one man's realism is another man's rubbish, or Rot, as the accepted terminology of modern colloquial criticism has it. It is true that I can demonstrate nothing beyond this; but I can at least commit myself to a variety of opinions upon which novel-readers—if there be any present—may raise a discussion. I may say then, that the least real novels are to me those which contain one of the tales which have been empirically found to be peren-[n]ially interesting to the majority of readers. You take a lay figure—male—and tack on to him a certain assortment of virtues. To a second male figure you tack on a certain bundle of vices. Then you take a third figure—female—and tack on to it all the graces you can think of. These are your hero, heroine, and villain. You can give play to your ingenuity in making them seem natural by such individualizing touches as making them unusually short or tall, giving the villain peculiar eyebrows or primrose gloves with very broad black stripes on the back, making the heroine like some famous picture, or dwelling on the hero's taste for salmon. You will also introduce—or may I say chuck in?—parents, solicitors, doctors and other necessary agents. The hero and heroine will love one another; and the villain will be jealous, and will stop at nothing to prevent their union. He will succeed in postponing it the whole length of the book. Then he will be killed or imprisoned for his crimes and the hero and heroine will get married. The story will proceed strictly according to those views of duty and conduct which the majority of readers accept, and with which all readers are at least familiar. Of this the public never tires. It reads over and over again this tale which has been told so often that the very names and phrases are as hackneyed as the "sentiments" addressed to the gallery in transpontine melodramas,[34] or the speeches in which votes of thanks are moved to lecturers. Paltry as this sort of work seems beside the masterpieces of literature, it is by no means easy to produce it successfully. Everybody in this room has tried to write a novel at one time or another; and therefore we know by experience that the thing is not to be done offhand; though doubtless we aimed higher than the writers whose works I have just described. But, in spite of our higher aim, how many of us have produced anything half so readable and sensible as the average novels by Miss Braddon[35] or the late Mrs. Henry Wood,[36] whose life work is nevertheless only the telling over and over again, without ulterior purpose, of the child's tale of love and villainy? The writers of the serials in the penny weekly journals of fiction, and of the tales in the "shockers" and "dreadfuls"[,] do the same thing, only not so well—that is, not so naturally; for even in this real of the Unreal, there are grades of unreality. With them may be classed the boys' stories of adventure[37] which are equally unnatural and equally without purpose except to amuse the reader without a thought as to the after effects of the amusement [or the truth of the features presented to his imagination].[38]

The next grade of fiction shews a decided awakening of conscience on the author's part. In such novels as those of the late Anthony Trollope[39] and his successor Mr. Norris,[40] with such members of the same school as Mr. James Payn,[41] we find the old story told with a scrupulous adjustment to the actual experience of the writers, and a sincere desire to use their art as a means of making that experience instructive and helpful to the younger readers. You find two new things in their books—didacticism and naturalism. The didacticism is intermittent, and seldom let slip openly without an apology or a mock-cynical affectation of not being too much in earnest. It is also kept subordinate to the romantic interest of the story. But it is there; and the book is more real for it. The naturalism consists in the substitution for the lay figure with its tacked-on bundle of virtues, vices, or graces, of figures carefully studied from nature. Compare the parsons of Trollope with the vicars and rectors of Mrs. Henry Wood; or the selfish and crooked gentlemen of Mr. Norris with the murderers, forgers and felons of Miss Braddon.

In the next grade to this, the purpose of story-telling to kill time practically disappears from the writer's consciousness; and the novel assumes a purely scientific and didactic character. At this point naturalism ceases to be a virtue: it becomes a necessary condition of the work. An actor may claim some credit for naturalism when he plays Othello with a real sword instead of an imitation; but the soldier goes into battle with a genuine blade as a matter of course—that is, if the contractors do their duty. No one dreams of calling George Eliot a naturalist, because she never dreamed of being anything else. She is purely didactic: we read her novels as part of our education. No human being has ever read "Lady Audley's Secret" as part of a scheme of self culture by reading; but "Silas Marner"[,] "Middlemarch" and "Daniel Deronda" are always read with that view, and are dreaded by the people who cannot conceive that learning is compatible with enjoyment. At the summit of purely didactic fiction we have such works as Bunyan's "Pilgrim's Progress", Dante's "Divine Comedy", Goethe's "Faust" and the Shakspere tragedies written after 1600. None of these men thought of themselves as the idle singers of an empty day.[42] They were teachers, seekers, speculators, critics, urgent propounders of the eternal riddle, and strugglers, above all, towards reality. They are no longer naturalists; for they strive to get at the realities underlying even naturalism. In my opinion, which is not peculiar, they are among the greatest writers of fiction. They are all didactic; and their method of criticizing life transcends naturalism as naturalism transcends the unnaturalism of Miss Braddon and the story tellers.

I propose now to read you a short piece of what I consider very realistic fiction. You will either know it very well, or not know it at all.

(Read the 4th Memorable Fancy from Blake's Marriage of Heaven & Hell)

That is from "The Marriage of Heaven & Hell", by William Blake, who passed for a madman, and so escaped persecution for his opinions. If realistic poetry is to your taste, but you find Blake too apparently extravagant, you can fall back on Shelley, whom I suspect of being the greatest Englishman of our century; though he died at an age which, even for an ordinary writer[,] is immature, and for a great realist poet is babyhood.

A classification which takes as its types Mrs. Henry Wood and Miss Braddon, Anthony Trollope and Mr. Norris; and George Eliot, without a word as to the place of Sir Walter Scott, the elder Dumas, Charlotte Bronte, Dickens, Thackeray, Mr. George Meredith and Zola, will not strike you as a specially complete one. But neither my knowledge nor your patience is unlimited. You may provisionally put these writers wherever you think they will fit whilst I say a word about the naturalism of M. Zola.

We have seen that the mere story tellers of the lowest grade—the "Art for Art's sake" people, as I may call them, are essentially copyists of previous tellers of the same story. They and their readers have the child's intolerance of any change in the nursery tale; and so it eventually comes about that the materials of this class of fiction not only get absurdly out of fashion, but from being copied at second hand, or rather second hundredth hand, lose all resemblance to the natural object, living or dead, which the original story teller described. This revolts the writers who have some conscience, some sense, and some independence; and sends them to Nature to study their materials afresh. Trollope did this in his novels, just as the pre-Raphaelites did it in painting. Mulready,[43] as Mr. F. G. Stephens[44] has recently pointed out, did it long before the pre-Raphaelites; and the so-called Impressionists[45] are doing it today years afterwards and finding that their particular form of Naturalism is as old as the century. It is in fact a reaction that is constantly going on; and it only makes a noise when some very sacred convention is attacked. The naturalism of the Impressionists, for instance, seems new only because they have suddenly become conscious of the fact that atmosphere is a visible and paintable phenomenon; and we, accustomed from childhood to see pictorial scenes represented as occurring in a vacuum, are put out by the shock to our habits.

The omission of the all pervading atmosphere in painting has its analogy in the traditional omission from English fiction of the influence of sex on the character and destiny of men and women, and that too on grounds which make its introduction not only an innovation but an indecency. The result was that our best novels—those of Dickens and Thackeray, for example, were simply left deficient on this side, whilst on the other hand novels like those of Ouida,[46] which dealt almost entirely with love affairs, shewed the evil effect of obscurantism by the irrational, unscientific, and indeed immoral treatment of them. Thackeray complained that it was impossible to describe a young man truthfully as Fielding had done. Mrs. Grundy[47] and Mr. Podsnap,[48] with their ideas in a hopeless confusion of early Christian asceticism with modern social reserve, would not hear of naturalism applied to love affairs, although coarse jesting was considered allowable. The official censor of plays reflects Mr. Podsnap exactly in his refusal to allow on the stage a single earnest allusion to the relations on which most dramas turn, whilst he licenses Criterion comedies[49] every point in which would be resented as an insult by an audience trained to real delicacy of thinking upon the matters in question. Mr. Podsnap is as impervious to reason as the Church was in France in the eighteenth century. The result was that the reasonable men left the Church to Voltaire, who set to work to profane it, outrage it, ridicule it, defy its threatened excommunications, leprosies, and lightnings, and exhibit himself to the awestruck believers not one penny the worse for the exploit. Mr. Podsnap has found his Voltaire in M. Zola, and his Tom Paine in Mr. George Moore.[50] Instead of saying politely, "There are certain things which you must really allow me to mention, Mr. Podsnap", M. Zola brutally says, "You are a pestilential and uncleanly minded old fool; and I am going to mention everything that you say I must not mention, including several things which nobody would have dreamt of alluding to if you had held your tongue, but which I will now stuff into your ears for the express purpose of teaching the world to despise your opinions". Accordingly, you will find M. Zola's books not only outspoken on the subject of the corruption of modern French society, but freely sprinkled with deliberate and apparently gratuitous nastinesses. And at the same time you will find plenty of those novel readers who take the most serious view of fiction, defending M. Zola as its most potent regenerator. For my own part, I wish I could believe that there are more ways of killing Mr. Podsnap than by choking him with filth; but since he has successfully resisted all other methods, I leave him to his enemy as a nuisance which must be got rid of somehow.

Now, M. Zola's method has made such a scandal,[51] as it was of course expressly meant to do, that his naturalism has come to be regarded as naturalism *par excellence*. It has even been called realism; but that is a mere blunder which need not detain us. Realism *in excelsis* transcends naturalism as far as Shelley transcends M. Zola. And I would contend that the lowest, merely fanciful fiction must advance towards Naturalism, whilst naturalistic fiction must advance towards Realism.

Thus Realism is the Goal; but it is a goal that recedes as we advance. If we examine the work of two of our greatest English fictionists— Shakspere and Dickens, we see that they both journeyed upward far from their starting point; and that the view from their final elevation broke upon them quite suddenly. From "Love's Labor Lost" to "Henry V", Shakspere produced a rare sheaf of plays; but if he had died then, not one Englishman in a hundred would now know his name. From "Pickwick" to "Bleak House", Dickens produced an extraordinary set of books; but had he died before "Little Dorrit" there might now be some question as to whether Thackeray was not as great, or even a greater writer. But Shakspere wrote an odd little play called "Troilus & Cressida" and then began to write great plays. Dickens wrote an odd little book called "Hard Times", and then began to write great novels. Yet we already have Darwin reaching a point at which he cannot be bothered reading the great plays; and the growth of social consciousness, though it has shewn us that Dickens's so-called caricatures of Society were nearer the reality than those of any naturalist of his day, is also making us feel that even novelistic fiction has much further to go than he brought it at his greatest. The Goal has receded since his time, and is receding still. So that though Realism is the Goal of Fiction, Ladies and Gentlemen, Fiction will never reach it.

Notes

1. All the quotations are drawn from Bernard Shaw, *Collected Letters 1874–1897* (London: Max Reinhardt, 1965): Macmillan's reader's report, undated (late January 1880); Shaw to Macmillan, 1 February 1880; John Morley to Shaw, 22 May, 13 and 15 June 1880; pp. 26–27, 30–32.

2. Shaw made at least three shots at the opening sentence of the paragraph, the first beginning with the words "In giving a brief sketch," which was scratched out and replaced by "In implying by the. . . ." before its final version, "In so stretching a story as to imply. . . ."

3. Henry Baden Pritchard (1841–84), English photographer and novelist, was employed in the chemical department at the royal arsenal in Woolwich, 1861, conducting the photographic department until his death. Pritchard also wrote *A Peep in the Pyrenees* (1867), *Tramps in the Tyrol* (1874), *Dangerfield* (a novel, 1878, adapted into a three-act play in the same year), and *Old Charlton* (a novel, 1879). But his most popular work seems to have been in the area of photography: he was proprietor and editor of the *Photographic News* from 1878 to 1884; and his book *The Photographic Studios of Europe* (1882) ran to two editions.

4. August Bebel, *Woman in the Past, Present and Future*, trans. H. B. Walther, International Library of Social Science No. 1 (London: Modern Press, 1885), p. 48.

5. One is reminded of Shaw's Eliza Doolittle who, in the opening moments of *Pygmalion*, declares loudly, "I'm a respectable girl: so help me, I never spoke to him except to ask him to buy a flower off me." Later, she repeats no less than six times that she is a "good girl."

6. William Morris, together with several others, including Edward Aveling, broke away from H. M. Hyndman's Social Democratic Federation in 1884 to found the Socialist League. Although Shaw remained on friendly terms with its members, he reminded their secretary, Henry A. Barker, when it came to debating with Charles Bradlaugh on their behalf in 1887, "I am a member of the Fabian Society only, and am not bound by the manifesto of the Socialist League." The journal of the Socialist League was *The Commonweal*, which may have been influenced in its rejection of this review in March 1885 by Shaw's expressed irritation with the League's manifesto (*Collected Letters 1874–1897*, p. 165).

7. Shaw's belief that "When Socialism is realized . . . every woman will be able, should she wish it, to die a virgin after a life of comfortable independence" had been pragmatically modified by the time he came to write *The Quintessence of Ibsenism* in 1891. There he states, "The domestic career is no more natural to all women than the military career is natural to all men; although it may be necessary that every able-bodied woman should be called on to risk her life in childbed, just as it may be necessary that every man should be called on to risk his life in the battlefield" (*The Quintessence of Ibsenism* [London: Walter Scott, 1891], p. 125).

8. "Laon Ramsey" was a young clergyman, Ramsden Balmforth (1861–1941), who for more than fifty years published a large number of works on religious and literary subjects, including studies of ethics, Wagner's operas, the problem play, and *Jesus—the Man* (1935).

9. Samuel Johnson, *A Dictionary of the English Language* (1755).

10. Robert Hunter (1823–97), lexicographer and theologian, whose principal work was the *Encyclopædic Dictionary* (1879–88).

11. In spite of his initial admiration for H. M. Hyndman (1842–1921), the English pioneer Socialist and founder of the Social Democratic Federation, Shaw soon became irritated by the latter's rancorous and revolutionary speeches and, preferring an evolutionary to a revolutionary approach, joined a splinter group of the SDF, the Fabians, in

September 1884. The two societies were not initially rivals, and Shaw was for a time a "candidate member" of the SDF. In later years Hyndman, in his politics, was to mellow somewhat.

12. The leading commercial lending library in London, founded in 1842.

13. Although a "Utopian" Socialist, Robert Owen (1771–1858) was more practical in his approach than François-Marie Fourier (1772–1837), who simply published a number of Utopian Socialist works containing his plans for a reorganization of society based upon a principle of harmony among the material universe, organic life, animal life, and human life. Shaw always contrasted such Utopian Socialists with their Scientific counterparts, exemplified by Karl Marx. Seven months after writing the above, in a review of Marx's *Das Kapital* in the *National Reformer* on 7 August 1887, Shaw again linked Owen and Fourier, declaring, "Twenty years ago, when this first instalment of Karl Marx's now famous work was published, arose the claim that Socialism, formerly a dream, had become a science. Thenceforth Robert Owen, St. Simon, and Fourier were to be regarded as well-intentioned Utopists, and Lassalle as one who saved himself by plagiarizing Marx, whose book is a revelation."

14. Want and destitution had made the Irish peasantry desperate in County Clare in 1831 and, in the wake of ensuing riots, founding of secret societies, and a resultant fear for the lives of his family, John Scott Vandeleur, late High Sheriff of County Clare, decided to establish a cooperative farm there. In England he sought help from a young businessman, Edward Thomas Craig (1804–94). In spite of initial opposition and threats from the local peasants, in November 1831 Craig organized the Ralahine Agricultural and Manufacturing Co-Operative Society, whose objects were common capital, mutual assurance of its members against poverty, sickness, infirmity and old age, better housing, mental and moral improvement of members, and the education of their children. For nearly three years the scheme prospered, quite revolutionizing the lives of the laborers, before Vandeleur, addicted to gambling, lost a fortune in his Dublin club. The cooperative was ruined, the estate sold, and Craig (and his wife, who had been induced to join him) were evicted and returned to England.

15. William Stanley Jevons (1835–82) published his *Theory of Political Economy* in 1871, in which he rejected the Ricardian view on the question of value and substituted a theory of exchange that claimed that the utility of a commodity is not proportionate to its quantity, but diminishes as the possessor becomes satiated: in short that the problem of exchange is one of quantities, and that, as dealing with quantities, it should be treated mathematically.

16. The followers of David Ricardo (1772–1823) objected to Jevons's theory of exchange, and the Irish economist John Elliott Cairnes (1823–75) gave voice to their objections, prompting Jevons to remark, "I much regret that Cairnes should have raised such absurd objections to the theory, proceeding entirely from misapprehension" (Jevons, *Letters and Journals*, 1886).

17. The Liberty & Property Defence League, founded in 1884 by Wordsworth Donisthorpe (1847–1912?), preached Individualism, which, both philosophically and economically, was the polar opposite of Socialism. Shaw reviewed Donisthorpe's *Individualism, a System of Politics* in *The Star* on 14 December 1889, admiring the author's courage and independence while lambasting his principles.

18. The Monument, to commemorate the Great Fire of London in 1666, was built in 1671–77 from designs of Christopher Wren; it has 311 steps from gallery to ground.

19. The work of J.M.W. Turner (1775–1851) foreshadowed Impressionism, and being thus ahead of its time was largely misunderstood. John Ruskin (1819–1900), who met the neglected Turner in 1840, championed his work in *Modern Painters* (Vol. I, 1843), and helped to turn the critical tide in his favor.

20. Shaw was fond of this quotation from Shakespeare's *Richard III*, which reads, in full,
    bid [Stanley] bring his power
    Before sunrising, lest his son George fall
    Into the blind cave of eternal night.
                                    (V.iii)

21. On 6 August 1763, Boswell reports of Dr. Johnson, "[W]e stood talking for some time together of Bishop Berkeley's ingenious sophistry to prove the non-existence of matter, and that every thing in the universe is merely ideal. I observed that though we are satisfied his doctrine is not true, it is impossible to refute it. I never shall forget the alacrity with which Johnson answered, striking his foot with mighty force against a large stone, till he rebounded from it, 'I refute it *thus*.' "

22. Gammon—the seventeenth-century nautical term for the lashing of the bowsprit—became in the nineteenth century initially thieves' slang for keeping someone occupied while his pocket was being picked, and finally a word meaning "humbug, rubbish, or ridiculous nonsense" [*OED*].

23. "General" William Booth (1829–1912), founder of the Salvation Army, was the polar opposite of Charles Bradlaugh (1833–91), freethinker and founder of the National Secular Society.

24. Henry Hawley Smart (1833–93), who served in the Crimean War and the Indian Mutiny, wrote over forty novels, mostly on horse-racing themes. He was described as unequaled as a recorder of sporting life, manners, and matters.

25. *Mind: A Quarterly Journal of Psychology and Philosophy*, started in 1876, continues to the present day, now subtitled simply a "quarterly review of Philosophy."

26. The portion in brackets was deleted by Shaw.

27. John Ruskin spoke thus of George Eliot's *Mill on the Floss:* "There is no girl alive . . . whose life has not at least as much in it as Maggie's, to be described and pitied. Tom is a clumsy and cruel lout . . . while the rest of the characters are simply the sweepings out of a Pentonville omnibus." "Fiction, Fair and Foul," Section V, in *Nineteenth Century* 10 (October 1881): 521.

28. Robert Browning's *Soul's Tragedy* (1846) is a play in two acts about a pretended patriot, Chiappino, the first act representing the poetry of his life, the second its prose.

29. W. M. Thackeray's *Book of Snobs*, satirical sketches of early Victorian snobbery, appeared originally in the pages of *Punch* as "The Snobs of England" (1846–47); it was published (revised) in book form in 1848. His novel *The Newcomes* (subtitled "Memoirs of a Most Respectable Family") appeared in twenty-four parts between October 1853 and August 1855.

30. George Cruikshank (1792–1878) was an English political caricaturist and book illustrator of Dickens, notably *Oliver Twist*.

31. Paul Gavarni was the pseudonym of Sulpice Guillaume Chevalier (1801–66), French illustrator and caricaturist, a witty, mordant observer of life.

32. George du Maurier (1834–96) was a French-born British artist, cartoonist, and romantic novelist, whose *Trilby* (1894) was enormously popular.

33. The "Choral Symphony," Beethoven's Ninth and last, was composed in his "transcendent third period," between 1821 and 1824.

34. The "sentiments" addressed to the gallery were pieces of improving advice, sententious sayings, addressed to a largely illiterate audience. The term "transpontine" [literally "across, or over, the bridge"] dates from c. 1844 and refers to the Victorian "Surrey-side" theaters on the south of the Thames, which were famous for sensational melodramas.

35. Mary Elizabeth Braddon (1837–1915), English novelist, became famous on the publication of *Lady Audley's Secret* (1862), and subsequently authored some eighty novels.

36. Ellen (Mrs. Henry) Wood (1814–87), English novelist, is noted for her novel *East Lynne* (1861), which became enormously popular, was translated into many languages, and adapted as a very successful drama.

37. Certainly Shaw's comment on children's literature is reinforced by his comment in "The Books of My Childhood," *T. P.'s Weekly* (19 December 1902): "Children's books . . . I always loathed and despised for their dishonesty, their hypocrisy, their sickly immorality, and their damnable dulness." But his review of children's books in the *PMG* on 29 November 1887 is a little more generous.

38. The portion in brackets was inserted by Shaw in pencil.

39. Trollope died in 1882.

40. W[illiam] E[dward] Norris (1847–1925), English novelist, wrote over a score of novels, including *My Friend Jim* (1886) and *Major and Minor* (1887), favorably reviewed by Shaw in the *Pall Mall Gazette*.

41. James Payn (1830–98), English novelist, supported his family by journalism, the editorship of *Chambers' Journal,* and a great many now-forgotten novels.

42. Shaw here quotes without acknowledgment the choric utterance "the idle singers of an empty day" from *The Earthly Paradise* (1868–70), the poem that established William Morris as one of the leading poets of his day.

43. William Mulready (1786–1863), Irish painter.

44. Frederic George Stephens (1828–1907), biographer of William Holman Hunt, Laurence Alma-Tadema, and Sir Edwin Landseer. At this date he edited and annotated the Grosvenor Gallery catalogues.

45. The term "impressionist," first used by a Parisian journalist to describe derisively Monet's painting *Impression: Soleil Levant,* and later accepted by many members of the movement as expressing the element common to their work, was officially adopted for their third exhibition in 1877.

46. "Ouida" (Marie Louise de la Ramée) (1839–1908), English novelist, spent part of her childhood in Paris, where she early displayed an ability to write. Most of her forty-five novels deal with fashionable life and exhibit a rebellion against the moral ideals displayed in much contemporary fiction. Shaw, reviewing *Othmar* (1885) for the *Pall Mall Gazette,* at first praised her clearsightedness: "she insists on the naked truth concerning the hordes of wealthy vagabonds who spend their lives unprofitably roving through Western Europe in pursuit of pleasure. She perceives that the society they form breeds monsters—that it is impervious to all healthy emotions and interests, and responsive only to coarse stimulation of its lower instincts." He went on, however, to complain about the novel's diffuseness, finding it "overloaded with worthless mock sociology, perceptibly tainted by a pervasion of the sexual impulses, egotistical and tiresome, and yet imaginative, full of vivid and glowing pictures, and not without a considerable moral stiffening of enthusiasm—half-reasoned but real—for truth and simplicity, and of protest against social evils which is not the less vehement because certain emotional and material aspects of it have a fascination which the writer has not wholly escaped." Notwithstanding Shaw's final verdict on it, Ouida's work may have furnished him with an idea or two for his early dramas, particularly *The Philanderer* (1893).

47. "Mrs. Grundy" originated in Thomas Morton's comedy *Speed the Plough* (1798), where, although she never appears, she is the neighbor of Dame Ashfield, who incessantly wonders what Mrs. Grundy will think or say. Hence she has become the symbol of conventional Victorian propriety.

48. Mr. Podsnap is the pompous, self-satisfied "member of society" in Dickens's *Our Mutual Friend,* swelling with patronage of his friends and acquaintances: "Mr. Podsnap was well to do, and stood very high in Mr. Podsnap's opinion."

49. So-called because the lessee and manager of the theater, Charles Wyndham (1837–

1919), had performed there in a series of popular comedies, commencing with James Albery's *Pink Dominoes* in 1877.

50. Shaw's review of George Moore's novel *A Mere Accident* (*Pall Mall Gazette*, 19 July 1887) reveals his irritation with one of Moore's "sham clinical lectures on morbid sexual conditions" (the "mere accident" of the title is a rape). His later appraisal in the postscript to Geraint Goodwin's *Conversations with George Moore* (London: Jonathan Cape, 1937), although containing some grudging praise, concludes: "All the stuff about his being a great prose writer is nonsense. Beside Scott and Dickens, Ruskin and Carlyle and De Quincey, he was nothing: he had no heights and no depths except in certain descriptions of Ireland and certain scandalous passages; but his enormous industry, his honesty and fearlessness, and his good-humor, pulled his imagination through."

51. Henry Richard Vizetelly (1820–94), who had published inexpensive translations of Zola's works in England, was prosecuted twice for obscene libel. The first action against him in 1888, including the defense, the fine, and the loss entailed by the suppression of the books, cost him nearly £1,000. Shaw's letter to *The Star*, published on 2 November 1888, championed the right of an author to "expose to society its own wickedness."

Stuart E. Baker

On Politics

Shaw was a man of many passions. People who are passionate about things do not compartmentalize their interests, saving their religion for Sundays and forgetting it the rest of the week. The unpublished fragments of Shaw's long writing career that follow are classed for convenience as "political," but they touch on many of his varied concerns: political, literary, and even dramatic. In the first paragraph of the preface to his *Plays Unpleasant*, Shaw insists that he was possessed by a dramatic imagination before he ever began to write plays. There is a flavor of the stage or the pulpit in nearly all of his writing. If he is not shaping his prose around an imaginary dialogue between himself and another, as he does in the first piece, which begins and ends by evoking an interview with a "man of fashion" about the delights provided by London parks in the fall, he becomes one of the outdoor speakers he describes: talking, cajoling, startling, admonishing—always striving to reach our ears, hoping a bit of his message will get through.

The student of Shaw may find little that is new and nothing very surprising in these short pieces, but they do provide a kind of thumbnail sketch of Shaw's career as an orator and propagandist. One or two have a virtue characteristic of Shaw's shorter essays. When he was forced to curb his natural prolixity he could often state his case with a degree of rhetorical power and logical clarity not found in his longer works. The short speech called "The New Theology,"[1] for example, conveys Shaw's religious convictions more clearly and persuasively than either the preface to *Man and Superman* or *Back to Methuselah*, the best known statements of the Shavian theology.

If there is a thread that runs through all of these pieces it is Shaw the orator, a man seeking his voice, looking for a way to deliver his message to unwilling or unheeding ears. We can see Shaw searching for his voice in the first of these pieces. It is appropriate to begin the political Shaw with an essay on "Open Air Meetings" because it was in the public forums of London that Bernard Shaw really found himself. The orator incubated in the heat of many debating-society meetings fledged and found his wings at the corner of Hyde Park. Shaw's enthusiasm for the outdoor pulpit is clear from his short essay "How I Became a Public Speaker," in *Sixteen Self Sketches*, and "Dramatist, Socialist, and Orator: A Chat with Mr. Bernard Shaw," as well as from Dan H. Laurence's introduction to *Platform and Pulpit*.[2] In "Open Air Meetings" Shaw describes the outdoor forum with a wealth of detail absent in the later work. His purpose, however, is unclear. Digressions are common in his works, but here he seems to stray from the point before ever finding it. In a sense, this is not a political piece at all, except that Shaw entered the world of open-air lecturing as a socialist orator, and he is inviting the upper classes, normally oblivious to park activities outside of the "season," to join him. This is a very "Fabian" approach, and rather different from that of most of his fellow socialist lecturers. Fashionable London dwellers concerned themselves with Hyde Park only during the social season, when the landed and titled aristocracy were in London. There were two serious concerns of the season: Parliament was in session, and the serious purpose behind the many balls and social events was the institution known irreverently as the "marriage market." Shaw may be asking fashionable gentlemen to participate in the larger life of the nation, but this is not perfectly clear. In the end the essay is simply an invitation to stuffy minds to open themselves up to the invigorating fresh air of public debate.

Shaw the socialist emerges more clearly in the piece on Proudhon, which was "got up" as his contribution to a lengthy examination of Proudhon by the Hampstead Historic Society. If Shaw was frustrated by his inability to reach an uncomprehending public, he was exasperated by the extravagances of his fellow socialists. Instead of sticking to what were, for Shaw, the undeniable truths at the heart of socialism, they were perpetually distracted by impossible scenarios, hysterical assertions, and irrational arguments. His frustration with Proudhon's absurdities is palpable. Shaw would forever be quoting Proudhon's central assertion: property is theft. It is theft because it takes without giving. Proudhon's attempt to bolster his assertion with weak and even preposterous arguments (some are even more fantastic than Shaw makes them out to be) was simply to pile dross upon a nugget of gold. Shaw's attitude is like that of the Inquisitor in *Saint Joan*, who argued that it is folly to clutter up your case with bad arguments as they will call your sound ones into question. It is not that Shaw wished to shun the economic complexities of socialism: his comments on Proudhon's suggestion that the workers of inferior land should be indemnified show that he fully understood the concept of rent, that he knew economic law makes it inevitable, but that it need not simply go into the pockets of idlers. Shaw attempts to make

Proudhon seem more reasonable than he in fact is. Shaw's personal and concrete illustration involving the two dinners is a very Shavian way of presenting an economic argument and much easier to follow than Proudhon's rather abstract argument. Unfortunately, Shaw's clarity only makes the weakness of the argument more apparent: what in actuality would happen is that the landlord would tell the proletarians to stop providing the second useless dinner and give him something else: a luxury item the rest could not afford. This was certainly not desirable from Shaw's point of view, but Proudhon does not make it clear why. Despite the special occasion for this essay, it offers the same economic views we see in Shaw's later writing, from the *Fabian Essays* to *Everybody's Political What's What?*

If the Proudhon piece shows his frustration with the irrationalities of his fellow reformers, the next is a sample of his fury at the intellectual corruption of politicians who present themselves as reformers. Even more of an occasion piece, "Ten Reasons Why Women Should Support the Progressives" was intended strictly for private consumption: Shaw was blowing off steam (something we can see him doing often in his private correspondence). At the request of the Progressive Party Committee of the London Reform Union, Shaw had written a leaflet encouraging women voters to vote for Progressive candidates in the November 1903 Borough Council elections. While it was published (anonymously), some of the committee members objected to parts of it and tried to persuade Shaw to change it. Shaw sent this parody to the secretary of the Reform Union, Francis W. Galton, when asked to revise the leaflet, saying, as Galton paraphrases, "Your Committee are not really Progressives at all—they are a pack of old Gladstonian Whigs—I know what they want; the enclosed is what they would really like." The original pamphlet urged women to become aware and involved in Council business so as to force the councilors to behave responsibly. Shaw also insisted, "It is no use trying to reduce the rates: the sensible thing to do is to make up your mind that since you must pay the rates, you will take care to get good value for them." It is possible that this sentiment and others like it were what the Committee found objectionable. Then, as now, politicians catered to and exploited the prejudices and ignorance of the public. Then, as now, they were more concerned with getting elected than promoting a policy of public betterment. Shaw always insisted that elected public officials had an obligation to educate the public, to keep it informed. An involved and informed electorate would help to keep the officials responsible and responsive. Shaw argued that politicians who promise lower taxes deliver only reduced services, and the taxes stay the same. But selling that message is not the easy way to win elections. The way to do that, Shaw's parody implies, is to blame the opposition for everything that is upsetting the electorate, from bad weather to high prices; promise to lower taxes; and loudly embrace all the reforms of fifty years earlier. The last suggestion must have been particularly galling to Shaw; many of his "Reasons Why Women Should Support the Progressives" are really declarations that Progressives are no different from the Liberals of the 1860s. In effect, Shaw is saying that these "Progressives" are more like Roebuck Ramsden than Jack Tanner (*Man and Superman*, of course, was completed in 1902). He ends the pieces with several suggestions for what amounts to stuffing the ballot boxes. "Since you have thoroughly corrupted your policies," he seems to be saying, "you might as well finish by corrupting your practice!"

The fragment, "Lady Day, 1929," is clearly a speech intended to be recorded and distributed to support the Labor Party in the June General Elections, but it does not appear to have actually been delivered. By this time the Labor Party with its socialist policies was a real force in British politics although it had yet to achieve a majority in Parliament, and such power as it had was maintained at the expense of considerable compromise and backpedaling. Out of power before this election, it managed to win a plurality and formed another minority coalition government under Ramsay MacDonald (the first was of brief duration in 1924). The speech is mostly unremarkable, but one can hear distinct echoes of *The Intelligent Woman's Guide*, published in the previous year, particularly in the insistence that freedom is invariably limited, nowhere more severely than by poverty. On the whole, it is not surprising that it was not recorded or distributed. The accent is less confident and straightforward than in Shaw's earlier tracts; the tone of frustrated pleading has a note of petulance, as if to say, "Please, *do* try to be reasonable, despite your natural tendency to the contrary." This is not a tack apt to appeal to a party professional—of any party—striving to win an election. The assertion that he would be willing to support even a Fascist party that would give everyone a decent job at a living wage also may not have pleased the politicians. His logic is sound, but his rhetoric is weak.

Shaw always felt that the heart of his theme was the plainest common sense; he could not understand why it was so difficult for ordinary mortals to comprehend. He tried many techniques over his long career: direct statement, dramatic illustration, meaningful jest, startling paradox— none was fully successful, although all served to increase his fame and amuse his public. The better he became known, the less he seemed to be understood. To some extent this alienation from his public was mutual; assuming he knew better than others, he often failed to hear them when he could have learned from them. Having experienced the folly of xenophobic demonizing throughout his life, he dismissed warnings about the dangers of Hitler, Stalin, and Mussolini as hysterical jingoism. Trusting to his intellect and instinct, he could be reckless about facts. The base of his revolutionary platform was simply the logical application of two old and established principles—the principle of equality and the doctrine of Jesus that evil can only be overcome by good—which, for Shaw, were the same. We are all the children of one Father-Mother-God, and none of us has the right to judge another. He shocked his supporters by assuming that Hitler was his brother and believed that in Stalin he had finally found a soul-mate, someone who thought and acted as he did. He believed that Hitler's belligerence could be cured just as Bill Walker's was, and that once Germany had shaken off the humiliation of Versailles, there could be no war as there was no longer reason for war. His errors sprang from the same fountain as his most brilliant insights.

Open Air Meetings (1885)

[PROVENANCE: Unsigned holograph manuscript, undated (c. September 1885), foliated by Shaw: 1–2, 2a, 3–8. Stephen Winsten Collection, Harry Ransom Humanities Research Center, The University of Texas at Austin.]

How many parks are there in London? Two, you reply, if you are a man of fashion. Of what use are they? You do not know that they are of much use; but Regent's Park holds the Zoo conveniently; and you put the name of Hyde Park on your card if you live anywhere within two miles of its railings, besides promenading there, horse and foot, in the season. On reflection, you believe that you were wrong in saying that there are only two parks: there is a place called Battersea Park across the river. Did you ever hear of Victoria Park, Southwark Park, or Finsbury Park? You think you have heard of Finsbury Park—Finsbury Something-or-other at any rate.[3] Ever been there? Certainly not. The question restores your tone: you regard it distinctly as an outrage; and on being asked further whether you walk in Hyde Park in September, you set down your catechist (whom you have hitherto looked up to as a superior person, though somewhat intrusive) as a man lost to society, and inform him compassionately that noone walks in Hyde Park now, as the season is over.[4] Like most Londoners on the subject of London, you are wrong in every particular. Walk from Knightsbridge Barracks to the Marble Arch next Sunday afternoon, or through the avenue in Regents Park, and you will find at its height a season of intellectual activity evinced by clusters of public meetings, at some of which you will find that you, your property, and the best means of depriving you of it, are being discussed more or less coolly by thousands of people, not one of whom belongs to the criminal classes. You will be able to take your choice of lecture on food reform, a sermon, or a harangue on the distribution of wealth; and you will probably gather more concerning your body, your soul, and your economic position in half an hour, than you are reasonably likely to learn in a thousand walks from Hyde Park corner to Albert Gate between Eastertide and Goodwood. Do you like to take your lectures lying down? Here you may gratify your fancy. The green sward is the natural couch of man; and the people for whose sake you daily avoid everything natural are now out of town.[5] There is room for you in this circle of listeners, flat on their backs, with their feet converging towards one of Mr Henry George's disciples, who is content if his most stirring appeals to them to "nationalize" the land succeed in eliciting a lazy " 'Ear, 'ear, guv'nor" from some supine proletaire. The cockney labourer envies the landlord only very languidly: the large capitalist, his actual master, is his favorite game: him he loves to hear denounced, and his downfall prophesied. Hence, a little distance off, may be found a meeting at which the audience have neither inclination [n]or room to lie down. Here Mr Henry George is passed over with contemptuous pity as a man of half measures— probably a Conservative in disguise. The speaker is a Socialist, or, as he sometimes tempers it, a Social Democrat. He points with a comprehensive sweep to the mansions in Park Lane; assures his listeners that those palaces are their handiwork, and the riches squandered daily therein the coined sweat of their brows; and invites them to compare that select thoroughfare with the slums in which they themselves have to dwell. Murmurs of conviction follow, and swell to approving shouts when the orator reproaches his audience with their baseness in tamely submitting to the slavery which the present social order allots to them. They enjoy his denunciations of themselves much as the sitters beneath a popular preacher relish the rhetorical scourgings which he administers to their vices. Probably each person admires the accuracy with which the cap fits his neighbour. Oratory and epigram sometimes infect the audience. "There is a many Rotten Rows in London, as well we know", remarks a worn-out labourer; "but that ere is the rottenest of 'em all".[6] An attempt which is exceedingly well received. It is noteworthy that the tone of these socialist speakers is decidedly irreligious, not to say occasionally blasphemous; but it must by no means be inferred that they harmonize with the professedly anti-religious body of Malthusian Secularists or "Bradlaughites", who insist on individualism as opposed to socialism, though from the point of view of those who have anything to lose by a revolution, the difference between the parties seems to be founded on their jealousy of one another's influence over the working classes rather than on any discoverable contradiction in their principles. On social questions, however, there is a schism among the Secularists. On the religious question they are solid; and their meetings are mainly intended as counter demonstrations to those of the Salvation Army, the Christian Evidence Society, and the converts of Messrs Moody & Sankey.[7] After these rival assemblies, which are often so close together that the speakers do their best to shout each other down, the audiences disperse with reluctance. Many of them linger in the neighbourhood in hope of a chance discussion, which seldom fails to ensue. Unwary couples, exchanging a few words on the subject of the meeting, are suddenly surrounded by a crowd which eggs them on to differ and debate. If they withdraw in confusion, some bystander gibes at them; another takes their part; and the two presently fall to argument, if they are capable of it; or if not, to invective, which pleases the crowd better. Sometimes the discussion forms part of the meeting: a chairman presiding, and allowing ten minutes to each opponent who comes forward. Considerable latitude is allowed to the disputants, who not unfrequently begin, "I will now, sir, in the brief time allowed me, deal with the asinine objections of our friend on the right". This is delivered in good faith as the correct form of expression for public occasions; and our friend on the right seldom resents it. As a rule, religious questions provoke most discussion. Economics strike the average Briton dumb: the subject is one of the few which he mistrusts his ability to handle without previous knowledge. Politics, on the other hand, produce riots. The moment they are alluded to, all who have the gift of eloquence speak at once. The rest groan, cheer, countercheer, and groan again. The rough, basking in the sun a little way off (the rough is bored by quiet meetings, and, after listening for a moment, moves off and lies down to recuperate after the momentary strain on his attention), hears the disturbance; rises like a giant refreshed; hurries to the meeting; forms a chain hand in hand with his fellows who arrive simultaneously; and, uttering hoarse but stimulating cries, rushes backward and forward through the scene until the meeting breaks up in disorder. The solitary rough is not brave. He is restless and shamefaced until he meets with other roughs to keep him in countenance. He especially dreads that strange social reformer, the Hallelujah lass.[8] At first sight of her quaint bonnet, jersey, and upturned eyes, he rushes to the conclusion that chance has provided him with a rare lark. He hastens to the outskirts of her circle, and, after a few inarticulate howls, attempts to disconcert her by profane and often obscene interjections. In vain: he may as easily disconcert a swallow in its flight. He presently hears himself alluded to as "that loving fellow creature", and he is stricken with an uncomfortable feeling akin to that which prompted Paul Pry's protest, "Dont call me a phœnix: I'm not used to it."[9] But the Hallelujah lass is not done with him yet. In another minute she is praying, with infectious emotion, for "his dear, precious soul". This finishes him. He slinks away with a faint affectation of having no more time to waste on such effeminate sentimentality, and thenceforth never ventures within earshot of the Army except when strongly reinforced by evil company or ardent spirits. A battalion of Hallelujah lasses in action is a sight worth staying a minute to study. They stand in an exact circle, and deliver addresses in succession, one following the other without a moments delay or hesitation. They are so admirably neat in their dress and orderly in their demeanour, that it is rather a shock—an agreeable one, on reflection—to discover by their speech that they come from the classes in which decency is difficult to maintain, and culture is impossible. As long as they speak strenuously, they concern themselves but little about lack of matter, which forces them to repetiwearisome tions which, it must be confessed, soon become too tedious for anyone but an habitual salvationist to endure. The occasional quaintness of their utterances may be judged by the following sample. "Oh Lord, bless dear London; and for our enemies, oh confound 'em, only dont 'urt their dear 'earts".[10] Somewhat impatient of these emotional appeals are the scriptural specialists who stand, bible in hand, and with a coloured map of Palestine hanging to their little finger, tracing the descent of the British nation from the lost tribes of Israel, and ingeniously extracting from the prophetic books of the Old Testament references to the Tzar of Russia, the Khedive, and General Gordon.[11] But the British nation, though perfectly ready to listen to an amusing speaker on any subject whatever, does not seem to care much for its pedigree, and betrays a taint of the spirit in which Marshal Junot, when admonished to respect his ancestors, exclaimed, "Am not I also an ancestor?"[12] The people at large seem to prefer the ordinary prayer meeting, where the familiar hot gospeller, hardly less sensational than a column of the Police News, tells of the atrocities he committed before he came to be saved, and asks you menacingly how long you intend to delay before you do as he did, and whether you are aware that you may be carried home dead on a shutter in spite of the pride of heart in which you feel confident of being able to walk. As a relief to him comes the unctuous pastor who begins his discourse with a long drawn sigh, and a soft exclamation of "Ah! first 'Ebrews is very comfortin' ". And so on, past the more argute Unitarian or Christadelphian,[13] back into the secular atmosphere of the Anti-Vaccination man or the Vegetarian, who offers you a tract entitled "How to spend Sixpence a Day", which you refuse, never having experienced the slightest difficulty in spending that amount in a much shorter period. From a multitude of counsellors you will have learnt at least that the parks are seldom more interesting than late on a Sunday afternoon in the month of September.

Proudhon—Ch IV. Propositions I–V. pp 126–153 (1886)

[PROVENANCE: Report and commentary on Pierre Proudhon's Qu' est-ce que la Propriété? *(1840), Chapter IV, Propositions 1–5, pp. 126–153. Unsigned holograph manuscript, foliated by Shaw: 1–10, dated on final leaf "21ˢᵗ January 1886", beneath which is a shorthand note indicating it was read on 30 January to the Hampstead Historic Club. T. E. Hanley Collection, Harry Ransom Humanities Research Center, The University of Texas at Austin.]*

In the five propositions which I have had time to read since our last meeting,[14] I have found nothing that is remarkable nowadays except the extraordinary ingenuity with which Proudhon has made the subject as difficult and obscure as his natural liveliness allowed. It is easy for a student of Marx to perceive that Proudhon was right in his main contention; but it is impossible to conceive anyone being perfectly convinced by his way of putting the case without more shutting of the eyes and opening of the mouth than is consistent with a conscientious study of sociology. Many of his propositions, interpreted as they would be by any ordinary reader, are beneath confutation. For example, his first proposition (126) is "That property is idiotic, because it exacts something from nothing". What is more, Proudhon admits that it gets it: his whole book is a protest against that fact. But *ex nihilo nihil fit.*[15] Property cannot do what is impossible. Proudhon, in proving that it does, only disproves his own proposition by a reductio ad absurdum. Ergo, as he would say himself, "*l'ouvrage de Proudhon est impossible*".[16] This does not, however, demolish his first proposition, but only the sentence in which he endeavours to formulate it. By demolishing the sentence, we prove that Proudhon is not to be depended on for the final and accurate expression of his own meaning, much less of the cardinal propositions of Socialism. That much ascertained, and we duly warned against the danger of endorsing Proudhon unglossed, we can consider the gist of the ill expressed proposition. This is, to follow the author's phrase as nearly as possible, "That Property is unreasonable, because it exacts something and gives nothing". He begins by pointing out that the examination of this proposition is that of the origin of rent. He is moved to contempt mingled with anger by the spectacle of men seeking a rational and legitimate origin for what is, on the face of it, theft, malversation, and rapine. Such search must, he thinks, surely be the high water-on-the-brain mark of proprietary idiotcy and of the power of egoism and general cussedness to bewitch clear headed men. Having thus relieved himself of the eloquence which had been pent up within him for fully four lines of sober inexactness, he states Ricardo's law of rent as "the quantity by which the produce of the most fertile land exceeds that of lands of inferior quality", putting the superlative in the wrong place with his usual unerring instinct of error. According to Ricardo, the amount of any particular rent will be the quantity by which the produce of the land exceeds that of the least fertile land in cultivation.[17] This is of course not a definition of rent, which Ricardo accurately defined as "that portion of the produce of the earth which is paid to the landlord for the use of the original and indestructible powers of the soil". Proudhon now indulges in a diabolical juggle with the words "law" and "right", which are identical in French. Translating in his mind our phrase "Ricardian law of rent" as "Ricardian right to rent", he proceeds to smash Say, Ricardo, Mill, and MacCullough[18] by demanding (127) "How can the different qualities of the soil confer a right to property in it? How can the varieties of loam give birth to a political principle?" This is a very pertinent question, and a strong way of putting the case. Unfortunately, the impression of Proudhon's cleverness conveyed by it is weakened by the doubts of his thoroughness raised immediately before by his extremely commonplace assumption that Ricardo's law was offered to the world as a golden rule of ethics. His next remark shews that he understood quite well what rent essentially is, and how in any just social system it must continue to be paid, though not of course to private proprietors. (128) "The establishment of rent", he says, "might well have had for its principle the desire for equality, since, if all have equal rights to the possession of good land, no one should, without indemnity, be compelled to cultivate inferior land". He then points out to "le seigneur Malthus" that the law of rent extends beyond the farmer's business to that of the manufacturer, the professional man, and in fact to the whole industry of society. This, considering that it was written in 1840, places Proudhon well in the front rank of the economists of his day. He next deals with Say's contention that the landlord is entitled to the value which his land, as a tool or ingredient, adds to the product, and that but for the landlord the labourers would fight with one another for possession of the soil. Proudhon refutes the first point on the lines followed by Henry George; and refers to Chap[ter] II for the answer to the second. He shews in fact that what Ricardo called "the natural and indestructible powers of the soil" cost the proprietor nothing, and therefore he has no right to charge for them. In short, he exacts something and gives nothing.

The second proposition is that Property is unreasonable because wherever it is recognized, production costs more than it is worth. This way of stating the case probably displeased Marx. Proudhon asserts that it is an economic proposition as distinguished from the first, which was legislative—a distinction which I do not quite catch, as both propositions are as purely economic as any case of applied economics can be.

But in discussing it he makes a point which is of some interest as regards the Positivist proposal to moralize the capitalist and landlord. He points out that if the proprietor were to earn his own living like the rest of the community, a special share of the total produce set apart for him would be wasted, as he would have no use for it. For instance, let us suppose a community free and equal except for the existence among them of a single landlord who demands, in return for permission to use the soil, that the rest shall supply him with a dinner every day gratuitously. If this landlord becomes moralized, he will do his share of the social work and earn his own dinner. Consequently, when the rent dinner arrives, he will say to the bearer, "Thank you; but I have already dined: you may eat it yourself". To which the bearer will reply, "Thank you; but I have already dined. I dont want it". Everyone else is in the same state of repletion. Therefore the dinner has to be thrown out, and the labour of producing it is wasted. In producing it, the community have been creating what Proudhon calls a *"non-valeur"*.[19] The dinner, being useless, is not worth the labour of preparing it. The production, in short, costs more than it is worth. Q.E.D. Now the practical result of this will be either that the community will cease providing the useless dinner, in which case landlordism disappears, or the landlord will give up earning his own dinner, and so unmoralize himself again. Thus he *must* be an idler if he wishes to remain a landlord. When he ceases to be an idler he pays for his dinner and is no longer a landlord. (top of 137) "But", adds Proudhon, "as regards the mere supporting of idlers, there will always be the blind, the maimed, the maniacs, and the idiots. Society supports these: it can well support a few more idlers also if it pleases["]. This is his excuse for proceeding to slay the slain with fresh propositions.

The third is a beast of a proposition to the effect that "Property is unreasonable because the production from a given quantity of capital is in proportion to the number of labourers employed and not to the number of shareholders—to labour and not to property". Suppose two men working together can produce a pounds worth of product per day. Each gets ten shillings as his share. Suppose one of them asserts and enforces a proprietary claim to half the produce as rent. He now takes, first ten shillings as rent, and then five shillings as his half of the net produce, leaving the other man—the proletaire—five shillings as against his own fifteen. Note that his proprietorship has not increased the produce by a single farthing. Now suppose that the proprietor resolves to live on his rent alone and give up working. His fifteen shillings immediately falls to ten shillings because his proletary partner, deprived of his aid, can only produce ten shillings a day, and therefore another proletaire must be employed to produce the other ten shillings, out of which he keeps half for wages. Thus, (137) says P[roudhon], ["]the proprietor finds himself impoverished by his attempt to enjoy himself: in exercising his right, he loses it; so that property seems to decrease and vanish as we strive to seize it. The more we pursue it, the more it evades us". Proudhon now, pleased with himself, formulates an axiom. "Rent must decrease as the number of idlers increases". The only objection to this axiom is that it is not true. The idlers must increase faster than the workers, productive fertility remaining stationary meanwhile, in order to diminish each proprietor's share of l'aubaine.[20] Proudhon, it must be confessed, falls off in this third proposition. He finishes it by discussing rent as payment for the right of occupation, arguing that the proprietor has no right to exact more from the tenants than he, unaided, could have produced had he occupied the land himself. Further (139 foot), the rights of occupation being equal for all, the landlord owes the worker as much on that score as the worker owes the landlord, and so their reciprocal obligations cancel one another.

The fourth proposition is that property is homicide. This is exactly true; but Proudhon's way of illustrating it is not worth spending time over. The only point which arrests one's attention is the conscription paragraph on P. 142, in which there is a flavour of Anarchism.

The fifth proposition (145)—the last with which I propose to deal—is that Property is fatal because through it society devours itself. "When the ass is too heavily laden", begins Proudhon, "he caves in: man advances ever". After so eloquent a commencement, one is not surprised to find the author declaring himself on the next page a revolutionary socialist. Speaking of rebellion against landlordism, he exclaims "For my own part, I declare openly that it is in my eyes the first of rights and the holiest of duties, and my only wish now is that this profession of my faith may become public". As is usually the case with Socialists, however, Proudhon's eloquence and his reasonableness are in inverse ratio to one another. He ignores the fact that a worker can produce considerably more than his own sustenance. "To slake the cupidity of Proprietorship", he says (P. 145) the worker must produce more than what he needs for himself. * * * [Shaw's asterisks] But in order to do this, he must usurp the production of others". This does not follow. If five men can produce enough for six, they can make a proprietor of him without trenching on any product except their own. The economic law propounded at the top of P. 149[,] "The producer's salary must suffice to repurchase his product in order that he may live", is no law at all, but a blunder. In order that he may live the producer need only be able to retain or repurchase as much of his product as he can subsist on, which may be only a half or even a third of the whole. The rest he can surrender to his master without touching the product of any other man or doing himself any further injury than giving half his work for nothing. Nevertheless Proudhon is so pleased with his own statement to the contrary that he pauses to challenge any economist in France to find fault with his calculation, and pledges himself to retract, in the event of his challenge being successfully taken up, all that he has wrongfully and wickedly advanced against property. The longer Proudhon dwells on this, the more infatuated does he become. At the top of P. 151 he breaks out again. "When the whole society labours, it labours for the whole society: if, then, only a part of society consumes, a part must sooner or later give up working. But to give up working is to perish, for worker as for proprietor: you will never get out of *that*". We will certainly never get out of it because we will never get into it. In the next paragraph he calls his law "a mathematic necessity["], and exclaims against the desolating spectacle of mankind blindly struggling against it. The fifth proposition, then, fails. The human race is not slowly decaying by starvation. In spite of property, it is growing bigger and stronger. Proudhon's final résumé of his proposition is, however, correct. "Property", he says, "charges the worker more for his product than it pays him for it". This is a very neat way of putting the surplus value theory,[21] and one that shews how unreasonable it is to expect a workman to provide for his future except by becoming a proprietor. Incidentally P[roudhon] describes how competition produces alternate phases of overproduction and stagnation, subdivides interest, and so forth. He also makes the statement, now familiar (146), that admirable machines for making labour easy and rapid become under property so many infernal machines which kill the workers by thousands.

There is an appendix eight pages long to the 5th proposition; but this I am content to relinquish to the opener of our next discussion[.]

Ten
Reasons Why Women
should
Support the Progressives
at the
Borough Council Elections.[22] (1903)

[PROVENANCE: Unsigned holograph manuscript, foliated by Shaw: 1–6, undated (c. September-October 1903); written for the Progressive Party Committee of the London Reform Union. Department of Special Collections, University Research Library, The University of California at Los Angeles: Coll. No. 670, Box 2.]

1. Because the Moderates want to raise the PRICE OF BREAD to Four Shillings the Quartern Loaf, which was the price before 1844, when

Mr Gladstone

established Free Trade & founded the County Council[.][23]

2. Because the Moderates are pledged to force every child in London to attend Confession twice a month, and to establish the Compulsory Worship of the Virgin Mary at the expense of the rates (the Tory-Moderate Education Act fixes the rate for this purpose at TWO AND SEVENPENCE IN THE £[).][24]

3. Because all the Borough Councils with Moderate Majorities have forced their Town Clerks to wear Wigs made out of the scalps taken from Boers by the Canadian Contingent in the late war.[25]

4. Because the rates always go up when the Moderates are in power, whilst the Boroughs which return Progressives have no rates at all, and distribute a bonus of fourpence in the £ every three years to the householders.

5. Because Mr Chamberlain, as Moderate Secretary for the Colonies, took no steps to extinguish the terrible eruption in Martinique, which cost thousands of lives and led to the disastrously wet weather of last summer.

6. Because the Small Pox Epidemic of last year was purposely set on foot by the Moderates in order that your children should be poisoned by the impure lymph supplied by Tory contractors for use in South Africa.

7. Because the Progressives are the only sincere opponents of the Water Companies, whose shares are held almost entirely by members of the present infamous Tory Government.[26]

8. Because all the great Reforms for the good of the people have been introduced by the Progressives and opposed by the Moderates.

9. Because the Moderates are pledged to abolish the County Council trams if elected, and to substitute motor cars at shilling fares driven by Mr Balfour through the crowded streets at *a mile a minute* (for which he has been repeatedly fined by Progressive Magistrates).

10. Because the Progressives are pledged to Abolish the House of Lords, which struck women off the Borough Councils because Mr Balfour, Mr Chamberlain & Lord Salisbury sent a telegram to say that Every Vote Given to a Woman is a Vote for President

KROOJER[27]

Vote early.

Do not be intimidated by Tory agents who try to persuade you that your daughter must not vote in your name if you are busy.

Go round yourself & vote again if you have time.

Ride in a moderate carriage. The Ballot is SECRET.[28]

[Lady Day Speech, 1929]

[PROVENANCE: Untitled typewritten manuscript, foliated [1]–4, drafted on Lady Day (25 March) 1929; unsigned. Shorthand note at foot of final leaf: "8½ minutes". T. E. Hanley Collection, Harry Ransom Humanities Research Center, The University of Texas at Austin.]

Dear Sir—or Dear Lady, as the case may be[:]

I take it that you have turned on this record to find out what I have to say on current politics in view of the General Election now pending. By the way, I had better date my communication: this is Lady Day,[29] nineteen hundred and twentynine. But the date does not greatly matter, because parliamentary politics have settled into a competition for your votes between the Labor Party and the Conservative and Liberal parties, both of which offer to save you from the Labor party. And when you ask them what harm the Labor Party will do you, they reply, that it will introduce Socialism, which will make your life miserable by a strict regulation of all your actions, dictating what you shall eat and drink, what you shall wear, how you shall work and for how long, what you shall believe, how much you shall get: in short, make a mere puppet of you instead of the free British citizen you now are.

Well, ARE you? If a Labor Government, or any other Government, made a law that you, sir, should wear collars, or that you, madam, should wear silk stockings, would that make any difference to you? It would not make any to me, nor to my wife. The only country in which people can wear what they please and leave off what they please (provided they are clean and decent) is Russia, which is held up to us as a terrible example of the slavery of Socialism. When I had to earn my living as an employee I should have lost my job immediately if I had not dressed and behaved as my employer thought proper, or if I had professed political or religious opinions offensive to him, or if I had not submitted completely to his control and disposal of my work and time during the all day and every day. I do not call that being free: do you? I should have been better off in that respect in a government office or a nationalized industry; for if I had a grievance I could have written to the papers about it or induced some member of the Opposition in parliament to ask a question about it; but being in private employment I had no such safeguard against injustice: my employer could give me the sack if he happened to dislike the color of my necktie or to think that my manner of addressing him did not sufficiently express my sense of his social and moral superiority to me.

Can you wonder at all this platform gabble about the liberty of private employment and the slavery of Socialistic employment leaving me cold.

The only way to increase my liberty is to shorten my working day and thereby lengthen the part of my day during which I can do what I like and be where I please. I lately had a letter from a man complaining of the price of my books, which he could not afford.[30] He said he worked fourteen hours a day for three pound ten a week to support himself and his family. Now this man has absolutely no liberty at all; for the ten hours that are left to him out of the twentyfour are needed for sleeping and eating and dressing, which are as compulsory by the law of nature as the fourteen hours are by the capitalist law of contract. He is doing two men's work for less than a living wage for one man who has to bring up a family: say four pounds a week at least, at a time when more than a million men are unemployed and kept alive out of the rates and taxes. I call that foolishness from the national point of view; and I say that any Government, Conservative, Liberal, Labor, Fascist, Communist, or what you please, which will give that man employment at seven hours a day and pay him four pounds a week for it, and will make it illegal for any private employer to work him longer than seven hours as long as there is an unemployed man in the country eating his head off on the dole, will *give* that man liberty instead of taking it from him. I will not say that it will double his liberty because twice nothing is nothing: it will take a man who is now a complete slave and make him a free man for seven hours a day without counting his home life.

Now turn to the windbags who are prating about British liberty as if a Briton could be free all day flourishing Magna Carta and waving a Union Jack. No honest man can be free all day. We must all do our bit every day just as we had during the war. Those who are not contributing to the wealth of the country are stealing from it. We have to give our children credit whilst they are growing up; but they must pay that debt of honor when it becomes due, and provide for their old age into the bargain. The first business of a Government is to organize this honest dealing for us. I support the Labor Party at present because the Labor party at least promises to do this, and recognizes its necessity, whilst the Conservative and Liberal parties denounce it as a horrible slavery and promise to protect us from it. They assure us that if we will only return them to power there will be a revival of trade under their fostering care, by which they appear to mean that there will be more men working fourteen hours a day for three pound ten a week, more enormously rich ladies and gentlemen paying higher wages to poor people to wait on their pleasures, and so forth. What I want to see is not one man taking a big income without producing a farthing whilst four or five get paid by him for brushing his coats and shining his shoes and driving his cars whilst one unfortunate slave has to provide all the wealth they consume, but everyone doing his fair share of the necessary work of the nation and enjoying his fair share of its product and of the liberty that is available when the work is done. The representatives of the gentlem[a]n with the big unearned income shriek at me that this [is] Socialism, Bolshevism, Red Ruin, and all the rest. I do not care what they call it: if it is common sense and common honesty it is good enough for me. And as, I am sorry to say, you have rather a bad habit of voting for the gentleman with the big unearned income I wish you would just think it over a bit.

The oddest part of the whole affair is that I who am saying this to you am a gentleman with what you would probably call a big income: at any rate I am a supertax[31] payer, and that the chances are ten to one that you are not rich enough to pay even income tax. You may even be my correspondent with the three pound ten a week and the family to keep [on] it. Yet I am a Socialist and I am almost safe in betting that you are a staunch Conservative and would rather be seen in a shabby hat than at a Socialist meeting.

Funny, isnt it.

Goodbye.

Notes

1. Delivered on 16 May 1907. *Christian Commonwealth*, 23 and 30 May 1907; rptd. in *The Religious Speeches of Bernard Shaw*, ed. Warren Sylvester Smith (University Park: Penn State Press, 1963).

2. *Sixteen Self Sketches* (New York: Dodd, Mead, 1949); "Dramatist . . . " *Cassell's Saturday Journal* 19 (16 January 1901): 372; *Platform and Pulpit*, ed. Dan H. Laurence (New York: Hill & Wang, 1961).

3. Finsbury Park (115 acres) was opened as a municipal park for sport and recreation in 1869. Victoria Park (290 acres) was the first park opened in the East End of London, in 1845. Located in Hackney, it was the scene in 1848 of the Chartists' demonstrations. Southwark Park (63 acres), opened in 1869, is in southeast London near the Rotherhithe docks.

4. The "season" is the period during which the "gentleman of fashion" whom Shaw addresses would leave the sporting pleasures of his country estate to socialize in London. As it extended from sometime after the end of March until the beginning of August, it could be described as roughly bounded by Easter and the running of the Goodwood races in Sussex at the end of July. In theory, the social season coincided with the months Parliament was in session, but it would be more pertinent to say it began with the yearly end of fox hunting and terminated at the opening of the grouse season.

5. The implication is that Shaw is addressing, not a genuine member of "society," who would be gone grouse hunting in Scotland, but someone a bit on the periphery.

6. Rotten Row (a corruption of "route du roi," and now usually called simply "the Row") is an equestrian pathway through Hyde Park and was a favorite haunt of the

fashionable during the Season. Rotten Row is also a street name in a number of English towns (*OED*). The jest offered by the speaker was not very original.

7. The Salvation Army, founded by William Booth, a Methodist minister, in 1865, did not receive its familiar name until 1878. The Christian Evidence Society recruited speakers to rebut the increasingly visible and vocal Secularists, Positivists, and other heretics in the various public forums of London. Dwight Lyman Moody (1837–99) and Ira David Sankey (1840–1908) were American revivalists who attracted considerable attention when they toured England, in 1867 and 1872–75. Their popular *Sankey and Moody Hymn Book* was published in 1873.

8. A Salvation Army officer. The following passage strikingly anticipates the encounter between Major Barbara and Bill Walker and shows Shaw's early interest in the Salvation Army.

9. Paul Pry is the title character of a comedy (1825) by John Poole (1786?–1872), a popular playwright who specialized in low-brow comedy and farce. The amusement of the piece derives from the conflict between Pry, a coarse, vulgar busybody, with his refined and sensitive betters.

10. Twenty years later this phrase, as well as its sentiment of loving militancy, would be echoed in *Major Barbara* when Bill Walker describes his treatment at the hands of the Salvationists, one of whom pins him to the ground while another implores: "Ow Lawd brike is stabborn sperrit; bat downt urt is dear art."

11. All extraordinary men who had recently been brought low. Alexander II, the Tsar of Russia who had done so much to liberalize Russian institutions, including the emancipation of the serfs in 1861, and who had escaped numerous assassination attempts, was killed by a bomb-throwing revolutionist on 13 March 1881. Ishmaïl Pasha (1833–95), the Khedive (viceroy) of Egypt, who had worked for the modernization of Egypt and was instrumental in the development of the Suez Canal, was deposed on 25 June 1879. General Charles George Gordon (1833–85), known as "Chinese" Gordon because of his military exploits in China, was killed on 26 January 1885 by the Mahdi in the fall of Khartoum after ignoring orders to evacuate his garrison.

12. Andoche Junot, the son of a farmer, became Duc d'Abrantès in 1807 because of his military victories as a general under Napoleon. Upon receiving the title, he is said to have replied to a member of the established aristocracy who asked him to name his ancestors: "Moi, je suis mon ancêtre" ("I am my own ancestor"). Shaw's version of the remark and its circumstances significantly changes its meaning.

13. The Christadelphians ("Christ's Brothers") were a strict apocalyptic sect founded (1848) in America by John Thomas (1805–71). They were markedly different from the liberal and rational Unitarians.

14. The Hampstead Historic Club devoted a number of meetings in the fall of 1885 and spring of 1886 to reading and discussing Proudhon. Shaw noted in his diary for 20 January 1886 that he "Read Proudhon's [*Qu' est-ce que la*] *Propriété* and began analysis of Chapter IV for Thursday" (*The Diaries, 1885–1897*, ed. Stanley Weintraub [University Park: Penn State University Press, 1986], I: 140). The page numbers in the text refer to Proudhon's book, of which there were a number of French editions (it had not yet appeared in English). Shaw appears to be using the first edition (Paris: J.-F. Brocard, 1840), but given Proudhon's schematic way of developing his argument and Shaw's systematic treatment of the five propositions in strict order, it is easy to identify the references in any edition that happens to be available.

15. "Nothing comes from nothing." The sentiment, if not its exact expression, probably originates with Lucretius.

16. "Proudhon's work is impossible." The expression that Proudhon uses throughout is: "*La propriété est impossible*," literally, "Property is impossible." Shaw translates this as "Prop-

erty is idiotic," or "Property is unreasonable," which are acceptable meanings for the French phrase, but Proudhon clearly has the stricter meaning in mind when he claims that property is "physically and mathematically impossible." In turning Proudhon's phrase back on him, Shaw may also be deliberately conflating the different meanings: "Proudhon's argument is impossible," and "Proudhon's work is exasperating."

17. This may not be clear. Proudhon seems to be saying that rent is the difference in yield between the *most* productive lands and all the others in a given market. Shaw correctly points out that the rent of a particular property is the difference between its yield and that of the *least* productive land. The farmer of the least productive land receives only subsistence; the owners of more fertile fields provide the same investment of labor, etc., yet get more back. That means the rich farmer can lease his farm to someone who will work for subsistence, and the property owner collects the difference: rent. Whether he works the land himself and gets the whole return, or "rents" the land to another, he receives a windfall, and the windfall is technically called "rent."

18. Jean-Baptiste Say (1767–1832) popularized and promoted the theories of Adam Smith in France. David Ricardo (1772–1823), a British economist of Dutch-Jewish parentage, refined and elaborated the ideas of Smith, bringing to political economy a degree of rigor and scientific method that made him one of the most influential economists ever. John Stuart Mill (1806–73), while not best known as an economist, refined Ricardo's ideas in his *Principles of Political Economy* (1848). He studied socialism, was sympathetic to many of its goals, and questioned the "sacredness" of private property, but never embraced socialism. John R. McCulloch (1789–1864) was a disciple of Smith and Ricardo, but was more sympathetic to the needs of the poor (he rejected Malthus). His name is spelt McCulloch or MacCulloch; Shaw's misspelling finds some excuse in the fact that Proudhon refers to him as "Maccullock."

19. A valueless or unexchangeable commodity.

20. Windfall.

21. A theory developed by Marx from Ricardo's labor theory of value, and on which much of Marx's argument depends.

22. A spoof on Shaw's own pamphlet, "A Word to Women Electors about the Borough Councils." The MS is accompanied by the pamphlet itself and an explanatory note from Francis W. Galton that is printed in Dan H. Laurence, *Bernard Shaw: A Bibliography* (Oxford: Clarendon Press, 1983), I: 56. Galton explains that at the request of the Progressive Committee, Shaw wrote a pamphlet addressed to women electors explaining why they should vote for Progressives. When committee members took exception to some of the arguments Shaw used, he responded with a parody of what he thought they really wanted, allegedly adding privately to Galton, "But don't let them see it or they will go frantic."

23. This fantastic assertion establishes the tone of what is to follow. The current debate on free trade had been stimulated by the declaration of Joseph Chamberlain (1836–1914), a member of the Conservative cabinet of Arthur James Balfour (1848–1930), that he favored the revival of tariffs. Always the pragmatist, Shaw agreed, although most socialists did not. The establishment of free trade refers to the abolition of the Corn Laws in 1846; the Local Government Act of 1888 established the County Councils. William Gladstone (1809–98), four times Prime Minister for the Liberal Party, was a supporter of free trade.

24. Shaw ran for County Councillor as a Progressive in the March 1904 election. His defeat was partly due to his endorsement of state support for parochial schools on the ground that half of the country's children had no real alternative to church schools.

25. The South African War, much of it guerrilla combat in which the distinction between combatant and noncombatant was blurred, was bloody and acrimonious, producing bitterness and charges of atrocities. The Liberals, who were out of power, blamed the Conservatives.

26. The supply of water through metal pipes was an innovation of the second half of the nineteenth century and was still in the hands of private companies.

27. The House of Lords did prohibit women from sitting on Borough Councils, a circumstance that Shaw mentions in his published pamphlet. Robert Arthur Talbot Gascoyne-Cecil, 3rd marquess of Salisbury (1830–1903), headed three Conservative governments, the last from 1899 to 1902. He resigned in favor of his nephew, Arthur Balfour, who was Prime Minister from 1902 to 1905. The reference to President Kruger of the South African Republic is an allusion to the fact that while Liberals blamed the Conservatives for the brutal conduct of the war, Conservatives charged that the war came about because Liberals permitted the creation of the South African Republic in the first place.

28. As today, political parties provided transportation to the polls for those of their partisans who found it difficult to get there otherwise.

29. Outside Britain, Lady Day is known as the Feast of the Annunciation.

30. Shaw's books were consistently priced beneath the general market level. A volume of Shaw's plays sold for six shillings in 1929, the same price as for *Three Plays for Puritans* in 1901. In 1931 an "omnibus edition" of his complete plays was priced at twelve shillings sixpence; if ordered with coupon vouchers from the socialist paper the *Daily Herald* in 1934 it could be obtained for three shillings ninepence. His *Intelligent Woman's Guide*, an expensive book to produce, was published in 1928 at fifteen shillings. A year later Shaw issued the 500-page work in a popular edition, in cloth, for five shillings. He was also the first major author to make his works available to the masses at sixpence when Penguin/Pelican books first appeared in 1937.

31. There was a flat rate for taxes up to a specified amount, above which a graduated surtax was applied. Through much of the decade of the thirties, the personal exemption was £100 and the supertax began at £2,000.

John A. Bertolini

Shaw Family Values

Near the end of *John Bull's Other Island* (1904), Peter Keegan elaborates a central Shavian metaphor, "this earth of ours must be hell," by explaining that the world is a place "where children are scourged and enslaved in the name of parental duty and education."[1] Keegan's idea that the family is a scene of oppression and that children are subject to parental tyranny animates the speech, "Socialism and the Family," which Shaw delivered to the already sympathetic Fabian Society on 1 October 1886, eighteen years before he wrote his Irish play.

In 1886, Shaw was thirty years old. He reviewed regularly for the *Pall Mall Gazette*. He published his fifth and last completed novel, *An Unsocial Socialist*. He was carrying on romantic affairs simultaneously with Jenny Patterson and Annie Besant, but was far from any notion of establishing a family himself. He had grown up in the Victorian world, surrounded by multitudinous sentimentalities about family life and affection, together with mountainous evidence of the mistreatment of children by their parents. When he became convinced, therefore, by his reading of Marx and other socialist thinkers that the way society governs and organizes itself must be altered radically, it was only logical that he should look upon the family as an organization in need of overhauling. Shaw's speech is full of hyperbole and paradox, designed to attack what he regarded as the false familial platitudes and pieties that camouflaged the tyrannies and even horrors inflicted on children by parents.

As always, Shaw's method of drawing attention to a problem is to outrage his audience's sense of the truth by interpreting some social practice as meaning the opposite of whatever people had understood it to mean, and using that interpretation to justify his proposal for a new way of living. For example, to justify his suggestion that the State take charge of all children who are "not absolutely infants," he observes that the State would only be doing for parents what parents themselves are always seeking: having someone else look after their children. As proof that he is right about normal parental desire in this regard, he urges that his audience consider, not the behavior of middle- or lower-class parents, but the behavior of wealthy parents who, because their wealth enables them to choose freely whether they like being with their children or not, are the test case. And since parents with the means always hire others to care for their children or send them away from home as early and for as long as possible, it must be true that all parents wish to be rid of their children. Consequently the State, in removing children, would only be fulfilling the true wishes of parents.

Now Shaw well knew that to propose such a thing, even to the Fabian Society, was like setting off a flare in the middle of the marketplace: it would attract people's attention to the plight of many children in late nineteenth-century Britain—exploited, mistreated, neglected to the point of suffering, when not downright abused. That Shaw fully realized how provocative his remarks would be can be gauged from Stanley Weintraub's gloss on Shaw's diary entry for the day he delivered the paper: "In the margins of the Fabian Society's minutebook, G. B. S. noted, 'This was one of Shaw's most outrageous performances.' "[2] In other words, Shaw himself conceived of it as an act of provocation. The playwright of the *Plays Unpleasant* is in rehearsal here.

The true object of Shaw's attack is people's self-centered refusal to look the problems of society in the face—what Shaw calls in this speech "our existing Individualist system"—and the concomitant obscuring of those problems by a cloud of pious niceties about natural familial bonds. Having thrown his grenade, Shaw is then willing to sit down at the peace table and concede that "philoprogenitiveness" (parents' love for their own offspring) "when it is duly moralized . . . probably adds to the happiness of both children and grown people." In contrast, "the life of terror and pain which many children live" will not bear thinking of for Shaw, and he therefore concludes his speech with an extraordinary personal denunciation of the Family: "I hate the Family. I loathe the Family. I entirely detest and abominate the Family as the quintessence of Tyranny, Sentimentality, Inefficiency, Hypocrisy, and Humbug." Again, Shaw offers such extravagance as an antidote to the poison of pious pretense about the family, not as a firebombing of the very idea of family.

Shaw's plays are, in fact, full of intense family feeling and affection: *You Never Can Tell, Major Barbara, Mrs Warren's Profession*, and *Man and Superman* all depict with insight and even poignance parental love of children. Mr. Crampton feels himself incomplete without the affection of his daughter and wishes to reclaim custody of her and her brother after many years of separation. Barbara Undershaft cannot really search for heaven until she acknowledges herself as her mother's daughter as well as her father's: at the end of her play Barbara emancipates herself from her mother by agreeing to marry Adolphus, then renews her connectedness to her mother by asking for her help in finding a house. The second act of *Mrs Warren's Profession* ends with Vivie affirming an emotional admiration for her mother, while the fourth act ends with Vivie drowning her emotional life in actuarial calculations, the price she pays for freedom from her mother. And John Tanner only discovers his true destiny when he feels that there is a "father's heart" within him.

There is hardly a play by Shaw that does not emphasize parent-child relations (*Saint Joan* is the exception, as it is in so many other respects). One of the great joys of *The Devil's Disciple* is seeing Mrs. Dudgeon relentlessly refuse to have any feeling whatsoever for her offspring. Henry Higgins's mother-fixation determines not only his eternal bachelorhood but even his choice of phonetics as a profession, which allows him to rival his mother's fertility by creating duchesses out of squashed cabbage leaves. Candida's attitude toward her father remains a central mystery in the play. Certainly, all the differences between her and Burgess in accent, manners, looks, and intelligence point to a daughter who has remade herself as distinct from her family as she possibly could. *Fanny's First Play* more lightheartedly depicts the necessity for children to free themselves from the deadening effects of the middle-class household—by becoming playwrights or suffragists and choosing their own fiancés.

But the play that occasioned in its preface Shaw's most profound and sensitive observations about family was *Misalliance* (1909), written twenty-three years after Shaw's "outrageous performance" before the Fabian Society. Gone are cries for the abolition of the Family; in their place are observations about the painful relations between parent and child: "The child cannot conceive that its blame or contempt or want of interest could possibly hurt its parent, and therefore expresses them all with an indifference which has given rise to the term *enfant terrible* (a tragic term in spite of the jests connected with it); whilst the parent can suffer from such slights and reproaches more from a child than from anyone else, even when the child is not beloved, because the child is so unmistakably sincere in them."[3]

Within the play itself, however, Shaw has distributed several sentiments from the Fabian Society speech. For example, he has Hypatia almost replicate his personal denunciation of the family (quoted above): "Oh, home! home! parents! family! duty! how I loathe them! How I'd like to see them all blown to bits!"[4] Shaw also has Hypatia's father, John Tarleton, wish the family to "be rooted out of civilization!" Neither Hypatia nor her father speaks for Shaw any more than his other characters do. But she does speak for the child to whom the family has become a stifling restraint. Hypatia wants to be an "active verb," and Family inhibits her, especially insofar as Family affects whom she marries. She is a comic version of Blanche Sartorius in *Widowers' Houses*, whose father's unsavory business of slum-landlordism makes her wish, "Oh, if only a girl could have no father, no family, just as I have no mother!"[5] But Shaw allows her father a corrective to Blanche's outburst: "What would you be now but for what your grandmother did for me when she stood at her washtub for thirteen hours a day?"[6]

Generally, Shaw's later objections to the Family fall into two categories. He objects when it limits rather than liberates. He considers the middle-class family unit artificially segregated, and therefore (in the preface to *Getting Married*) a constraint upon free social intercourse, or (preface to *Androcles and the Lion*) an impediment to political and communal involvement. Shaw also objects (preface to *Misalliance*) to imposing emotional burdens on family members that are separate from mere human feelings. In all of these concerns, Shaw battles for the freedom of children from any artificial tyrannies, such as parental interference with children's marriages or social involvement, or demands for filial displays of affection that are not genuinely felt.

In Shaw's last major pronouncement on the family, *The Intelligent Woman's Guide to Socialism and Capitalism* (1928), Shaw allows that there has been some progress in the protection of children from cruel parents, but he criticizes the system by which children who have been harmed by their parents are returned to the custody of those very parents, after the parents have been punished for their cruelty. This is, of course, the main problem welfare authorities have to deal with at present, and Shaw's alertness to it in 1928 shows his familiarity with current social problems as well as his prescience.

Shaw's speech to the Fabian Society on Family may be partly a grumbling against experience with his own family, for Shaw knew both the bitter shame of a child humiliated by the public drunkenness of a father he had affection for and the odd uneasiness of a neglected son whose mother brought her voice teacher home to live with the family. But the speech is really a fireworks display to capture the attention of his audience. And given his flexibility in adapting his views to changing facts, I cannot help thinking that were he alive today and contemplating the utter breakdown of the family in our society and the consequent social chaos and suffering of children entailed by it, he would, far from endorsing his 1886 opinion, be saying (with Barbara Dafoe Whitehead in *The Atlantic*, April 1993), "Dan Quayle Was Right."

Socialism and the Family (1886)

[PROVENANCE: *Holograph manuscript, foliated by Shaw: 1–11, with unfoliated cover title on which is written, "Read to the Fabian Society at 19 Avenue Road. 1ˢᵗ October 1886."; signed "G.B.S." and dated "29ᵗʰ Sept. 1886." at foot of final leaf, beneath which is a shorthand annotation: "Can be read slowly in 21*

minutes." T. E. Hanley Collection, Harry Ransom Humanities Research Center,
The University of Texas at Austin.]

A Socialist cannot define his attitude towards the Family without great
risk of placing himself in a false position. Historically considered the
family is a belated relic of primitive Communism. As such, it seems to
claim the admiration of the party which is striving to hasten the second
coming of Communism one turn higher in the spiral path of Social
Evolution. But practically, and therefore in the true sense philosophically, the Family is a petty despotism; a hotbed of Individualism; an
example of everything that is intolerable and Bismarckian in State-
Socialism; a school in which men learn to despise women and women to
mistrust men (much more than is necessary); a slaughter house for children (the firstborn succumbing to unskilled treatment—the lastborn to
neglect); and an effectual extinguisher of the promise of early manhood
and womanhood. Unfortunately, we cannot as yet do without it; and
therefore we put a good face on the matter by conferring upon it the
conventional attribute of sacredness, and impudently proclaiming it the
source of all the virtues it has well-nigh killed in us. It is said that children
instinctively recognize the truth of the Bible; and there can be no doubt
that the explanation of this is to be found in the correspondence between
the child's experience of the home and the family, and the stories of Cain
& Abel: Joseph and his brethren: Abraham and Ishmael: David and
Absolom. If anyone doubts the hypocrisy of those views of English home
life and family feeling which bishops and respectable laymen are expected to profess, let him consult any woman who has married into a
large family and has three or four sisters-in-law. If he thinks that parents
can safely be trusted to be even merciful to their offspring, let him study
the records of the Society for the Protection of Children. Or, if he rejects
that as a record of mere aberrations, let him observe the eagerness of the
ordinary youth to get free from his father's roof, and the strained relations which exist between him and his parents until these finally abdicate
and admit his independence. Let him count the number of women of his
acquaintance who are willing to marry or who have married any man—
however uncongenial—in order "to get away from home." That very
phrase "married to get away from home," is perfectly familiar to us all;
and the significance of its familiarity can hardly be exaggerated. It
should never be forgotten that the parental and filial instincts are not
distinctively human. Our domestic animals are just as much parents and
offspring as we are; and no sacredness can possibly attach to the relation
between a mother and her child that does not attach equally to the
relation between a cat and her kitten. For reasons of state, we do not
hesitate to make extremely short work of the maternal feelings of our

cats; and if we are more careful of the lives of children and the feelings of women, we are so because children are scarcer and more useful, and cost their mother much more suffering and sacrifice than kittens do. But both in human kind and brute kind from the time that the offspring can exist independently—from its weaning, in short, the object of the parent is to drive it away and see as little of it as possible. This sounds, at first, like a tremendous libel on thousands of middle and working class homesteads. But I contend that the point is one that must be settled by the conduct of parents who can afford to do as they please, and not by that of middle and working class people who are forced to keep their children about them whether they like it or not. Go among those who have the means to delegate their parental functions, and you will find them doing so without remorse. The rich woman's child is suckled by a hired nurse; left in charge of servants until the time comes for sending it to a boarding school; and kept there with holiday intervals (which the parents dread) until the son goes to the university, and thence into life as an independent man, whilst the girl returns to her mother, who sets to work at once to marry and get rid of her, and takes it very ill indeed if her daughter refuses on grounds of personal dislike a suitor who is eligible in point of rank and money. Such parents are said to be unnatural; but their conduct exactly resembles that of animals in a state of nature; and there is no reason to doubt that their poorer neighbors would, if they could, act in the same manner. The model domestic class of middle class people with slender incomes do so as far as they can afford to. Among them, the marks of the servant's influence are usually stronger than those of the mother's in the nursery phase of the children's career; and schooltime is hailed as a respite from the discomfort caused by the waving of the olive branches. I need go no further to prove that if the State, in fulfilment of its duty, were to remove children not absolutely infants from the custody of their parents, it would, far from inflicting a hardship, be doing exactly what the parents have always tried to bring about for themselves as far as was possible without State-Intervention. And even in the case of infants, the objection, if raised at all, would come from the mother alone. We may without hesitation take Rousseau as the typical father in this respect. And to many highly intelligent and sympathetic women, maternity is so far from being a delight that it is as a duty solely that it is submitted to.

Under our existing Individualist system, the family, objectionable as it is, must remain untouched—in other words, the necessary human crop must be raised by private enterprise, with only such violations of the laissez-faire principle as are absolutely demanded by the preservation of the race. When the State adopts children, it must give them equal training, and throw them without discrimination of classes into one another's society. Parents would not tolerate this at present. Our various "standards of comfort" involve various standards of manners, language, cleanliness, and, in short, civilization. The nineteenth century child of the west end squares must not be placed beside the unfortunate little savage of the slums, lest both should be unfitted for the place they must subsequently fill in society. Besides, a child is the property of its parents; and as this form of property, like others, produces profit, the parental sense of it is very strong indeed. There are many ways of turning a child to account. Insuring its life when an infant and then allowing it to die of neglect or apparently accidental exposure, may seem a proceeding against which Nature cries out in horror. Nevertheless medical officers of health assure us that infant mortality and infant insurance go hand in hand. The uninsured, and the exceptionally hardy children who disappointingly survive, can fetch the beer and do small jobs until they are old enough to earn wages. Most of us know the atrocities of the system of employing young children in factories and mines which led to the passing of the Factory Acts. We hear somewhat less of the desperate efforts which the parents made to deprive their children of the protection of those Acts. The *ideal* mother would give her own life to shield her children from harm. The *actual* mother will, if not forcibly prevented, drive her child into inhuman drudgery, involving abominable physical and moral contamination, for the sake of a few shillings a week. There are women who would not do this to their own children; but these women would not do so to any children. It is the moralized *woman* in them—not the *mother*—that revolts against such barbarity. The upper classes do not enslave their children because they are too rich to need their earnings, and too well attended to need their personal services. But the instinct of the parent-proprietor in them peeps out through their efforts to sell their daughters advantageously in the marriage market. Let the State propose to adopt its growing citizens tomorrow, and high and low would protest against being "robbed" of their children. Observe the expression robbed. It is not that of the ideal bereaved parent: it is that of the real defrauded proprietor.

But there would be another feeling at work. Those orphans whom the State now adopts are treated so shabbily by it that they lose the advantages of orphandom, and even have reason to envy homebred children. Consequently we think of the child of the State as a hideously dressed, stunted, emotionally starved, disreputable charity boy or girl, immured among paupers in a prison for the poor, or "boarded out" among the black beetles in a back kitchen. Now a parent's respectability would be compromised by his child occupying such a position; and however little he may care for the child, he always clings to his respectability. Therefore he will not hear of State nurseries and child communities. Again, many people have a curious instinct which they describe as "love of children," just as a fancier speaks of his love of pigeons or dogs. Such people are practically baby fanciers. They are not happy unless they are surrounded by children. Sometimes they pet them and indulge them: sometimes they beat them, starve them, and neglect their permanent interests. They dress them up and exhibit them without regard to their health and comfort; they turn to new pets when the old ones grow too big to be played with; but still they are, they say, "fond of children." This, the "philoprogenitiveness" of the phrenologists, is to moralized maternity what lust is to love. It is as possible for a passionately fond mother to be savage, cruel, self-indulgent, capricious, and treacherous to her children, as it is for a woman who regards her maternal duties as an unwelcome burden, and who never really likes her children until they are old enough to form rational friendships with her, to sacrifice her welfare to theirs so heroically as to become a stock illustration of the moral grandeur of the system of which she is the victim. Now, the philoprogenitive people would not submit to be cut off from the children any more than the fanciers—who are often, by the bye, extremely cruel—would suffer their dogs and pigeons to be torn from them. And here we have an objection which would not disappear in a socialist community. The sense of proprietorship and the dread of disreputable associates might be safely ignored by a collectivist administration; but philoprogenitiveness, if baffled, would bring about a revolution. For we all have our share of it, and when it is duly moralized, it probably adds to the happiness of both children and grown people. Another, and more important objection to the seclusion of children is, that intercourse with their elders, as far as the elders will stand it, is an indispensable part of a child's education. But the separation of children from adults is not a necessary consequence of State adoption. A child within the precinct of a State nursery need be no more inaccessible than a barrister in chambers in the Temple or a boy at Eton. Parents might see much more of their children than they ever do at present if they can help it, without interfering with the duties of the State. Children might be permitted to spend all their disengaged time at their parents' houses, provided both parties preferred that arrangement. It is in the extremest degree improbable that any such preference would last for more than a week on either side; and it is likely that people would invite other people's children quite as often as their own; but the possibility of having the children home in this fashion would completely meet the demands of the philoprogenitive, without in the least bringing the child back under the yoke of an irresponsible private master. At present any father can imprison and barbarously torture a child at his own pleasure with impunity, either for his amusement or as a penal infliction with respect to which he is judge, jury, bar, witness, and executioner, with the usual results as to the culprit's chance of either justice or mercy. The life of terror and pain which many children live under this system will hardly bear thinking of. It is true that most men are too humane or too lazy to abuse their power, though very few are too conscientious to neglect their responsibility or delegate it carelessly. It is also true that most men are too honest to bilk their creditors or pilfer; but the State does not therefore permit the dishonest minority to steal with impunity; and it should not permit the cruel minority to maltreat children with impunity. When it is considered that to our future citizens the good nature of easy going parents, and the incompetence of timid ones, are only less injurious than the harshness of the domestic tyrant (whose authority is always partly evaded by precocious lying and cheating) it is hard to see in our institution of the Family anything but a foolish individualistic makeshift, or to regard it otherwise than Swift did, or than Plato and Aristotle would assuredly do if they could pay us a visit.

An incidental inconvenience of the institution is the spurious personal relations to which it gives rise. Instead of leaving us free to form congenial ties with those who attract us and who respond to our impulse towards them, our very affections are prescribed for us. We are taught that it is our duty to love our brothers, sisters, aunts, and uncles, and even in a minor degree our cousins, although these persons, in whom we probably recognize all our vices, may and very frequently do excite our hearty aversion. Except in tribal communities, it is neither natural nor desirable that people of near kin should be thrust into any factitious relations with one another. Family quarrels are only in part due to disputes about inherited property. They are just as bitter among propertyless people, among whom the jealousies, rivalries, and favoritism of home life produce all the rancour that prevails in the average county family: a rancour which is not the less odious because it underlies a certain clannishness which will combine the family as one man against an intruder by marriage. It is the exceptionally unlucky people who tell you that their childhood was the happiest time of their life. More commonly the date at which we begin to enjoy life coincides with the date of our escape from home; and our troubles recommence when we set up a home of our own.

It is, then, my opinion and my hope that Socialism must prove fatal to the Family. I hate the Family. I loathe the Family. I entirely detest and abominate the Family as the quintessence of Tyranny, Sentimentality, Inefficiency, Hypocrisy, and Humbug. I use these unphilosophic expressions to indicate how lightly I regard the evil consequences which many people anticipate from its abolition, and my disbelief in the genuineness of Family cohesiveness. Remove the external pressure of the Individualist system; and the people whom you think bound together by sacred ties will start asunder like the charge of a bursting shell. We shall then be free to study the next phase of the question, which will be the scientific and conscientious breeding of the human race instead of the shocking promiscuity that prevails at present. And I shall, if I live to see that day, propose, as a preliminary step, the summary execution of all poets and romancers as persons by all human experience proved guilty of keeping in repair the mask of sham purity under which our system has hitherto concealed its essential indelicacy.

Notes

1. Bernard Shaw, *Collected Plays with Their Prefaces* (London: Max Reinhardt, 1970–74), 2: 991.

2. Stanley Weintraub, ed., *Bernard Shaw, The Diaries 1885–1897* (University Park: Penn State University Press, 1986), 1: 202.

3. Shaw, *Collected Plays*, 4: 110.

4. Shaw, *Collected Plays*, 4: 182.

5. Shaw, *Collected Plays*, 1: 109.

6. Shaw, *Collected Plays*, 1: 111.

Sally Peters

Shaw and the Seamy Side of the Ring

"Went to the Museum in the afternoon and began article on prize fighting for *Star*," recorded Shaw in his diary on 19 January 1888. He finished the piece the next day and sent it in to the newspaper, which had commenced publication three days earlier. It never appeared. Perhaps if Shaw had written under his own name instead of drafting his piece in the form of a bogus interview it would have fared better, for by then Shaw was an acknowledged expert on pugilism, having cast a prizefighter as the hero of *Cashel Byron's Profession* five years earlier.[1]

Shaw's fourth novel, a joyous romp that was supposedly "an attempt to take the reader behind the scenes without unfairly confusing professional pugilism" with its "blackguardly environment," originally was serialized in *To-Day*, Henry Hyde Champion's socialist monthly. Champion liked the novel so much he put out a shilling edition in book form in 1886, giving the fledgling novelist a taste of success. "The world never did know chalk from cheese in matters of art" was Shaw's mock disclaimer of the work brimming with playful autobiographical resonances—his warrior hero is a blue-eyed, auburn-haired, middleweight antivivisectionist. In 1901, to protect his novel from piracy, he transformed it in one week into a play. *The Admirable Bashville* is written in blank verse, "so childishly easy and expeditious (hence, by the way, Shakespear's copious output)"—the literary contender being unable to resist jabbing the literary champion.[2]

But Shaw's knowledge of pugilism was not limited to literary fisticuffs. In the early 1880s, Shaw regularly spent Sunday evenings at the home of the poet and dilettante Pakenham Beatty. "Paquito" aspired to a boxing title and was happy to coach a sparring partner. To supplement Beatty's training, Shaw read about boxing at the British Museum, where he discovered Pierce Egan's classic, *Boxiana*, which praised cool judgment and elegant position. He also read *Fistiana*, published by the editor of *Bell's Life in London*. Along with its lists of champions, rules of the ring, and hints on sparring and health, it stressed the importance of courage and "science," as opposed to slugging. Such views of boxing were furthered by Beatty's instructor at the London Athletic Club, where Shaw soon found himself developing his sparring skills. Ned Donnelly, an acclaimed "professor" of boxing and the author of *Self-Defense*, had developed a scientific approach to the manly art based on defensive parries for every offensive move. He achieved his modicum of immortality not for his system of glove-fighting, however, but as the chief model for Ned Skene in *Cashel Byron's Profession*.[3]

Admitting that there is something in pugilism "that appeals irresistibly to the romantic coward that is in all of us" and having gotten "an imaginary reputation" as a boxer, Shaw entered the Queensberry Amateur Boxing Championships in March 1883 in both the middleweight and heavyweight divisions. Looking "like a tall man with a straight left," he weighed in his six-foot one and a half inches at barely over ten stone (140 pounds, like the former fighter in "The Seamy Side").[4] But the bell sounded prematurely on the title aspirations of the Fighting Irishman from the British Museum: his name was not drawn. The only souvenir he took home that day was the program, which he annotated and saved. Disappointed or not, Shaw continued to follow the sport with avid interest, commenting on boxing and its figures in a number of journalistic analyses. In addition, characters talk with their fists literally or metaphorically in *How He Lied to Her Husband* (1904), *Major Barbara* (1905), *The Fascinating Foundling* (1909), *Overruled* (1912), *The Millionairess* (1934), and *Shakes versus Shav* (1949).

For Shaw, the born prizefighter—like the world heavyweight champion Gene Tunney or his own Cashel Byron—expresses himself as instantaneously and unconsciously as the born arithmetician or the born writer. Shaw admired the elegance of strategy, thought, and will demonstrated by such a natural genius, while he detested the vulgar third-rate slugger. When reigning world heavyweight champion Joe Louis's tour made no money, Shaw observed to Tunney that "our sporting crowds know nothing about boxing. What they pay for is bashing."[5] At that time (1948), Shaw was still so closely identified with boxing that upon Louis's arrival in London, it was announced that the only people he wanted to visit were Shaw and Winston Churchill.

"The Seamy Side" treats the betting side of boxing, which Shaw always disparaged. The piece resembles a longer article on the Georges Carpentier-Battling Siki (Louis Phal) fight that appeared in the *Sunday Chronicle* on 10 December 1922. In both articles, he treated the topic of corruption using the format of a mock interview. Admiring the "sweet science" glorified by both the ancient Greeks and contemporary thinking practitioners, Shaw repeatedly denounced the unsavory atmosphere surrounding boxing, while revering the elements of manliness and discipline that lay behind boxing's romantic aura as "the noble art."

A Prizefighter on Prizefighting: The Seamy Side of the Ring (1888)

[PROVENANCE: Unsigned (but name and address on reverse of final leaf) holograph manuscript, on slate-blue paper, seven leaves foliated by Shaw: 1 (truncated), 2, 2a, 3–6, dated at top of first leaf "Jan 1888". Shaw's diary indicates it was drafted on 19 and 20 January. Henry W. and Albert A. Berg Collection, New York Public Library, Astor, Lenox and Tilden Foundations.]

Several correspondents having written to us to protest against the countenance given to prizefighting by the article in our first issue, we sent our representative to call on a zealous member of a small local congregation, formerly well known in the ring as a very clever fighter at ten stone and thereabouts, with a view to ascertaining his opinion of the profession to which he was once an ornament. The negotiations began with a letter sent through the minister of the congregation; and the ex-pugilist's reply was as follows:—

Kind Friend: In answer to your earnest enquiry as to my past, I have to inform you that though well knowing myself to be a miserable sinner I should be well content if I could say that prizefighting was the worst I have to answer for. I have had great experience, having from the age of 17 to 35 been open to any likely looking business for £15 a side and upward. In compliance with your directions, and understanding from the Rev Mr — that your desire is to do good, I shall answer your questions as close as I can free of charge; and express myself in the manner of this world so that the fear of being preached at may deter none from reading my words.

On receipt of this, our representative lost no time in hurrying to the residence of the old gentleman, whose white locks concealed the inroad made on his left ear by his adversary's teeth in a celebrated fight nearly forty years ago. His appearance was venerable, and his manner a little sanctimonious at first; but this speedily wore off, and "the manner of this world" came back to him as naturally as possible.

"To come to the point at once, Mr —", said we, "what sort of fellows are prizefighters, as a rule ["].

"Respecting the general character of professional men", replied our host, with a touch of dignified reproof in his tone, "I will say that I have known greater blackguards out of the ring than ever I knew in it. Them that have the heart to fight and the self denial and sense of duty in them

to train are far better spiritually than them that do but bet on the fight-
ers, and live with an oath ready to the inside of their lips and a glass to
the outside. Dont think that a man can rise to great eminence in the ring
by ruffianizing".

"Why?"

"Because the competition is too severe".

We kept our countenance, and inquired as to the qualities of a first
rate fighter.

"They can be cultivated, but not put into a man, by teaching. They are
a born aptitude for hitting, strength in the right places, bottom [endur-
ance]* [,] certain favorable proportions of the body, quickness, good aim,
good judgment of distance, nerve, and a resolution to win your backers'
money for them in spite of your feelings. Then sobriety and patience in
training are needful; and a turn for business is of great assistance to a
man who gets his bread by his fists["].

"What is the largest sum you ever got for winning a fight?["]

"£14.12.0 and my training expenses. The fight was for £50 a side. The
most I ever got over a single fight was £150. I lost the fight on that
occasion. The other man's principal backer made a heavy bet with my
brother Ted that I was going to win; and I could not see my own flesh
and blood beggared over me. But I found such difficulty in getting
backed again after that that I gave up those evil courses; and from that
day forth I can honestly say that I never lost on purpose without straight-
forwardly arranging it with my own backers first["].

["]Have you ever been cheated by your backers?["]

["]Always. How could I help myself? A poor lad cannot find the money
to back himself. Suppose his friends fancy him and see their way to
making something out of him, they challenge some established professional man in his name for so much a side, and make a deposit. If the
challenged man's friends think it good enough, they agree to back him
and cover the deposit. The balance of the stakes must be scraped together out of the friends of both parties; and of course they expect to
stand in to get something extra back if their man wins the stakes. They
have no more human feeling for him than if he was a racehorse or a
fighting cock; and when everyone else is satisfied, there is precious little
left for him except the honor and glory and a few glasses of champagne.
If he gets beaten when fighting to win, he soon finds out what his friends
are worth."

"Then prizefighting does not pay?"

"Well: that depends on how badly the man is off to start with. It wouldnt
pay anyone that had much to lose; but a labouring lad, working all day and

*Shaw's square brackets.

half the night to earn anything from six to fifteen shillings a week, dont see how he can very well change for the worse so long as he keeps out of trouble. If he is a good lad with his hands, he begins to pick up first a few pence and then a few shillings by sparring. Then he finds himself made a bit of a hero, and let drink with gentlemen; and that goes a powerful way with a young fellow that never was treated with consideration since he was weaned. The idea of being a champion gets hold of his imagination. He mostly goes to the bad then. He gets into the thick of a parcel of the primest blackguards in London; and if he wants to keep in with them and not be called a Juggins,[6] he must drink with them, keep their hours and habits and company, give in to their notions of knowingness—which is just always trying to get the better of somebody and nothing else—and stand in with them all round in the service of their master the Devil. Do you, sir, just take up with professional boxing, and keep your eye on it for three or four years; and you will see a string of young uns go into it rosy, healthy, well looking, spirited lads and come out of it seedy, stale, bragging, broken down drunkards and loafers, as regular as if it was done by machinery. But a few are too stubborn or too sensible to be led away; and a few more have constitutions that will stand anything. If a clever glove fighter has a turn for teaching, and knows how to be decent, civil, and obliging when it's his interest to be so, he may come to have a gymnasium of his own at the west end, and have a swell connexion. If he is only good for the ring, and can keep within reason as to liquor—though he's almost bound to drink too much if he drinks at all, then I would say that if he sticks to some regular occupation between his fights, and gets to be known as a trustworthy man that will take real trouble to win his backers' money, he may, by being careful of his winnings and getting to find some of the money for himself, retire when his time's up in a far better position than others of his family who have worked all the time as ordinary laboring men. So I wouldnt say that it never pays; but the chances are a hundred to one against it".

"But men like Mace & Sull—"[7]

"What have they got to do with it: they are one in a thousand. Such men as they cant help being pugilists: the work comes looking for them instead of they looking for the work. If the Archbishop of Canterbury had had Mace's genius for it, he'd have been in the ring in spite of himself. I am only speaking of men like myself, with a good professional standing, but no great name. People get too much led away by thinking only of the cracks.[8] Read Fistiana; and see how many of the names in it ever came to your ears. Not one in five hundred".

"May I take it then, Mr —, that you dont recommend the Star to encourage prizefighting?"

"No: I dont want to have my words taken in that way, unless it would be to make way for more serious subjects—for all sport is only the crackling of thorns under a pot. But it is the opinion of all decent and respectable professionals that the ring would have a better name if the papers would send real gentlemen to come and see fair, and if the law was altered so that a prizefight would not be the only place in England where bad characters are safe from meeting the police".

"Do you think that the practice of choosing sporting reporters to act as referees at fights conduces to the fairness of the proceedings?"

"It is always hard to get a dependable referee—one that has honesty and judgment and is not to be intimidated. In my time, when, besides the champions, Baldock, Boss Tyler, Travers, McKelvy, Ned Donnelly, Green, Jerry Noon[9] and others were before the public, Bell's Life was the great boxing authority; and the reporter used to be made referee. I remember Bob Travers punching his head for one of his decisions. I remember Boss Tyler doing it another time; and if he hadn't I'd have done it myself—for I was full of sin then, and it was a foul as plain as could be. I've acted as referee myself, and had the sleeves pulled out of two coats off me; but I always refused to give my decision until the day after".

"What effect has a fight on the spectators?"

"They carry on to no end, especially the ones that have money in it. Yelling, swearing, screaming at you by every name they can lay their tongue to to go it and do all manner of things to the other man. Not a place to bring a lady to, I can tell you. Some lots are worse than others; but even the best are something choice. They go for a win, a tie, or a wrangle, as the saying is. No man likes losing".

"But does not fighting make a man plucky, and less likely to use knives and revolvers and such weapons?"

["]If you can use your hands, you are less likely to be frightened into carrying a knife, but more likely to get into mischief. Real fighting takes the pluck out of you. As a rule, there's never enough difference between you and anybody that can get backed to stand up to you, but that he'll give you even if you beat him, more than it would be worth your while to take unless you were paid for it. By the time you know your business you lose the heart for it. The only strength that lasts in this world comes from above".

"Surely Tom Sayers[10] never knew what fear was?"

"Sayers was very plucky; and well he might, though I could always make a fool of him with the gloves. He could stand anything and last out anybody—could take the worst you could give him and finish you when your bolt was shot. But he learned from Ned Langham that it's better to lay down to a quick hitter than to stand up to him. He played Heenan that way, just as old Nat played him. And he didnt care to fight Mace at the end. No more didnt Mace care to fight Sullivan. No: the young 'uns for pluck, I say: not because they're young, but because they dont know as much as we old uns. Youre bound to lose at last; and how do you know but it may be next time?"

"One question more, Mr —. Did you bring up any of your sons to your old profession?"

"No, sir: I should be sorry to. No more would any of us that could do better for the lads".

"Thank you for a very pleasant chat. I think, if I meet Jem Smith[11] on my way home, I shall recommend him to put by what he can for a rainy day, and get out of the ring as fast as possible".

"That's it, sir. Ask him who he thinks will be afraid of him in twenty years time from this, and whether his appetite will be any the smaller. And if you would kindly mention to him the address of our little meeting hall, he might find himself some Sunday with nothing to do, and the fancy might take him to come. There has been a many joined us since me and Bendigo[12] chose the better path".

We promised to mention it if we had the opportunity, and, wringing the veteran's hand, returned to Stonecutter St a little disenchanted with the ropes and stakes.

Notes

1. *Bernard Shaw, The Diaries 1885–1897*, ed. Stanley Weintraub (University Park: Penn State University Press, 1986), 1: 340–41. Even though the interview was bogus, Shaw's piece had its roots in a world he knew well. In regular attendance at boxing matches and training sessions, he must have chatted with a number of old timers, retired pugilists eager to share anecdotes and reminiscences about the ring. Shaw's creation of the "born again" pugilist he sketches here resurfaces in *Major Barbara* in the off-stage Todger Fairmile, who has given up boxing for religion. Shaw's vivid insight into the world of his religious ex-pugilist suggests a real-life model, perhaps even William "Bold Bendigo" Thompson (1811–80), the English champion who is mentioned in this piece.

2. Preface to *Cashel Byron's Profession* (New York: Wm. H Wise, 1930), pp. xiv, x–xi; preface to *The Admirable Bashville*, in *Collected Plays with Their Prefaces*, ed. Dan H. Laurence (London: Max Reinhardt, 1970–74), 2: 433.

3. For a sketch of Beatty, see Dan H. Laurence's headnote in Bernard Shaw, *Collected Letters 1874–1897* (New York: Dodd, Mead, 1965), pp. 19–20. Shaw cites Donnelly as the source for Skene in "64 Years Later," typescript preface added March-April 1946 to the manuscript of *Cashel Byron's Profession*, on presentation to the National Library of Ireland, published in *Shaw: An Autobiography 1856–1898*, ed. Stanley Weintraub (New York: Weybright & Talley, 1969), p. 98 (hereafter "64 Years Later," *Shaw: An Autobiography*). A model for Byron was Jack Burke (1861–97), a scientific English pugilist whose opponents included English boxer Charley Mitchell and American John L. Sullivan. Burke, "the Irish Lad," ruined his health by getting his weight down to 154 pounds for a match with the

middleweight champion Ted Pritchard and was forced to retire soon after. There has been much confusion in tracking Shaw's Burke because it has not been previously recognized that there were *two* Jack Burkes. The scientific pugilist engaged in contests of brief duration and for several years fought matches in Australia and South Africa, returning to England in 1894. There was also the 130-pound "Young Jack Burke" (c. 1863–1913), born in Galveston, Texas, who, in an 1893 contest for the lightweight championship of the South, fought Andy Bowen to a draw in New Orleans in the longest recorded glove fight in boxing annals—110 rounds, lasting seven hours and nineteen minutes. The Burke of marathon fame, born George Campbell, subsequently toured in vaudeville with a popular gymnasium and sparring act, as Burke and McAvoy (later as Burke and Finn).

4. *Sunday News* (London), 10 July 1927; "64 Years Later," *Shaw: An Autobiography*, p. 98.

5. Shaw to Gene Tunney, 9 June 1948, Bernard Shaw, *Collected Letters 1926–1950*, ed. Dan H. Laurence (New York: Viking, 1988), p. 821.

6. Juggins is slang for fool, simpleton, idiot, or the victim of a swindle. The term, used by Benjamin Disraeli in *Sybil* in 1845, had found its way to the popular pages of *Punch* by 1882.

7. James "Jem" Mace (1831–1910) used a scientific method that has earned him praise as a nineteenth-century father of boxing, inheriting the laurels the eighteenth century bestowed upon James Figg (1695–1734), the first recognized bare-knuckle champion, and on champion Jack Broughton (1704–89). Mace won the British title in 1861 and became the first world heavyweight champion in 1866. He advocated glove fighting after the Marquis of Queensberry rules appeared in 1867, is credited with improving boxing's image, and was a proficient violinist. John L. Sullivan (1858–1918), known as the "Great John L." and the "Boston Strong Boy," was not only the most popular sports figure of the nineteenth century, he was also an important American cultural hero who seemed to epitomize both manliness and the unbridled energy of American life. In July 1889, he went seventy-five rounds against Jake Kilrain in the sweltering Mississippi sun, successfully defending himself by a knockout in what turned out to be the world's last bare-knuckle championship fight, an event that poet Vachel Lindsay celebrated in "John L. Sullivan, the Strong Boy of Boston." Despite his bare-knuckle championship bouts, Sullivan preferred gloves and wore them in forty-four of his forty-seven matches, popularizing glove fighting and the Marquis of Queensberry rules. In at least this sense he was the first modern boxing champion. However, in a championship glove fight in 1892, James J. "Gentleman Jim" Corbett handed Sullivan his only defeat, and Corbett's victory immediately captured the popular imagination as a triumph of scientific skill over brute strength.

8. A crack is a first-rater, one who excels in skill and performance.

9. Jake Baldock was an English boxer from the Pelican Club. He and Jake Kilrain acted as seconds to Charley Mitchell in his illegal contest against John L. Sullivan on 10 March 1888, secretly held at the estate of the Baron de Rothschild outside Paris. With both Mitchell and Sullivan suffering from a drenching icy rain, the fight ended in a draw at Baldock's suggestion after three hours and ten minutes. Bob Travers, "The Black Wonder," was born Charles Jones in 1836, in Norfolk, Virginia. He fought between 1854 and 1864, using the surname of the master whose death had released him from slavery. Boss Tyler probably was Bob Tyler, winner of a bout in Essex Marshes in 1850, according to *Fistiana*. McKelvy possibly was Boston's Johnny MacKey, who opened a sporting saloon in the 1850s in Chicago, one of a breed of ex-boxers who immersed themselves in boxing activities in and out of the ring. Green appears to be Alf Greenfield, who was born in Northampton, England, in 1853. His 1884 match with John L. Sullivan in New York City was stopped and both boxers arrested for violating the state's prohibition against prizefighting. Jerry (Jeremiah) Noon, British champion in 1827, is identified in *Fistiana* as a young Greek, five foot eight inches tall, weighing nine stone six (132 pounds).

10. English champion Tom Sayers (1826–65), "The Little Wonder," also known as "Napoleon of the Prize Ring," was a 152-pound London bricklayer who met opponents of all weights. Nat Langham, a farm laborer from Leicestershire who trained Bob Travers, was the only man ever to beat Sayers. U.S. heavyweight champion John Camel Heenan (1835–73), "The Benicia Boy," who was five inches taller and heavier by two stone, challenged Sayers. One of the most famous sporting events of the century, the bare-knuckle match took place in a field in Farnborough, Hampshire, on 17 April 1860. Constables rushed the ring to stop the fight during the thirty-seventh round. Five more rounds were fought with a crowd in the ring. Then, with Sayers being strangled on the ropes, a draw was declared. Among those at ringside was William Makepeace Thackeray, who celebrated "that great fight of HEENANUS / With SAYERIUS" in his poem, "A Lay of Ancient London," supposedly recounted by an ancient gladiator. Writing in 1927, Shaw thought dullness and blackguardism the reasons for boxing's decline, not brutality, "for the spectacle of Sayers bunging up Heenan's eyes as Nat Langham had bunged up his own, cannot have been so very dreadful" (*Sunday News* [London], 10 July 1927).

11. Jem Smith (1863–1931), reigning heavyweight champion, won the British title with a bare-knuckle knockout against Jack Davies on 17 December 1885, in Surrey. On 9 December 1887, Smith paired off against Alf Greenfield in an exhibition match (followed by Sullivan and Jack Ashton) for Edward, Prince of Wales. Ten days later, exactly one month before Shaw wrote "The Seamy Side," Smith and Jake Kilrain fought to a draw in a marathon fight of 106 rounds at Isle de Souveraines, France.

12. William "Bold Bendigo" Thompson was taught to box by his mother. He beat James "Deaf" Burke (1809–45) in 1839 for the championship; in 1845 he defeated the much larger Ben Caunt (1815–61) in a 93-round championship bout; five years later he successfully defended his title against Tom Paddock (1824–63) in forty-nine rounds. After being jailed twenty-eight times for various infractions of the law, Thompson reformed, becoming an evangelical Methodist and preaching to huge crowds in London. A memorial to him was erected in Nottingham, his birthplace.

Alfred Turco, Jr.

ON WAR AND PEACE

Shaw's attitude toward war and peace can be simply summarized.[1] Although war is a human abomination that no amount of romanticizing or heroics can justify, nonetheless, Shaw believed, "when war overtakes you, you must fight. . . . One does not trouble about the danger of damp sheets when the house is on fire" (*WRW*, pp. 234, 232). The best outcome that can be hoped for from the "colossal stupidity of modern war" (*WRW*, p. 27) is a concluding peace conference capable of creating structures of international cooperation banning war as an instrument of future policy. Pacifism, while admirable in theory, is not practicable because "we must face the fact that pugnacity is still a part of human nature, and that civilization is still in its infancy" (*WRW*, p. 236). The foregoing précis hardly does justice to the nuances of Shaw's thinking, but is meant to convey the gist of views to which he adhered for a lifetime.

The seven pieces that follow do not markedly alter the picture we already have of Shaw on war. Still they are worth bringing to light because, despite his reputation as a man who frequently repeated himself, Shaw never made the same point in exactly the same way. Hence the impression this group of selections gives is not merely of recyclings (or precyclings) of known pronouncements, but of interesting variations on a theme in which familiar opinions are seen in new shadings.

The first piece (1899) predates the Boer War; the last (1950) postdates World War II. The "Great War" (1914–18)—to which Shaw devoted by far the most attention in print—is represented here by a single selection. Having already made his own encyclopedic gathering from this period, Shaw left slim pickings for scholarly sleuths. For this reason, it seems appropriate to comment in this space on his controversial *chef-d'oeuvre*: *Common Sense about the War*, originally published as a supplement to the *New Statesman* on 14 November 1914. Even to sympathetic friends, *Common Sense* at first blush seemed the utterance of a courageous but foolhardy man; today the first adjective seems more valid than the second. Few of the English citizenry were in a mood for common sense, preferring fits of patriotic indignation that Shaw afterward compared to "a man working himself up to a Berserker orgasm in a pillow fight" (*WRW*, p. 164). That Shaw criticized the British did not make him pro-German: as he commented later, "Whenever I point out a flaw in any case, its advocates instantly cry out frantically that I am a supporter of the opposite case" (*WRW*, p. 120). Granted, Germany had violated a treaty of 1839 guaranteeing Belgian neutrality, but how many treaties had Britain abrogated since then? No doubt Germany had built up her fleet into that of a major naval power, but where was it written that "the domination of the sea belongs to British commerce" (*WRW*, p. 37)? One claim that so outraged his critics—that Britain shared blame for the war because "we did not say straight out . . . that if Germany invaded France we should fight her" (*WRW*, p. 45)—is now a commonplace of the history books.

Shaw's admiration for certain achievements of German *culture* did not preclude his condemnation of German militarism: "The Kaiser and his ministers . . . made their dash [at France through Belgium] and put themselves in the wrong at every point morally besides making victory humanly impossible for themselves militarily" (*WRW*, p. 42). But in contrast to some of his compatriots, Shaw distinguished between defeat of the Kaiser and the destruction of Germany. He favored the former only. Far from desiring the latter, he looked forward to Germany's taking the "sooner or later inevitable step into the democratic form of government to which Europe is visibly tending" (*WRW*, p. 66). Granted that some of Shaw's later political allegiances have justifiably come under attack, what is there to object to here except his refusal to join a frenzy?

In annotating these texts, I have not thought it necessary to cite chapter and verse for information about persons and events that can be found repeated in dozens of standard historical reference works. Among many secondary sources I consulted, two of the most useful were the *Norton History of Modern Europe*, general editor Felix Gilbert (New York: Norton, 1971) and *English History: 1914–1945* by A. J. P. Taylor (New York and Oxford: Oxford University Press, 1965). In contrast to footnotes, the headnotes to each piece express my own attempts to come to terms with the man whose sometimes self-contradictory pronouncements reveal him to be anything but a simple human being.

ON SHAW'S "WHY NOT ABOLISH THE SOLDIER?" (1899)

Written five months before the advent of the Boer War in October 1899, Shaw's unfinished letter has nothing to do with that subject. Indeed, the occasion of Shaw's riposte is hard to pin down. The *Daily Chronicle* of 20 April does contain an editorial concerning the difficulties of army recruiters in attracting soldiers; the newspaper's solution to the problem is to offer better wages and conditions of work. Conscription, however, is mentioned neither there nor in a previous week's article on inept recruiting. England did not in fact resort to the draft until 1916, after the initial surge of volunteerism in World War I had subsided.

In any case, Shaw's point does not concern conscription, but soldiering. He believes that men should be able to join the military without sacrificing their rights as civilians. With great good sense, he debunks the notion that severe restrictions of civil liberties and the summary imposition of condign punishments are justified by the need to maintain "discipline" in the army. There are many areas of civilian life (the signalman's control of railway traffic or the manufacturing of explosives) where a breakdown in "discipline" would be every bit as disastrous as its equivalent in battle. If the dangers inherent in such employment are sufficient deterrent to negligence, the same is even more true of service in the military. No one openly proposes that civilian workers be denied basic rights, subjected to cruel penalties, or reduced to machines by their choice of a trade.

Shaw's response to soldiering's importance for national survival is to appropriately reward those who choose to become soldiers. In *Common Sense*, Shaw would advocate that the policy of "the Labor Party is to abolish the Militarist soldier . . . and substitute for him a trained combatant with full civil rights, receiving the Trade Union rate of wages proper to a skilled worker in a dangerous trade" (*WRW*, p. 52). For other passionate Shavian protests against inhumane treatment of enlisted men, see the section called "Flogging in the Fighting Services" in *Doctor's Delusions, Crude Criminology, Sham Education* (Standard Edition, 1931, pp. 260–81), as well as the chapters from *WRW* entitled "Compulsory Soldiering" (pp. 188–96) and "The Conscientious Objectors" (pp. 197–212).

Shaw's unsent letter, although dealing with a quite different subject, resonates interestingly with current bogus arguments in the United States defending prejudicial treatment—or outright exclusion from the military—of gay persons whose behavior (or mere presence) is considered a threat to morale and "discipline." Progress since Shaw's time seems to consist of the problem's having been shifted from sadism to bigotry.

Why Not Abolish the Soldier? (1899)

[PROVENANCE: Holograph draft letter, in pencil, to the editor of the Daily Chronicle, *foliated by Shaw: [1]–6, signed "G. Bernard Shaw" and dated "Hindhead, 20 April 1899." on final leaf. British Library: Add. Mss. 50693, folios 264–69, with additional holograph passages on 266b and, inverted, on*

267b. Three extracts published in Shaw—"The Chucker-out," *ed. Allan Chappelow (London: Allen & Unwin, 1969), pp. 357–58.]*

To the Editor of the Daily Chronicle

Sir

So conscription is coming at last. Your representative thinks that the Government that introduces it will be dead in a week. That is a very poor consolation for the conscripts, since it is quite certain that the succeeding government will not repeal the Act. Conscription is inevitable if we persist in the imbecile habit of believing that a nation can only be defended by soldiers. Let us see whether it is not possible to find a fresh English idea to rescue us from a stale continental one.

I am a timid civilian, detesting war as sincerely as anybody can; but in extremity I should take my part in the defence of the community if I were permitted to do so on honorable terms: that is, if I could do so without becoming a soldier and thereby surrendering all the rights and liberties of a British subject. A soldier is above all things an outlaw and a slave. If he dislikes his trade, he is not free to leave it. If under great provocation he attempts to correct his sergeant's manners and language by hitting him on the nose, an indulgence which would cost a civilian £2 in a police court, he is deprived of trial by jury, and sentenced, by officers all professionally bound to back the sergeant, to the punishment of a garotter. Once in prison he is flogged frequently and mercilessly. If he hits a commissioned officer (which costs a civilian £5), it is considered a signal mercy that he is not shot out of hand, as he would be in some foreign armies. Freedom of speech and of the press do not exist for him; and his fellow countrymen, very naturally and properly despising him for selling his birthright for the Queen's shilling, demand that soldiers in uniform shall not be admitted to places where gentlemen assemble to drink. All this is said to be indispensable for the maintenance of discipline. Now every argument that proves the need of "discipline" for the soldier proves it tenfold for the officer. The Chinese, ever logical, have always flogged their admirals and generals as conscientiously as their seamen and privates, with the remarkable result that their "thoroughly disciplined" forces are the only ones in the world which it is absolutely impossible not to beat. In England we do not flog and enslave officers, because all the unanswerable arguments in favor of doing so have to give way to the plain fact that no English gentleman would accept a commission on such terms. Just so will the arguments for flogging and enslaving the soldier have to give way to the fact, deplored by you in recent issues, that the English working man will not serve on such terms either. Formerly he was an illiterate bumpkin who was practically kidnapped by false representations: nowadays he reads the papers; has plenty of discharged & starving short service men in his social circle; and knows all about it. He can no longer be even cheated into the degradation of soldierdom.

Further, the civilian worker, by his experience in trades far more hazardous than that of the soldier, knows that the alleged necessity for military discipline is the excuse of the incompetent officer & the delusion of the bellicose civilian. Our commanders, naval and military, ask us to consider the frightful consequences that would ensue if a regiment, or the crew of a battleship, were suddenly to refuse to do their duty. I am unable to see any probable consequences half as frightful as would certainly follow the sudden refusal of the signalmen on the London & North Western Railway to do *their* duty. These mentally disabled gentlemen talk about the need for discipline in a ship. Do they know what the need for discipline in a cordite factory is? Yet cordite is manufactured by civilians with all the liberties of ordinary citizens. It is not necessary to take elaborate precautions against fatal consequences: such consequences themselves are sufficiently deterrent. The real object of the demand for discipline is to make soldiering so stupidly mechanical that it can be worked by officers without sufficient brains and character to make them respected and obeyed. The theory of discipline is that soldiers & sailors are naturally insubordinate, and full of original ideas & plans of campaign which they are only restrained from carrying out by an iron discipline. Coleridge, for instance, was once a trooper; and the War Office seems to have accepted him ever since as the normal type of cavalry soldier, insisting always on the danger of men thinking for themselves. Now even Coleridge, though he thought for himself, could not act for himself.[2] The truth is that men, until they are goaded into insurrection by unbearable ill treatment, will follow any leader who will save them the trouble of thinking and acting for themselves. It is, in fact, one of their worst faults. The English workman in particular is as arrant a sheep and hero worshipper as any man alive, as you will see by his conduct in the trade-unions which he has organized with the most jealous reservation of his democratic rights. According to the disciplinarian theory, the captain of a cruiser ought to be the most absolute autocrat, and the secretary of a trade-union the most abject slave in England. As a matter of fact it is the captain who is the slave and the secretary who is the autocrat. The "discipline" which only makes the seaman grumble, condemns the unfortunate captain to solitary confinement (lest familiarity with his subordinates should breed contempt), and occasionally drives him melancholy mad, and leads him to give orders which his slaves must (theoretically) obey as dutifully as the gentleman who was recently ordered by his admiral to ram the flagship, and obediently did it, and sent hundreds of men, including the admiral himself, to the bottom.[3]

If a parliamentary return could be made of the number of ships that have been saved by disobedience to officers who have been disciplined out of their wits, we should have a reaction in favor of positive Anarchism.

However, nobody wants Anarchism, least of all the British workman, with his superstitious docility. The way to provide for the defence of the country is either to abolish the army, or else retain it only as an organization of brilliantly equipped beadles, for exhibition outside the Horse Guards & other public buildings, and for forming processions and walking out with the nursemaids who so patriotically supply our warriors with pocket money. Also, of course, for keeping our silly War Office harmlessly occupied. In the meantime employ a number of ordinary English civilians to do the actual fighting, subject to no special legislation, and free to leave at a week's notice if they do not think the situation and pension worth having. Let their officers have precisely the same authority over them as a station master has over a railway porter, and no more. Pay them well; treat them honorably; give them cartridges enough to learn shooting; and there will be no difficulty about recruiting: on the contrary, the police will probably have to be called in to regulate the crowd of applicants. The plan is not novel in its essence: Cromwell tried as much of it as was necessary in 1645; and he immediately went over his opponents, thitherto victorious, like a steam roller.[4] The fact is, the British Empire has now come to a pass at which it needs men, not soldiers, to defend it. The military idea is a superstititon; and the future, as far as it depends on fighting, belongs to the nation that first abolishes the soldier[.]

Our present forces could be retained temporarily as an organization of . . .[5]

G. Bernard Shaw

[Added paragraph on verso of folio 267, with no indication here or in the text as to place of intended insertion.]

Hitherto we civilians, not being personally incommoded by discipline, have managed our own business and left these silly military people to mismanage theirs. But now that they have reduced the condition & prospects of the soldier to such a point that even railway shunters & Sheffield screw [?] grinders will not enlist, they actually have the audacity to propose a revival of the Pressgang and the reinforcement of the army by simple slavery. It is therefore necessary to tell them bluntly, first (in order to make them listen attentively) that they are fools, and second, that there is no more difficulty in procuring a practically unlimited supply of men of any desired quality for national defence than the Great Central Railway found in staffing its extension to London. It is a question of pay, treatment, & prospects: nothing else.

ON SHAW'S APPEAL FOR THE SECOND AMERICAN LIBERTY LOAN (1917)

The British "War Loans" and the American "Liberty Loans" were government appeals to the public to underwrite the costs of the war by investment, to be repaid with interest: in other words, war bonds. There were four Liberty Loans in the United States during World War I (as well as a Victory Loan drive after its conclusion). The first of these was offered on 15 May 1917, more than a month after the U.S. entered the war on 6 April; the last concluded on 18 October 1918. Total subscription for all four loans was more than 24 billion dollars; by the war's end, Britain alone owed the United States $3,696,000,000—more than pocket money by the standards of the time.

Shaw had apparently been asked by an American newspaper syndicate (an appeal possibly made to other noted persons as well) to provide an advertisement/encouragement for the second loan appeal floated on 1 October 1917. Perhaps the candor with which he acknowledged why some Americans might *not* wish to assist in another loan campaign dissatisfied the syndicate; in any case the piece appears to have been filed and forgotten.

Surely Shaw's advocacy would have helped the cause among thoughtful citizens of this country. Too much has been made of Shaw's unpopularity in Britain during World War I—how there were calls that he be tried for treason, how his entrance into a public gathering would trigger departure of the right-minded. But it should not be forgotten that at this time Shaw was by far the most famous man of letters in the world, describing himself without immodesty as "one of the few writers whose words cross boundaries" (*WRW*, p. 98). He could in 1914 publish "An Open Letter" to President Woodrow Wilson without seeming pretentious or silly (*WRW*, pp. 106–11). Douglas Haig, then Commander-in-Chief of British forces in France, invited Shaw to visit the western front in 1917, a gesture it is almost impossible to imagine being extended today by a military leader to a mere *writer*. Shaw's dispatches from the field—printed in *WRW* under the title "Joy Riding at the Front" (pp. 213–39)—are vivid reportage, offering acute perceptions of how this conflict had changed the nature of war forever, often in unexpected ways ("Modern war is appallingly tedious"—*WRW*, p. 215).

It should also be noted that, however controversial a figure Shaw may have been in his adopted country, his attitude toward the United States at this time was as close to deference as he ever came to that unShavian trait. He saw this country as the least compromised of the great powers in the war and the one in the best position to expedite international machinery of cooperation after the armistice. His view that "Washington is still privileged to talk common humanity to the nations" (*WRW*, p. 110) is a far cry from earlier jackanapes gibes or the later "Look, You Boob" pugnacity to which he would come in the early 1930s (see *Platform and Pulpit*, pp. 226–34).

[Appeal for the Second U.S. Liberty Loan, 1917]

[PROVENANCE: Untitled holograph manuscript, foliated by Shaw: 1–3, signed "G. Bernard Shaw." and dated "Parknasilla | 12ᵗʰ Oct. 1917." on final leaf. Huntington Library, San Marino, California.]

The second Liberty Loan will have to be dug out of a harder streak of American human nature than the first. In every country there are crowds of people who will give money for bad reasons. In England, when the war began, excited Britons rushed feverishly through the streets offering money to anybody for anything that professed a connexion with the war. It was collected largely by professional swindlers, some of whom are now in prison with the shutters up on their bogus anti-Hun societies.[6] Quite a lot of it was taken by attractive young ladies who discovered that if they stood in the streets with a tiny Union Jack in one hand and a money box in the other, men with patriotic lumps in their throats would just rain coin into the box. The police had to put a stop to it; but it gave the contributors the happiness of believing that they were doing their bit; and it is quite likely that the girls spent the money as usefully as the lumpy throated men would have done.

And yet so much of these spoils of the sentimental and fatheaded got honestly handed in, that a Prince of Wales's Fund with no discoverable purpose rolled up to millions, and had to be frankly plundered by the Government because there was nothing else to be done with it.

It was just the same with the first War Loan and with the first Liberty Loan in the United States. People felt that they had to give their distressed country money or burst. I did not feel like that, and did not give any. Besides, I thought my money would be worse wanted later on. It was. I waited for the Second Loan, and put my shirt on it. From the point of view of impressing the enemy, and reassuring the timid folks at home it was important that the Second Loan should be a greater success than the first. A falling-off would have been worse than a defeat in Flanders; and the situation could only have been saved by resorting to the bankers: a plan by which the Government incurs much more debt than it gets money for; and the difference has to be made up in the long run by the working people, who ought to have taken up the stock and kept the bankers out of it.

Just remember that the Government of the United States must get this money anyhow. If it gets it from you, it will pay the interest to you. If it gets it elsewhere, *you* will have to pay the interest, and pay it on more money than the Government will really touch. Let me repeat: no tax-payer or consumer of taxed goods in the United States (and this means you and everybody) can keep out of this Liberty Loan. There is no Liberty about it for you: the Germans will see to that. But those who get into it by finding the money will be on the right side of it instead of on the wrong side.

There are still a good many George Washingtonians in America, who believe in America keeping out of European politics.[7] And they are as right as ever they were—if America only could. Do they suppose that Wilson did not try to keep out? Do they suppose that he does not know that Europe must achieve democracy for herself as America has done, and that there are Junkers[8] in England as well as in Russia who would use a victory to confirm their own privileges and destroy the liberties of the peoples just as ruthlessly as if they were all Hohenzollerns? He knows it quite well; and that is just exactly why the United States had to come in. In Europe diplomacy is still left to the Junkers: the British Foreign Office is as exclusive a preserve for them as it was in the days of George III. The French Republic would have sought its natural ally in the United States instead of in the Russia of the Tsar, and there would have been no war, but for the foreign policy of Lord Salisbury,[9] to whom all republics were contemptible and ephemeral disturbances of the perma-nent divinely appointed order of Court and Country Gentlemen. A settle-ment of this war with America left out would be another Holy Alliance with another Metternich dominating it by the right of the most reaction-ary.[10] Revolutionary Russia could not prevent it: she has enough to do in liquidating the bankruptcy of the Tsardom. France would not prevent it, because both her commercial interests and her natural resentment of the devastating attack she has suffered make it impossible for her to consider the large interests America and the neutrals have in trade with the Cen-tral Empires.[11] To put it shortly, Europe, angry and jealous, wants to destroy Germany. America wants to democratize Germany, and to de-stroy nothing but the anti-democratic constitution of Germany. America knows that a nation of 60 million people cannot be destroyed; but she knows that a militarist monarchy of robber barons can be destroyed, because she has done it before and can do it again. George Washington, if he were alive today, would be the first to recognize that the Atlantic is no longer an ocean, but a bridge, and that the work of the founders of the United States will not be done until Germany is a Republic. So make the second Liberty Loan a greater success than the first. Any other result would mean that America was taking her hand from the plough.

One word more. War is a horrible business; and to contribute money to its prosecution wrenches the best instincts of the best men as no other sort of financial transaction can. But there is no way out of war but the fighting way until the establishment of a supernational court of justice, a supernational legislature, and a supernational police, makes an end of the existing international anarchy. America did not make this war; but she cannot stand by and look on it as if she had no interest in its issue. Her interest is as deep as that of any of the original belligerents; and the more powerful her inevitable interference, the sooner will the horrors that are revolting her conscience be brought to an end.

ON SHAW'S REPLIES TO QUESTIONNAIRE FOR *THE WORLD OF TRADE* (1920)

No run of this journal has ever been located, and no press cutting of the questionnaire has surfaced. Even in the unlikely event that the piece was published in Germany, it is useful to have the original English text as evidence of the soundness of Shaw's political views in the period directly following the war. Posted on 1 February 1920, his replies to the four questions can be condensed into three points that today seem unexceptionable. First, that the humiliating terms of the Versailles Treaty bore the seeds of the next war with a resurgent Germany: as he had already warned, "A head with the brains of sixty millions of people in it takes more sitting on than we have bottom for" (*WRW*, p. 179). Second, that more will be gained by including a democratic Germany in the family of nations than by making her a defeated pariah. Third, that international cooperation by the League of Nations should replace the outdated "balance of power" politics of national rivalries. Shaw was of course not alone in offering such counsel; the fact is that it was not followed in time. (The Dawes Plan of 1924 and the Locarno Pact of 1925 did soften the effect of the original sanctions imposed on Germany.) Shaw turned out to speak more truly than he would have wished when he warned, near the end of *Common Sense*, that without constructive political measures, "the cessation of hostilities will last only until the belligerents have recovered from their exhaustion" (*WRW*, p. 95).

To understand what drove Shaw from this basically reasonable position to his support of totalitarian regimes in the 1930s, one needs to consider the economic situation in England during the 1920s. The country that saw itself as having fought to save the world for democracy and achieve a better life for its people found itself by 1921 in a severely worsening economic depression that at one point left 23% of its workers unemployed and dependent on a humiliating "dole." Promised social reforms to diminish poverty and improve housing and health care were not effectively implemented because Lloyd George, himself a Liberal, headed a coalition government (1919–22) dominated by Conservatives who frustrated the implementation of progressive policies promised in the post-armistice elections of December 1918. Ramsay MacDonald, in his brief tenure during 1924 as the first Labour prime minister in a coalition government, scored several successes in foreign policy; but in matters of domestic reform MacDonald's hands were as effectively tied by the Liberals as Lloyd George's had been by the Conservatives. The dominant British statesman of the 1920s was the less than energetic Stanley Baldwin (Conservative prime minister, 1924–29), whose lack of a consistent program or clear ideas provoked historian A. J. P. Taylor to quip: "There was to be no Protection [contrary to Baldwin's earlier pledge], no class war; if possible, there was to be nothing at all" (*English History: 1914–1945*, p. 221). The ten-day general strike of 1926, arising out of a crisis in the British coal industry, resulted in defeat for the unions and further alienated the working classes. The effects of an even more serious worldwide depression struck Britain in 1929; things fared no better in France and America, which had seemed to emerge from the war full of puissance and promise. Unfortunately, Shaw's palpably growing disgust during the 1920s with the floundering western democracies was simultaneous with the early rise—in Italy, Germany, and above all Russia—of strong men who "began by effecting some obvious reforms over which party parliaments had been boggling for centuries" (Preface to *Geneva*, 1947). Here was a new type of leader who could get things done; whether these "things" were worth doing seems not to have troubled him.

[Replies to Questionnaire, 1920]

[PROVENANCE: Typewritten questionnaire in English, submitted by the World of Trade, *86 Niedenau, Frankfurt am Main, with Shaw's holograph responses, unsigned. The manuscript is undated, but is accompanied by an envelope addressed by Shaw, postmarked "1 FE 20". Recorded as H17 in Dan H. Laurence,* Bernard Shaw: A Bibliography *(Oxford: Clarendon Press, 1983). Harold C. Ackert Theatre Collection, Washington University Libraries, St. Louis.]*

First: Do you believe that Great Britain and America will allow of Germany's seeking and finding relations with the Anglo-Saxon nationalities, in a fashion worthy of the German nation's dignity?

They must, if they have any regard for their own dignity.

Second: In what manner, possible for Germany and desirable for all concerned, should, according to your opinion, such relations be brought about?

Tear up the Versailles scrap of paper;[12] admit Germany and her Allies to the League of Nations; recognize the Bolshevik Government of Russia;[13] accept the *fait accompli* as to conquests; cancel the indemnities in consideration of the territories surrendered; and in other respects return to pre-war relations, provided Germany does not return to a less democratic constitution than the British.

Third: Which preliminary steps do you recommend to further such relations?

The first step—the rejection of M. Clemenceau as President[14]—has already been taken. The second would be an overwhelming defeat of the present London Coalition at a General Election.[15] This would be a sufficient mandate for an energetic Prime Minister to announce the willingness of the British Empire to proceed as above. The third would be the acceptance of and adhesion to the League of Nations (enlarged and made genuine as above) by the United States of America.[16]

Fourth: What would be your attitude at the present moment, were you of German nationality?

One of extreme courtesy to Russia, the United States of America, Scandinavia and Holland, with a view to restoring the political equilibrium of Europe and recovering the prestige lost by the conclusion of the war. Germany is the centre of gravity of the Protestant North in Europe; and its domination by the Latin-African South is dangerous for all parties until the League of Nations and the development of Internationalism supersedes Balance of Power diplomacy.

ON SHAW'S MESSAGE TO THE WORLD LEAGUE FOR PEACE, GENEVA, 6 SEPTEMBER 1928

This is one of more than a thousand original statements, all of them holograph, provided to the World League for Peace, of which about half (including Shaw's) were reproduced in facsimile and issued under the title *Pax Mundi: Livre d'Or de la Paix* (Geneva: Paxunia for the Ligue Mondiale pour la Paix, 1932) as loose broadsides in large printed cloth folders. The number circulated is uncertain; twenty-five sets accompanied the individual manuscripts when sold as a single lot by Charles Hamilton Autographs, Inc., at auction in January 1966 at the Waldorf Astoria Hotel in New York.

Uniquely in the present volume, Shaw's contribution (written while attending the ninth assembly of the League of Nations) is a hitherto published one. Yet this all-too-true testament, so little known and inaccessible, fits snugly enough into the context of Shaw's other utterances on war that it seemed worth rescuing as the kind of steely, humane utterance that will keep its author's name alive as a cultural force. For one such piece of terse eloquence, many lapses in political judgment may be forgiven! Later surveying Shaw's career in retrospect, non-disciple Aldous Huxley put the point best: "If, instead of just applauding Mr. Shaw's plays and chuckling over his prefaces, we had also paid some serious attention to his teaching, what remains of our civilization might not be lying under sentence of death. But, as usual, *homo amans, credens,* and *bellicosus* has proved to be a great deal stronger than *homo sapiens*" (*G.B.S. 90,* ed. S. Winsten [New York: Dodd, Mead, 1946], p. 270).

[MESSAGE TO THE WORLD LEAGUE FOR PEACE, 1928: facsimile issued 1932]

Peace, in its most general sense, is neither possible nor desirable. Life is strife: strife with our own ignorance, with our ferocity, and with the material circumstances which limit and cripple our aspirations.

But the physically violent method of strife which we call war is dangerous because it is the method by which the worst men can most easily destroy the best. By it the fools destroy the sages, and the criminals the men of good intent.

Therefore let it be ruled out as dishonorable between nation and nation as between citizen and citizen. It is possible to strive without violence; and in renouncing war we make no truce with evil, which war always professes to destroy, but which in fact it always engenders and reinforces.

This will not convince the soldiers and diplomatists. They know that war is effective. But let them study history, and learn that its effects are never those intended by those who resort to it.

ON SHAW'S SELF-DRAFTED INTERVIEW AT DURBAN (1935)

Written during Shaw's second visit to South Africa in 1935, the envoi to this draft suggests that Shaw composed it as a press interview (although the possibility of a radio talk cannot be ruled out). In either case, the piece represents the nadir of Shaw's political thought in this collection. It would be hard to imagine a worse howler than his opening sentence, unless it be his subsequent assertion that "the greedy dogs of

Europe . . . are not yet safely chained up except in Russia." To have been pro-Bolshevik in 1920 was one thing; to be pro-Stalinist in 1935 was quite another. The first of Stalin's purge trials took place the following year.

On one point, Shaw was precisely on target: his prediction of impending war in Abyssinia. Italy was to attack Ethiopia (as it is now called) in October 1935 and annex that country in May 1936. But Shaw's position toward Mussolini's aggression is both emotionally and intellectually confused. On the one hand, Shaw appears to reject imperialism. When he writes that "in a war between white and black[,] Europe cannot very well take the black side," his ensuing gloss makes clear that this remark is meant as a prediction (alas accurate) of what would happen, not a prescription for what should happen. But Shaw's apparently laudable advocacy of a policy of "Africa for the Africans" is compromised by his failure to distinguish between the interests of native Africans and those of European settlers of Africa. He in fact supported Mussolini's illegal takeover of a sovereign state as a triumph of civilization over savagery—in part because of his revulsion at native Danakil warriors' fondness for taking the testicles of slain enemies as war trophies (see *CL 1926–1950*, pp. 424–25).

Shaw's concluding paragraph is both prescient and myopic. Perhaps beguiled by the proclaimed Stalinist policy of "socialism in one country," he fails to foresee the expansionist agenda that would turn Russia into yet another empire. Nonetheless, Shaw does have a glimmering of why such an agenda would ultimately fail. While doubtless the perfect form of government for everybody everywhere, "world socialism" cannot be imposed successfully by one country upon another; each nation must realize the communistic ideal for itself. It took more than another half-century for the deadly drama nascent in Shaw's prognosis to play itself out. What would his reaction have been to Moscow newspaper headlines in 1991: "Supreme Soviet Suspends Communist Party"?

[Self-Drafted Interview at Durban, 1935]

[PROVENANCE: Untitled, self-drafted interview, typewritten from shorthand draft, leaves numbered [1]–3, unsigned, dated by Shaw "Durban | 1935." at top left of first leaf. (Shaw visited Durban from 28 April to 22 May.) British Library: Add. Mss. 50698, folios 24–26.]

"I have been telling the world for weeks past that there is not the least likelihood of war in Europe. Now that Germany is on her feet again, and all pretence of limiting her military strength is at an end, there is nothing to fight for. I have said so again and again. I have also said that there is a strong probability of war in Abyssinia. A considerable part of that country is salt desert hundreds of feet below the level of the sea and enjoys a temperature of 150°F. to work in. Signor Mussolini may think twice before he decides that it is worth annexing as part of Italy's share in the partition of Africa among the European Powers; but if he decides in the affirmative, he will snap his fingers at the League of Nations unless it saves the situation by giving him a mandate before he asks for it; and in the ensuing war between white and black[,] Europe cannot very well take the black side. And will you please note that though the European question is settled as far as Germany is concerned, and settled in Germany's favour thanks to Hitler, the African question is not. At present Germany is excluded from the partition of Africa among the white Powers. She dare not go to war yet to recover her lost colonies, especially as the African Germans would expect to be as independent of Berlin as South Africa is of London; but when her restored power is fully developed, it may not be easy to resist her claim to a share in the partition. Until the white Africans, to say nothing of the black ones, develop their internal organisation to a point at which Africa can effectively resist any attempt to meddle with her with the object of exploiting and laying tribute on her, there will be a danger of her becoming a bone of contention between the greedy dogs of Europe, who are not yet safely chained up except in Russia. What you will need in Africa is a Monroe doctrine for Africa. The Afrikanders and the British, with the Portuguese, the Italians, the French, and all the rest of them will finally have to combine against Imperialist Europe as Africans with the slogan 'Africa for the Africans.' "

"That has a nationalistic sound, Mr. Shaw. Does it mean that you think as a Socialist that the future of our civilisation can best be safeguarded by striving towards the attainment of national socialism in each country individually before fighting for international socialism? Let me put it to you this way. Would it [be] best for each country to strive to attain the present Russian ideal instead of the ideal of world socialism?["]

"The Russian ideal *is* world socialism. But Russia has had to begin with her own bit of the job under her own conditions and not in the air. We shall all have to do the same. Russia has achieved miracles of social organisation whilst we have been telling one another silly lies about her. Her statesmen are the ablest and honestest in the world. But they are cleaning up their own shop, not everybody elses. World socialism must be built with socialised States, not with profiteering ones. You must build with bricks, not with sand. Good morning."

ON SHAW'S "HOW TO TALK INTELLIGENTLY ABOUT THE WAR" (1940)

Drafted in July 1940 for an unknown source, this essay shows Shaw in a better light by supplying further proof (for those who need it) that he was not pro-German once World War II had begun in 1939. Far earlier than that, his enthusiasm for Hitler had pointedly excluded the latter's racial theories. To his own discredit, however, Shaw tended to treat the Führer's anti-Semitism as an aberrant crack in the head of an otherwise sound statesman. But, while bizarrely retaining admiration for certain aspects of *Mein Kampf,* (*CL 1926–1950,* p. 643), Shaw repudiates the megalomaniacal ambitions of its author. "This is not a war for Xtian civilization," he wrote in 1941: "It is a war to disable an aspirant to the government of the earth, by name Adolph Hitler" (*CL 1926–1950,* p. 605).

"How to Talk Intelligently" is nonetheless marred by some muddled thinking. Shaw posits one of Hitler's cardinal sins to have been discrediting "National Socialism" by identifying it with mere "Hitlerism." Shaw tries to rescue the former term by interpreting it—as if spelled with small letters—to mean simply the organization of a nation's economy along socialistic lines. His inability to grasp that the Nazi party was not merely the Berlin branch of the Fabian Society provides an important clue to the main weakness in Shaw's later political thinking: his application of useful nineteenth-century assumptions to twentieth-century circumstances they no longer fitted. Julian Kaye, in his very underrated and still important book, *Bernard Shaw and the Nineteenth-Century Tradition* (1958), argues convincingly that Shaw came to intellectual maturity during a late-Victorian era when it was assumed that the growth of democratic institutions was all but inevitable. Hence any government's resort to coercive measures could be at most a temporary expedient impelled by emergency; totalitarianism itself was a thing of the past. From this perspective, Mussolini, Hitler, and Stalin were not perceived by Shaw as genuine threats, but rather as drastic tonics for the ineptitude of do-nothing democracies.

Such thinking results in a peculiar blindness for a man who cannot be excused on grounds of being senile or stupid. When Shaw boasts to his imperiled Austrian Jewish translator, Siegfried Trebitsch—"As for silencing me, that is not possible" (*CL 1926–1950,* p. 337)—he seems not to realize that whatever truth this claim may have is contingent on his living in a society where freedom of expression is protected by law and tradition. (Speaking his mind openly in the Stalinist Russia he so admired, how long would Shaw have lasted?) Begging the important question, Shaw equates freedom with mere *free time* a worker has left over after performing the duties of his job. This quantitative measure—expounded below in paragraphs six and seven—is obviously not an adequate ideological definition of liberty, but Shaw would cling to it in his later years: "Where 90% of the people have all the work and no leisure, and 10% all the leisure and no work . . . Liberty is a will-o'-the-wisp: Magna Carta, . . . the American Constitution, and the French motto of Liberty and Equality are mere scraps of paper" (*Everybody's Political What's What?*, p. 351).

An analogous instance of a misapplied nineteenth-century assumption is Shaw's defining "Communism" to mean state-funded water systems, street lighting, police forces, sanitation, libraries, medical care, and so forth: in short, public services "paid out of the common stock made up by our rates and taxes . . . for the benefit of everybody indiscriminately" (see the chapter, "Communism," in the *Intelligent Woman's Guide*, pp. 11–13). Of course in *this* sense of the word, practically the entire civilized world may today be described as "communist"; Shaw's perversity was to fancy that the Russia of the 1930s was an implementation of Fabian proposals for social reform in the England of the 1880s. While on many subjects— occasionally even political questions—the elderly Shaw could write as illuminatingly as ever, this essay shows him as well-meaning but out of his element: a progressive Victorian who had outlived his premises.

How to Talk Intelligently about the War (1940)

[PROVENANCE: Typewritten (carbon) manuscript, with typed signature "G.B.S." at end of text, revisions in ink, leaves numbered 1–7, with eight-line typewritten insertion affixed to top of third leaf. Bernard F. Burgunder Collection, Division of Rare and Manuscript Collections, Cornell University Library. The Cornell copy is undated. The shorthand draft in the British Library (Add. Mss. 50698, fols. 128–30) is dated 15 July 1940, as is a carbon of a typewritten transcription (fols. 131–35). A revised carbon transcription typewritten on blue paper (fols. 136–41) is dated "19/7/40" at foot of final leaf. Another carbon transcription (fols. 142–49), presumably the final draft, is undated.]

Before giving the necessary instructions I must warn you that I am not advising you to talk intelligently about the war. It may be dangerous, partly because our official censors are not all intelligent, their pay not being sufficient to secure the great public capacity their work requires, and partly because intelligent remarks on the war may be more useful to the enemy than to ourselves. But in any case it is just as well that you should understand what you are talking about, as that will enable you to judge for yourself when you should not talk about it.

When you feel moved to eloquence on the subject of Hitlerism, Aggression, Democracy, National Socialism, or Communism, be careful. It is Mr. Hitler's business to persuade the world that Hitlerism is National Social-

ism, which we practise ourselves, and will have to practise much more
extensively in the future. It is greatly to his credit that he has done so
much of it in Germany purposely, intelligently, and quickly, whilst Western Governments have been doing it reluctantly and slowly under pressure of social needs that have forced their hands. Now if he were really
fighting to establish National Socialism in Europe and we were fighting
to prevent him, we should be entirely in the wrong and he entirely in the
right.

What, then, is our quarrel with him? It is that he has attached to
National Socialism some mischievous things that do not belong to it.

First, a claim to government of the world by the Germans as a Chosen
Race, and a resolution to impose this on us by physical force as the first
steps in civilization are imposed on Waziris, Danakils, and other "savage"
tribes who kill white men at sight.

Second, a personal autocracy which might be good for all of us if he
were God Almighty. But as he is only a man of like passions with ourselves, and may at any moment take to drink or go mad, we will see him
in heaven before we will allow him to muck about with sixty millions of
central Europeans to impose his single will on the rest of us.

As to Democracy and Liberty, do not forget that when Adolf Hitler
said that British Democracy is a lie, and Benito Mussolini called Liberty a
stinking corpse, the people cheered them. They have both been poor
men; and they knew what they were talking about. How much liberty
have men—even independent British yeomen who call themselves "their
own masters"—when they have to work sixteen hours a day to pay their
rents and mortgage interests and keep alive?

Keep off this subject until we have achieved a share of such liberty as
the tyranny of Nature allows us for nine-tenths of our own people. Most
of us would prefer some comfort and security. Even Marshal Pétain has
found out that much.[17]

Real Democracy means that the country shall be governed in the interest of everybody and not of a privileged class. It does not mean parliaments on the British Party model elected by overwhelming majorities
whose political ignorance is discrediting and destroying democracy. It
means government by whatever method will really secure its ends. We
should fight, not to save democracy, but to begin it. So take care how you
shout the word.

Aggression is a word very much in vogue just now; but you had better
think twice before you use it. We are not the terrified victims of Mr.
Hitler's aggression: quite the reverse. He did not declare war on us: we
declared it on him, and must live up to that proud position. He has taken
up our challenge undauntedly, and won the opening round with so
much to spare that if we stop fighting before we have at least got even

with him we must go out of business as a first rate power. He, as the attacked party, and so far the victorious one, can without discredit propose an armistice or a peace conference; but the least suggestion of such a thing on our part would be a "Hold! Enough!" for which there would be no excuse, as we are not yet within sight of the end of our resources. There must be no more nonsense about our being certain to win, and God being on our side, as in that case we have nothing to do but sit down in our armchairs and let God win. God helps those who help themselves; and Mr. Hitler helps himself so energetically that he will knock us into a cocked hat as he has knocked France unless we put the last ounce of our weight into the fight with him. When we do, God help him.

Say as little as possible about the blockade. If we cannot fight Germany squarely and have no chance unless we can starve her, so much the worse for us; for it is not certain that we can starve Germany, and quite certain that we could do it only by starving her neighbors enough to make us extremely unpopular on the Continent. Last time, the blockade business very nearly brought America into the war against us;[18] and it may bring the whole world against us if we push our claim to command the sea further than an internationally limited claim to police it. The subject is a dangerous and historically a very disagreeable one; and the more we hold our tongues about it the better. In a blockading match the casualties are women and children first and soldiers only in the last extremity; and unless we win or draw in a clean fight victory will be worthless and leave us without a friend in the world.

When you feel that you must let yourself go against the enemy, abuse him as much as you like; but do not imagine that you are abusing him when you call him a Communist or a Fascist, or some other word that you do not understand. Civilization could not exist for a fortnight except on a basis of Communism: communal streets and their lamps, roads, bridges, police forces, fire brigades, drainage systems, water supplies, parliaments, municipalities, courts of justice, armies, navies and air forces, with hundreds of public services of which you know nothing. Persons who denounce Communism may be classed with our grandfathers who were afraid of ghosts and fresh air, especially at night.

Everybody has the use of communal machinery; but the value of that use can be appropriated as rent and interest by the owners of the land and of the vast capital sums that arise from the ownership of land, leaving the rest of us working as hard as we did before for a bare living. Take the new motoring roads for example. They are a great convenience and save a lot of money. But the landlords of the roadsides take all that money in frontage and neighboring rents. If you doubt it, take a bungalow or open a shop on them and try. The State makes the road; and immediately the contiguous land which was worth perhaps less than a pound an acre becomes worth hundreds of pounds an acre. The rich become richer and the poor relatively poorer until private individuals have bigger incomes than hard-working Queen Elizabeth ever dreamt of, while millions of less lucky people are thrown out of employment. Consequently the landlords and capitalists, who used to use their political power to prevent the State doing anything but protect their property now use the whole power of the State to build up great private fortunes with capital raised by taxing and rating everybody, and skim the cream off the results as rent and interest. They are "all Socialists now."

Socialist production combined with landlordism in this way is called Fascism in Italy and Nazi-ism in Germany. In England we call it Freedom, Liberty, Civilization, What Our Fathers Bled For, and other agreeable names which encourage us to bleed for it. This is how the Nazi Führer and the Fascist Duce can always find powerful allies even in the countries they are at war with. These allies constitute what we call the Fifth Column. All the Nazis, Fascists, and Fifth Column fight among themselves for the possession of more land and markets (this is called Imperialism) but they all agree heart and soul in a common abhorrence of Soviet Russia, where landlordism is not tolerated. The landlords naturally regard Soviet rule as an unbearable tyranny. But it has built so many cities, roads, canals, and huge industries in its vast dominions that a partition of Russia is a bait that no capitalist or financier can resist.

If you have taken in all this you are probably astonished to find yourself no longer an ordinary man or woman in the street talking nonsense about the war by echoing the Noodle's Orations[19] which you hear on the wireless, or repeating the phrases you have picked up from whatever newspaper you take in. You have been all along an ardent Fascist or Communist or National Socialist or Fifth Columnist without knowing it. But do not be alarmed. As far as this war is concerned it does not matter a rap what you are if you are a British subject. If you speak English or wear a British uniform no German soldier will stop to enquire into your politics before he thrusts his bayonet through you, or showers bullets on you from his Tommy gun, or drops a bomb down your chimney. If you do not kill him he will kill you. It may be that this monstrous state of things should not have been brought about; but it is too late to argue now that it has been brought about. When we have convinced the Germans that they cannot smash the British Empire, and can easily ruin themselves in trying to do it, then it will be time enough to give our political opinions a turn.

We shall need highly intelligent opinions when the settlement comes, or we shall make as hopeless a mess of it as we did last time. Victory alone will not save us. The great German victory over France in 1870–71 brought a ruinous financial crisis on Germany and provided a first rate investment for the hoarded gold of the French peasants.[20] Our victory in 1918 and our determination to make Germany pay ended in unemployment on a scale never before dreamt of, and millions of brave Britons on the dole.

And all because we talked through our hats and never understood what we were talking about.

ON SHAW'S DESIRE FOR PEACE (1950)

However one may judge Shaw's political judgments in his later years, this late essay—written for an unknown Russian paper by a man of ninety-three—shows that his ability to produce vigorous and lucid prose remained undiminished to the end. The body of the piece is a digest of Shaw's assessment of Marx's greatness and his limits. As early as the Fabian tract, *The Illusions of Socialism* (1897), Shaw had explained the ways in which he both was—and was not—a Marxist. He credited Marx with being a great social prophet who grasped the truth that most cultural questions are at bottom economic questions, but he disagreed with such specific Marxist doctrines as the class war or theory of surplus value. The current discussion is as cogent as any he had offered previously.

The article's coda reveals Shaw's awareness of the counterforces that would later produce the Cold War. It had been long apparent that the alliance of Europe and America with Russia had not survived the end of World War II. Characteristically, Shaw rationalizes Russian militarism as the result of her justifiable fear of the combined might of the United States and the countries comprising NATO. Hindsight can easily see flaws in his argument, which is nonetheless not a bad prescription for 1950 in stressing the advisability (ignored as usual by the parties concerned) of avoiding tensions capable of leading to a third world war.

Bernard Shaw on Peace (1950)

[PROVENANCE: Typewritten (carbon) manuscript, unsigned and undated (1950), leaves numbered [1]–6. Recorded as H24 in Dan H. Laurence, Bernard Shaw: A Bibliography *(Oxford: Clarendon Press, 1983). Dan H. Laurence Collection of Bernard Shaw, Archival and Special Collections, University of Guelph Library, Ontario. There is a top copy of this manuscript in the British Library, Add. Mss. 50699, folios 194–99, as well as an earlier version (folios 188–93) partially put together with scissors and paste, on both white and blue paper. Both of the British Library manuscripts are undated.]*

A hundred years ago Thomas Carlyle described the British nation as "40 millions of people, mostly fools."[21] Now as it is impossible to foresee what fools will do, only fools will pretend to be prophets in the matter of peace or war.

It will be asked whether I, writing as I am for a Russian paper, dare describe the population of the U.S.S.R. as "200 millions of people, mostly fools." Well, why not? As I am out of their reach they cannot tear me to pieces. Russians and Britons are human beings; and though no two human beings are exactly alike (the difference in political capacity between Stalin and an average moujik[22] is almost a difference of species) yet every million of mankind is exactly like every other million. On this scale equality is real. On the scale of personal individuality it is a delusion. And if Nations are mostly fools, and are helpless without the leaders and rulers whom Nature produces only at the rate of five per cent of births, questions of peace and war depend on the selection of this gifted five per cent as rulers. Fools do not select them: they instinctively fear them: and fear always breeds hatred. Therefore, if all nations are "mostly fools," wise selection of rulers is not compatible with Adult Suffrage. The mob will never vote for the *élite*. Jerusalem slays the prophets.

Besides, authority turns the heads of men not born to it. Nero, John of Leyden, Paul I, Hitler and Riza Khan were so corrupted by it that they had to be murdered by their courtiers or forced to abdicate; but Cromwell, Washington, Masaryk, Lenin, and Ataturk kept their heads and held command until they died by their sheer mental ability and realistic common sense, just as Stalin does now.[23] Lenin, when any constituency elected a dunderhead, sent him back and told the voters to behave sensibly and elect a qualified candidate, usually naming one for their choice.

We have to face these facts. Hitler was right when he called Adult Suffrage sham democracy. None the less his election of himself as Allerhöchst for life turned his head. He went the way of Paul I.

Karl Marx divided society into bourgeoisie and proletariat, waging a civil war of classes, which he thought would end with the victory and dictatorship of the proletariat, and the subsequent fading-out of the bourgeois State. He expected that this dictatorship would occur first in the State in which modern industrial Capitalism was most developed, and last in Russia, where it was least developed. But having no administrative experience, and being himself a bourgeois born and bred, he made mistakes, great as he was. Feudal barbarous Russia was not last but first. Sasha Kropotkin[24] said to me 30 years ago, when she was the most beautiful child of the Revolution, "Russia will save the soul of the world." Sasha was right and Marx was wrong. Communism is Capitalism *in excelsis*. What we Communists call Capitalism is not Capitalism. It is Plutocracy, and should always be called so. It is anti-State. Communism is pro-State.

Communism is neither a melodrama in which every Communist is a hero and every Plutocrat a villain, nor a Utopia in which everything is done by the State and nothing by private enterprise. There is more private enterprise in Russia than in England. Only when it is financed by the State and exploited by plutocratic private owners does it call itself The Corporate State or National Socialism. Its popular name is Fascism. Though it is associated in our minds with the anti-Semite mania of Hitler and the imperialism of Mussolini, it has no logical connexion with either. Many activities may be quite wisely left to controlled petty Fascism. Criticism, Art, and Science had better be free from all control except that of the common law.

Marx was sometimes pragmatically right when he was theoretically wrong. His doctrine that labor creates value works well enough in modern industrial practice, just as Newton's erroneous first law of motion worked well enough in astronomical practice before Einstein upset it. The truth is that value creates labor.

Marx, like Ruskin before him, failed completely to understand rent and interest; but here again, by lumping them together as surplus value (Mehrwerth), he took them into account as hard facts and came out pragmatically right.

In short, Marx, though he changed the mind of the world, and ranks among the greatest of prophets and Mahatmas, was not God Omniscient, and must not be idolized. About Equality, a fundamental subject, he tells us nothing except that men able to manage industry will, like the ancient Roman *Villicus,* accept a lower wage for exercising their peculiar ability than do manual labor for a higher wage.[25] This is true; but it is not enough for administrative practice. Equality of political ability does not exist, nor can it be manufactured by equality of education or any other known anthropometric method. But equality of income is quite feasible, and is essential under Communism. Yet in plutocratic England it has been carried much farther than in Communist Russia. I, formerly a rich capitalist playwright, have now hardly a pound sterling to spare. The Kremlin must follow suit by prescribing a Basic Income for everybody, sufficient for a cultured home and the best education, and raise all incomes or reduce them to that basic level by redistributive taxation.

This does not mean that everybody shall have exactly the same number of kopeks every week, or that the Basic level shall be imposed by Ukase in one afternoon. Such a catastrophe would wreck civilization. The basic level must be worked up to gradually by increased production until the country is rich enough to make every couple in the land intermarriageable, thereby abolishing all plutocratic class divisions. Equalization need go no further. Millionairesses do not now marry railway porters nor millionaires marry washerwomen. Their habits are too different. But there are so few millionaires that if they did not marry thousandaires they could never marry at all, nor can they form different class habits. Consequently when the Basic Income has risen to thousands it will not matter if a few individuals of extra-talent or luck have ten times the basic income to play with. They cannot wear ten hats nor eat ten dinners. They can do nothing with their spare cash but endow new social experiments, found new institutions, make great collections of works of art, finance scientific research, or the like, all very desirable activities to be taken over later on, if successful, by the State.

And now I shall be asked what all this has to do with war and peace. What about Mr. Churchill and Mr. Bevin and President Truman and the hydrogen bomb?[26] I must reply that I never waste time by telling people what they already know as well as I do, nor pretend to know what I know no better than they. I prefer to give my readers something new to think about. Mr. Churchill honestly desires peace; but he is convinced that Stalin is waiting for a favorable opportunity to launch an aggressive war not only on the Western Powers but on the whole earth, and that he thinks of nothing else by day or night. Therefore, says Mr. Churchill, the Western Powers must arm to the teeth. Mr. Bevin and the Labor Party leaders, though they profess Socialism without knowing exactly what Socialism is, believe the same as Mr. Churchill. President Truman has to countenance this delusion, and go on making hydrogen bombs or lose his majority in Congress.[27] This explains why every British political speech begins with a pious declaration of peace on earth and goodwill to men, and ends with a declaration of defensive war against Russia.

As to the little group which calls itself the Communist Party without knowing what Communism means in practice (Lenin dismissed their dreams as measles) it is assumed that everything they do is dictated by Stalin; and when I say that I heartily wish it were, as they could have no better leader, this simple matter of fact is received as a monstrous paradox.

The question now open is whether and how far Russia, though dreading and not yet able to afford another war, is not convinced that the Western Powers, organized as The Atlantic Pact,[28] are not a gigantic Imperialist conspiracy to overthrow and decommunize the U.S.S.R. It is not for me to answer this question. Being a foreigner I can only say that if Russians, like Britons and white Americans, are "mostly fools" it is here that the danger of war lies. Only by dispelling this reciprocal hallucination can it be averted.

AFTERWORD

In Shaw's *Man and Superman* (1903) the Devil warns Don Juan, "In the arts of life man invents nothing ... his heart is in his weapons. This marvelous force of Life of which you boast is a force of Death: Man measures his strength by his destructiveness." Shaw was born more than four years before Lincoln's election as president of the United States. Bayonets and rifles were the dominant weapons, and the main means of military transport was the horse. Shaw died five years after President Truman ordered the dropping of atomic bombs on Japan, which made the once shocking new paraphernalia of World War I—poison gas, hand grenades, machine guns operated by foot soldiers—seem like outdated toys. Had the Devil been right after all? Given the staggering pace of a half century of "progress" in the technology of weaponry unaccompanied by any noticeable increase in the wisdom of its inventors, how did Shaw finally assess the human prospect? In a note of 18 December 1945 he replied to a query from *Stockholms Tidningen:* "Are you an optimist or a pessimist about international relations?"

> Neither. We have reached the point at which all our previous attempts at civilization have collapsed through the political incompetence of the human animal to solve its problems.
> Whether we shall pull through this time remains to be seen. The future is unpredictable, but full of possibilities both of prosperity and ruin.[29]

In *Shaw's Moral Vision* (1976), I described him as an optimist in the very long run—not necessarily a reassuring thought if one ponders that the "run" might involve the extinction of the human race and its replacement by a new experiment of the Life Force, described to fellow-socialist Sidney Webb as "some superFabian species capable of behaving decently" (*CL 1926–1950*, p. 757). "The bomb" had upped the ante, but not changed the game. As an eyewitness to the ravages of near-total war, Shaw had written in 1917, "Either the best is yet to be, or the sooner we all blow one another off the face of the earth the better" (*WRW*, p. 235). The overall cast of evidence suggests that Shaw leaned ever so slightly toward the positive alternative. In his last full-length play, *Buoyant Billions* (1947), the Priest avers, "The future is with the learners." At the beginning of the nuclear age, the question for Shaw remained open.

Notes

1. Persons wishing to acquaint themselves with Bernard Shaw's published views on war and peace might begin by examining (1) *Arms and the Man* and the follow-up essay

that reactions to that play provoked, "A Dramatic Realist to His Critics" (both 1894); (2) *Heartbreak House* (the play [1916–17] and preface [1919]); (3) letters Shaw wrote during World War I, many of which are available in *Collected Letters 1911–1925* (hereafter *CL*), ed. Dan H. Laurence (London: Max Reinhardt, 1985); (4) *What I Really Wrote about the War* (hereafter *WRW*) (New York: Brentano's, 1932)—Shaw's own omnibus collection featuring two major monographs, *Common Sense about the War* (1914) and *Peace Conference Hints* (1919), interwoven with briefer pieces and his later commentary; and (5) relevant sections from longer Shavian political texts such as *The Intelligent Woman's Guide to Socialism and Capitalism* (Standard Edition, 1932; orig. pub. 1928) and *Everybody's Political What's What?* (Standard Edition, 1944).

2. Samuel Taylor Coleridge ran away from Jesus College, Cambridge, in December 1793 to enlist in the 15th Light Dragoons, but was bought out of the army by his family four months later.

3. The flagship accident is treated with Shavian exaggeration, but presumably relates to the ramming of the *Victoria* by the *Camperdown* on 22 June 1893, to which he also alludes in his lecture "The Dynamitards of Science" (1900), published in *Platform and Pulpit*, ed. Dan H. Laurence (New York: Hill & Wang, 1961), pp. 31–36.

4. In 1643 Cromwell successfully recruited a regiment later known as the Ironsides that maintained remarkable esprit de corps as well as a perfect won/lost record in battle. At his instigation, Parliament reorganized the Roundhead army—purging it of leaders sympathetic to the king—to create a "New Model" army that routed Charles I's remaining troops at Naseby in 1645.

5. Inserted after the draft was completed and signed, this unfinished statement was an afterthought.

6. This description of wartime street swindlers is repeated in the Preface to *Heartbreak House* in the subsection entitled "War Delirium," annotated as follows in Shaw's *Complete Prefaces*, ed. Dan H. Laurence and Daniel J. Leary (London: Allen Lane, 1995): "The Commissioner of Police, in 1915, with the approval of the Home Secretary, promulgated regulations under the Streets Act of 1903 that gave him the power to issue or withhold permits for street solicitations, thus curbing unlawful collection of money for bogus charities. The regulations were effected on 12 August" (2: 326).

7. The reference is to Washington's Farewell Address (17 September 1796) in which he warned the United States against "entangling alliances" in the affairs of other nations. Well into the twentieth century this speech remained holy writ for Americans supporting an "isolationist" foreign policy.

8. Shaw's use of "Junker" in this sentence is sarcastic. Going back several centuries, the term technically refers to ultra-reactionary members of the Prussian landed aristocracy east of the Elbe, often responsible for brutal subjugation of peasants under their control. Shaw's point is that this class of landlords—conveniently demonized in British anti-Hun rhetoric—exists in many countries: "A Junker is not a fiend in a spiked helmet but the German equivalent of an English country gentleman" (*WRW*, p. 97). During World War I Shaw was fond of referring to Sir Edward Grey, Liberal foreign secretary, 1905–16, as a British "Junker."

9. Lord Salisbury was a British statesman (1830–1903) noted for his imperialistic policies. The Boer War was fought during the last of his three prime ministries.

10. The Austrian Prince Metternich (1773–1859) was a leading architect of the reconstruction of Europe along "balance of power" principles at the Congress of Vienna (1814–15) after the defeat of Napoleon. The Holy Alliance (1815)—an amorphously defined union that eventually included all European Christian states except England and the Vatican—sought to preserve ruling dynasties against liberal movements of all stripes. In fact the brainchild of Tsar Alexander I, the Holy Alliance was privately ridiculed as

meaningless by Metternich, whose name nonetheless (for other valid reasons) became a symbol of the reactionary politics that prevailed in post-Napoleonic Europe until challenged by the revolutions of 1848.

11. Shaw means the "Central Powers": the alliance of only four countries—Germany, Austria-Hungary, Bulgaria, and Turkey—that comprised the losing side in World War I.

12. In 1839 Britain and Germany signed the Treaty of London, which guaranteed the independence of Belgium. When Britain in 1914 declared war on Germany for invading Belgium, German chancellor Theobald von Bethmann-Hollweg asserted that Britain had entered the war "just for a scrap of paper." Shaw latches on to the phrase to imply that the British at this moment seemed blind to the possibility that one day Germany might wage war against Britain over another "scrap of paper"—i.e., the Treaty of Versailles. More than facile sarcasm is involved here, however, for Shaw was in fact disgusted by the Treaty's placing (in its Article 231) the entire blame for World War I on German aggression. While readily granting that war forces us to confront "a blasting glimpse of what human nature is capable of at its vilest" (WRW, p. 175), he found it hypocritical to single out one country for condemnation when "there is not a single state in the world at present with a presentable character" (WRW, p. 162).

13. Germany was admitted to the League in 1926 and Russia in 1934. The Bolshevik government of Russia was recognized by England in 1924 and by the United States in 1933.

14. Georges Clemenceau was premier (not president) of France, 1917–20. While here regarded by Shaw as an instance of nationalistic intransigence, Clemenceau's defeat in the elections of 1919 resulted in part from the feeling of his countrymen that he had been *too* willing to compromise French interest at the Paris Peace Conference. Clemenceau had at first insisted that the part of Germany west of the Rhine be established as an independent state, but was pressured by Lloyd George and Woodrow Wilson to accept a demilitarized Rhineland that would remain German but under Anglo-American guarantees of protection. While not a man of broad vision, on this point Clemenceau turned out to be right. When Hitler (in March 1936) marched German troops into the Rhineland, France and her former allies—who could have intervened decisively at that point—did nothing.

15. Wishful thinking on Shaw's part. Lloyd George's coalition government was succeeded in 1922 by a Conservative government led first by Bonar Law and then by Stanley Baldwin. However, during his ten months as prime minister in 1924, Ramsay MacDonald did significantly shift British foreign policy toward internationalism. MacDonald recognized Soviet Russia, strengthened British support of the League of Nations, and defused the question of German reparations by persuading the countries affected to support the Dawes Plan.

16. More wishful thinking: isolationist sentiment in Congress permanently blocked entrance of the United States into the brainchild of its own president, Woodrow Wilson. In *Peace Conference Hints* (1919), Shaw had praised (with premature optimism) this country for "producing at the right moment a man who, like Washington or Lincoln, easily dominated a colossal situation as spokesman for the highest ideals, whilst British and French demagogues could not rise above the rhetoric of the prize fight and the cinema 'sub-title' " (WRW, p. 271).

17. The eighty-four-year-old premier (1940–44) of the southern part of France unoccupied by Germany after Hitler's swift and stunning defeat of the French in 1940. The Vichy government (named after its capital) was an authoritarian regime that collaborated with the Nazis. A former hero at Verdun in World War I, Pétain was sent to prison for life after the armistice.

18. Somewhat of an exaggeration: America was not about to enter World War I on either side despite considerable pro-German agitation in the early years of the war and anger over Britain's violation of international law on the high seas. The United States

government in December 1914 issued a public note of reproof after American mercantile ships were boarded and searched by the British navy in its efforts to extend the naval blockade against Germany to include basic necessities of life, such as food and clothing, as well as military equipment and supplies. American public opinion shifted dramatically with the German sinking of the British passenger liner *Lusitania* in February 1915. Even so, Wilson did not break off diplomatic relations until Germany's announcement on 31 January 1917 of resumption (after a hiatus of two years) of unrestricted submarine warfare.

19. That is, political twaddle. Probably a reference to a character inclined to orotund pontification in Fielding's *Tragedy of Tragedies* (1731). Noodle and his cohort Doodle are described there as "courtiers in place, and consequently of that party that is uppermost."

20. Her defeat in the Franco-Prussian war permanently ended the institution of the monarchy in France and resulted in her ceding to Germany the territory of Alsace-Lorraine (returned only after World War I). Shaw understates the advantages of victory to Germany, which for the first time became a unified country, with Bismarck serving uninterruptedly as chancellor until 1890.

21. An allusion (and misquotation) from *Latter-Day Pamphlets* No. 6 (1850?), where Carlyle refers to "a Parliament speaking through reporters to Buncombe and the twenty-seven millions, mostly fools."

22. Alternate spelling of "muzhik," a peasant in Tsarist Russia. It may be objected that Shaw makes no mention here of the kulaks, an economically more successful class of peasant farmers whom Stalin exterminated by the millions in the 1920s when they resisted agricultural collectivization of their land. Shaw does elsewhere excoriate the Bolshevik expulsion of the kulaks (for instance, see the *Intelligent Woman's Guide*, pp. 467–68, 471). But was it enough for him to refer to this atrocity as "a stupid anti-Fabian blunder"—as if such "liquidations" were only a matter of a mistake in policy?

23. For those names that are no longer household words in 1996: John of Leiden (1509–36), a Dutch tailor who became fanatical leader of the Anabaptists, led a revolution in Münster in 1534, where he ruled briefly by terror in an attempt to establish a heavenly city; Paul I (1754–1801), son of Catherine the Great who undid many of his mother's reforms, was reactionary emperor of Russia, 1786–1801; Riza Khan was the original name of Reza Shah Pahlavi (1878–1944), shah of Iran, 1925–1941, when he was forced to abdicate (a fate shared by his son in the revolution led by Khomeini); Thomas Masaryk (1850–1937), distinguished intellectual and humanitarian, was the first president of Czechoslovakia, 1918–35, the only eastern European country to establish a stable democracy after World War I; and Kemal Atatürk (1881–1938), a prominent "young Turk" in the early twentieth century, overthrew the Sultan in 1922 and became founder and first president of modern Turkey, 1923–38.

24. Sasha Kropotkin-Lebedeff was the only child of Prince Peter Kropotkin (1842–1921), the famous anarchist and writer.

25. *Villicus* is used here in its general sense of "overseer": a person who works for less money in a position of authority over one of lesser rank who may earn more.

26. Ernest Bevin had served as foreign secretary in the Labour government of Clement Attlee since the defeat of Churchill's ministry in the general election of 1945. In *The Times*, from mid-1948, Bevin and Churchill (the latter no longer P.M. but still an M.P., whose word mattered) both figured prominently in articles about the possibility of a Western Alliance.

On 7 April 1949, three days after the formal signing of NATO, Truman publicly declared that "He 'would not' hesitate . . . to use the atomic bomb if it were necessary for the welfare of the United States, or if the fate of the democracies of the world were at stake." Churchill had urged Truman to make such a statement at a private talk at the White House between 25 and 31 March 1949. Martin Gilbert, *Churchill: A Life* (New York: Henry Holt, 1991), pp. 883–84.

Truman formally announced on 31 January 1950 that "I have directed the Atomic Energy commission to continue its work on all forms of atomic weapons—including the so-called hydrogen or superbomb." Earlier that month, news reports in *The Times* had connected Truman with plans to develop a hydrogen bomb. Despite rumors about a "superbomb" in Washington, D.C., newspapers in November 1949, Shaw could not have heard of the *hydrogen* bomb until January 1950—which may thus be assumed to be the earliest possible date for the essay's composition. (A grateful tip of the cap to Fred Crawford for spotting the clues enabling this essay to be dated as one of the last Shaw wrote.)

27. Although a Republican sweep in the elections of 1946 deprived Truman of the congressional majority that he had inherited from Roosevelt, the Democrats regained their majority in both houses in the elections of November 1948. Shaw is pointing to Truman's need to retain this majority in the November 1950 elections.

28. The Atlantic Pact, a forerunner of NATO, had been signed in Paris on 27 October 1948, by which time negotiations for NATO were already under way. Shaw, like many others, used the term "Atlantic Pact" after NATO formally came into being on 4 April 1949. According to the Index of *The Times*, it was some time before people consistently referred to this alliance as NATO or as the North Atlantic Treaty Organization.

29. Hitherto unpublished shorthand reply to a cabled query. Harry Ransom Humanities Research Center, The University of Texas at Austin.

Charles A. Berst

SUPERMAN THEATER: GUSTS, GALUMPHS, AND GRUMPS

However unlikely it may seem that dramatic materials by Shaw remain unpublished, here are three: a scenario for *Man and Superman* and two playlets. The rare scenario is extraordinary for lights it casts on Shaw's creative methods, especially in their early stages. The playlets epitomize Shaw's spontaneous creativity: each springs from a letter as a small flight of art when Shaw felt capriciously theatrical or found epistolary prose inadequate to express what a dramatic sketch could vitalize with humor and point.

The three pieces include a striking number of personal allusions that relate variously to Shaw's social, political, and metaphysical views and emerge colorfully through characters often based on individuals he knew. For the knowledgeable reader, such backgrounds give the pieces extra spice, while the pieces, in turn, give the backgrounds fresh life and interest.

Abundant fun in the three is accessible to everyone. Shaw is having a good time, to which serious aspects of his materials add pungency. Although the pieces are diverse in their subject matter and settings, they have at least one target in common: fanatics. In the scenario, fanaticism gusts from a compulsive social and moral revolutionary; in one playlet it galumphs from a pedantic political zealot; in the second playlet it grumps, against intimidating odds, from a stubborn rationalist who risks his manifest destiny by defying Manifest Deity.

Shaw takes impish delight in demonstrating how fanaticism hazards a fall. Perhaps its greatest flaw, he infers, lies in its inability to laugh at itself. But, when properly ground, those who cannot laugh at themselves at least offer laughable grist for those who can.

ON SHAW'S SCENARIO FOR *MAN AND SUPERMAN* (1901)

The scenario for *Man and Superman* is unique in Shaw studies. Since the manuscript of this important play has disappeared, the scenario is the primary evidence we have of the play's artistic evolution. The only other Shaw play scenario that has surfaced is a shorthand sketch for *The Devil's Disciple*, whose manuscript survives.[1] Then too, the scenario involves a contradiction: not only did Shaw never acknowledge it, but he often declared such plotting contrary to his creative methods.

On 12 January 1929, for example, he informed the journalist Hannen Swaffer, "You must regard me as a hardened old professional who is inspired all the time during working hours. My subjects come to me anyhow; and when I have chosen my subject the play writes itself. I can even begin without a subject with the same result: the characters come and talk and define themselves and explain their business; and there is your play for you. Thus my plays must be classed as inspirations, not as constructions. Hence their charm!"[2] No flashing eyes and floating hair; but no pedantic constructing either. Rather, creative energies attracting characters, dialogue, and action that evolve spontaneously.

Similarly, Shaw had written William Archer on 22 June 1923, detailing his instincts for inspiration over construction and citing *The Devil's Disciple* and *Man and Superman* as examples: "Ibsen's method was the vital method, not the mechanical one. . . . My way is not essentially different. I write my dialogue (which involves creating the characters and doing all the vital work), as it comes. I then go over it and arrange it for the stage. . . . But sometimes the thing begins with a situation or even a quite trivial repartee. Thus The Devil's Disciple began with the situation of the arrest of Dudgeon . . . and Man and Superman with 'I am a brigand: I live by robbing the rich' 'I am a gentleman: I live by robbing the poor'—a complete irrelevance. But these are only the first crystallizations of the magic fluid: I do not work constructively to them: they simply suggest people to whom they might have happened; and these people behave as God pleases" (*Collected Letters 1911–1925*, pp. 837–38).

Still, after a performance of *Man and Superman* in 1905, Max Beerbohm had commented, "I found that as a piece of theatrical construction it was perfect."[3] And Archer, not aware of Shaw's scenario, criticized him for his disinterest in plots, especially for letting his plays trail off into verbal conflicts. Neither Beerbohm's praise nor Archer's critique was far from the mark, but from Shaw's point of view both focused on concerns secondary to most fine drama and tertiary to his. To Archer he retorted: "My play grows until it stops, just as an animal does. . . . [Y]ou are a perfect idiot as a professor of dramatic Constructionism" (*Collected Letters 1911–1925*, pp. 838–39).

In some details *The Devil's Disciple* scenario looks like a trial run for its *Man and Superman* successor. Dated 14 April 1896, four pages are in shorthand, followed by slightly more than a page in longhand, apparently added to clarify later action. Three characters are identified by letter and briefly described at the start: the males as A and B (Dudgeon and Anderson), and the female lead as Z (Judith). Essie appears as Y in Act I. The *Man and Superman* scenario, in longhand except for many shorthand character descriptions, also has two portions (dated 2 July and 8 October 1901), suggesting that Shaw similarly dealt with later details as they emerged. Characters are identified by letters here too, but their names are also given in the cast list, which is divided in two columns, men A to K on the left, women Z to U on the right.

More significantly, the scenarios differ greatly in the fullness of their development and in their relation to their respective plays. *The Devil's Disciple's* includes neither Burgoyne nor Swindon and does not individualize members of the Dudgeon family. Its melodramatic values are bold and banal. Shaw took somersaults to undercut them in writing the play.

By contrast, the *Man and Superman* scenario offers an abundance that threatens to burst the play at its seams. Not counting the Hell scene quartet, seventeen characters appear in the cast list. Eventually Shaw eliminated four: Tanner's father and mother (who appear neither in the scenario nor in the play), a solicitor (briefly in the scenario but not in the play), and Ann's sister Rhoda (who becomes an offstage presence in the play).

Shaw clearly played with characters' names. He vacillated between Tenorio and Tanner, a quandary he solved by choosing the latter, which anglicizes Tenorio while retaining Don Juan associations. Besides, a tanner tans (beats/thrashes) hides, much as Tanner would tan Roe-buck-Rams-den (with "buck" and "ram" both nouns and verbs). Octavius Robin-son, in turn, flutters through the action in danger of being swallowed by a feline female, and amid allusions to birds netted, suffering, or dead. Then too, chloroformed by Mendoza's mawkish poetry, men doze off. "Balgarnie," an alternative for Hector Malone's surname, probably derives from Florence Balgarnie, one of Shaw's acquaintances in the Dialectical Society and secretary of the National Society for Women's Suffrage. Besides obstinacy, Ramsden's given name could reflect John Arthur Roebuck, an Independent M.P. who, in Henry Adams's words, "had been a tribune of the people, and, like tribunes of most other peoples, in growing old, had grown fatuous."[4]

What, then, about the "C.B." after Ramsden's name and the "(F.J.)" after Pytchley, the solicitor? "C.B." could stand for Commander (or Companion) of the Most Excellent Order of the Bath, an honor befitting one who resembles *"a president of highly respectable men, a chairman among direc-*

tors." Such a title, however, hardly jibes with Ramsden's description of himself as a man of advanced opinions: "I am plain Roebuck Ramsden when other men who have done less have got handles to their names, because I have stood for equality and liberty of conscience while they were truckling to the Church and to the aristocracy. . . . But I draw the line at Anarchism and Free Love and that sort of thing."[5] Without a handled name but with these convictions, Ramsden, according to the scenario's cast list, "affects a combination of Don Qux [Quixote] & Dr Johnson"—which would make him an extravagant idealist, individualistic moralist, and social reformer, an awesome composite suggesting that Shaw may have jotted "C.B." as a note to himself, signifying Charles Bradlaugh.

Born in 1833, editor of a free-thought weekly from 1860 onward, renowned for championing individual liberties, president of the National Secular Society, elected to Parliament as a radical but not seated for more than five years because he refused to take its religious oath, Bradlaugh, like Ramsden, considered himself an advanced man, yet shrank in Shaw's eyes because he adamantly opposed socialism. Like Ramsden, he was an obsolete liberal of the 1860s. Perhaps clinching Shaw's association of the two is a seemingly casual but revealing parallel. Shaw notes that "*Roebuck believes in the fine arts with all the earnestness of a man who does not understand them*" (2:534). Five years later in a letter to G.K. Chesterton, he comments that Bradlaugh "had never in his life, as far as I could make out, seen anything, heard anything or read anything in the artistic sense." Shaw had crossed swords with Bradlaugh on socialism, and regretted that a full-fledged debate between them had not materialized: "Bradlaugh was a most tremendous debater; and I should have made a very poor show with him in point of personal thunder and hypnotism; but . . . I could at least have said my say" (*Collected Letters 1898–1910*, pp. 762, 493).

Thus Shaw's well-known acknowledgment that he modeled Jack Tanner not only on the socialist leader H. M. Hyndman but also, more intimately, on himself, may be complemented by another composite source: "Roebuck Ramsden C.B." as John Arthur Roebuck and, more intimately, Bradlaugh, to whose ghost Shaw may at last have had "his say" by pitting Tanner against Ramsden. Given these sources, the play could even satirize the historic debates of Hyndman and Bradlaugh.

Obscure as it may seem, the "(F.J.)" following Mr. Pytchley, a solicitor, is easier to identify than "C.B." Signing "F.J." on letters to G.B.S. was a retired solicitor, Frederick Jackson, who will appear shortly (see *The Trinity v Jackson*) in a role so colorful that we can imagine Shaw pitching Pytchley from the play because he could hardly do his friend justice in a trivial part. Besides, he had already exploited the melodramatic device of a lawyer reading a surprising will in *The Devil's Disciple*. Less expendable, apparently, was Ann's little sister Rhoda, who, although absurdly passive, survives through three acts of the scenario. Shaw's note that she is in love with Octavius suggests his reason for retaining her so long: as a consolation prize for Octavius she could have complemented his Life Force parable, gently counterpointing Ann (originally Anne) and Violet.

Following Shaw's preliminary sketch of elements in the first two acts (some of which he soon dodged), the most remarkable aspect of the scenario is how closely he followed its gist and details in drafting the play. Nonetheless he did shift scenes, their relative weighting, or their emphases to render the play's dramatic action, characters, and comedy especially effective.

Because the scenario uses the classical Greek practice, later adopted by the French, of designating a new scene whenever characters enter or exit, comparisons between it and the play can be quite precise. For example, the following applies the scenario's format to the play's first act. If one matches these scenes with those in the scenario, Shaw's creative alterations become especially clear. Lengthy character descriptions have been eliminated from the page count, which may serve as a relative time count:

1. Ramsden-Octavius. 5 pp. Discussion of Whitefield's death and Octavius's prospects with Ann. Ramsden is indignant about *The Revolutionist's Handbook* and Tanner, and impressed with Ann's sense of duty to her parents.
2. Tanner enters. 5 pp. He despairingly reveals Whitefield's will appointing himself and Ramsden joint guardians of Ann, whom he finds uncontrollable, a boa-constrictor. Irritation and contention; Ramsden flings *Handbook* into wastebasket; Tanner says Octavius must fetch Ann so they may know what she intends for them. Octavius leaves.
3. Tanner-Ramsden. 2 pp. Tanner puts forward his impudence and truthfulness; Ramsden counters by asserting how advanced *he* is.
4. Octavius returns with Ann and her mother. 5 pp. Ann says dutifully she cannot set aside any guardian her father appointed. Abashed, both men agree to serve. Ann calls the men by childhood nicknames, captivating Ramsden and Octavius, not Tanner. She, her mother, and Ramsden leave.
5. Tanner-Octavius. 3 pp. Tanner calls Ann a lioness, part of nature's vital purpose, seeking to use men; warns Octavius that the artist-man in him must struggle with the mother woman for profounder realities of art and philosophy.
6. Ramsden and Ann return. 7.5 pp. They have discovered Violet is pregnant. Anguish. Ramsden and Octavius declare the unknown

scoundrel must marry her; Tanner ardently defends her and her child's rights. Octavius leaves to speak with her. Ann maneuvers Ramsden's exit.

7. Ann-Tanner, 12 pp. Recollection of their childhood romance that ended when Tanner's soul was born of a moral passion; Tanner calls it an unconscious love compact (9 pp.). Ann puts her boa, then her arms around his neck; he thinks she is in love with Octavius and only playing; she calls him a baby and a flirt.

8. Ramsden, Octavius, Miss Ramsden enter. 2 pp. They report that Violet is obstinate. She has sent for a cab.

9. Violet enters. 3.5 pp. Tanner congratulates her on her courage, worth, vitality, bravery, asserting the irrelevance of her not being married. Indignant, insulted, she reveals she *is* married; Ann knew. Tanner is crushed: "double crossed!"; now they must all "cower before the wedding ring."

Besides the substantial revision of Scenes 1 and 2, what is most immediately apparent in a comparison with the scenario is that the trauma over Violet's pregnancy has been moved backward and subordinated. While over half of the act's scenario is devoted to it, it takes a third less time in the play. More important here are less sensational but telling definitions of the major characters up to Scene 6, wrought through Shaw's orchestration of varied groupings.

The next major departure from the scenario is the length of the Ann and Tanner scene. One of the scenario's sketchiest, it becomes the longest in the play. In both it aptly follows Tanner's warning Octavius about women's pursuit of men, and its romantic qualities are fittingly sandwiched between scenes about Violet's pregnancy. In the play, however, it gains depth first through bittersweet recollections of youth, then through childhood's love surfacing boldly and metaphorically in Ann's boa embrace.

Scene 9 not only conflates the scenario's last two scenes but also deflates Tanner in a brilliant comic climax. Whereas the scenario ends the act with a mildly intriguing question—who is Violet's husband?—the play mischievously mocks Tanner's vulnerability: to be demolished by a debater would be embarrassing enough, but to be insidiously duped by a predatory woman, then utterly upended by a prig's wedding ring, is ignominiously flabbergasting.

In Act II the play follows the scenario so closely that several quotations are lifted from it almost verbatim, such as Ann's response to Tanner's witless urging that she declare her independence and come with him to Spain, in II.4: "Oh yes, I will come: since you wish it: you are my guardian: I think we ought to know one another better"; and Straker's response to Tanner's request that he put Octavius and Ann together, in II.8: " 'Not a bit o use . . . he may just as well give it up first as last'. 'Why?' 'Cos she's after someone else'. 'Who?' 'You' " (parallels in 2:601, 610). Apparently Shaw became so fond of Straker that the play's greatest departures from the Act II scenario involve his extra appearances. One detail not transferred is a title for the "favorite air" Straker whistles when Tanner mentions Ann. The scenario provides one: "Pop Goes the Weasel." There are many lyrics to this old English dance tune, but most feature a monkey chasing a weasel. The association seems apt, given all the animals Tanner identifies with Ann, her relentless pursuit of him, his trying to weasel out of entrapment, and the nonchalant wit with which Straker repeatedly one-ups him.

Shaw's note preceding Act III, Scene 3 in the scenario—"III - 1 & 2 as in old diary to end of the dream"—flags a manuscript for a second volume of *Unpublished Shaw*. While precise dates for the play's composition are few, this note reflects a chronology that started with the Mendoza-Tanner "robber of the rich/robber of the poor" exchange of Act III. In May 1900 Shaw began the diary's Hell sequence. The scenario followed, first with I, II, and III.3 on 2 July 1901, then with IV and V on 8 October 1901. By January 1903 revisions of the play were at last finished, and the Preface was under way.[6]

Elements in the scenario shed further light on this evolution. The play's departures from the scenario's first act and quotations from its second, along with the three-month gap between the scenario's two parts, suggest that Shaw started the play, testing various options before settling on details and completing the scenario. He might also have been working on the Hell sequence, but he had at least drafted its last line by 8 October 1901, since Tanner echoes this in the Act IV-V scenario of that date—"A father! a father for the Superman!"—precisely Doña Ana's cry that ends the Hell scene in the play. Shaw's continuing attention to the scenario appears throughout Act IV of the play, down to a near-transcription of Violet's note to Hector: "Dearest   They have all gone to the Alhambra—I have shammed headache . . . Jump into John's motor . . . Quick, quick, quick" (paralleled in 2:701).

Finally, the *Man and Superman* scenario reveals that despite his denials Shaw could be a constructionist. The scenario's scene-by-scene (group-after-group) format has special value not just as it offers clear points of comparison with the play, but also as it graphically shows how Shaw's creative process involved a coalescence of inspiration and structuring. This appears most strongly in his major alterations to the scenario's first act, where each change improves the act both dramatically and structurally. The closeness of the play to the scenario in Acts II and IV, by comparison, suggests the powers of Shaw's characters and comic texture over dramatic form. When the scenario leaves off before the end of the action, Shaw's inspiration takes over, yet does so in fine form.

As the scenario highlights the fact that Shaw wrote the play's Hell sequence before turning to its social comedy, it raises yet another issue of structuring: according to Shaw's creative progression, the play was a philosophy first and a comedy second, not, as the play's subtitle and primary action presents it, the reverse. This provokes a dilemma that physicists have discovered in the fourth dimension: a × b does not necessarily equal b × a. *Man and Superman* accommodates the dilemma with structural ingenuity: as the comedy followed the philosophy for Shaw, its very element was anticlimax; and as the comedy of Act IV follows the philosophy of Act III, much the same is finally true in the play. In toto, since the comedy of anticlimax is a comedy of truth for Shaw, *Man and Superman* gives off ambiguous sparks.

Ultimately Don Juan's heaven is formless, above scenarios, while Ann's world is fraught with forms; and although Jack Tanner aspires to Don Juan's heaven, he has to live in Ann's world. All is not lost if life can inform forms as much or more than forms inform life. Such was the process between Shaw's scenario for *Man and Superman* and the play.

The Superman,
or Don Juan's great grandson's grandson (1901)

[PROVENANCE: Holograph manuscript, unsigned, eleven unnumbered leaves (the first is a cover title), dated "2/7/01" at top of second leaf and "8/10/01" at top of tenth leaf; text on final leaf overlaps six inverted holograph lines of notes (for a lecture?): "Dullness now that Blasphemy is gone | 'Prophet of Nay' | 'Agnosticism' | Stallworthy-Levy | Kipling-Scott 'Temple of Holy Ghost' | Conceit out of us— Darwin". Henry W. and Albert A. Berg Collection, New York Public Library, Astor, Lenox and Tilden Foundations.]

2/7/01.
A.   John Tenorio or Tanner, author of The Young Revolutionist.
B.   Octavius Robinson A's friend, dramatic author.
C.   Roebuck Ramsden C.B.   Z's guardian. Soul of honor.
     Affects a combination of Don Qux & Dr Johnson.
D.   George Whitefield Tenorio [.] A's father.
                    Tanner
E.   Henry Straker, A's motorman. Of the new world. Has cut his
     cousin for marrying a lady. "The New Man"
                 ?Balgarnie
F.   Hector Malone, son of American millionaire who wants him to
     marry into the English aristocracy. Is secretly married to Y.

G.   Mr Pytchley, a solicitor. (F.J.)
H.   Mendoza—a Jewish brigand.
I.   Goatherd, hired by brigands to keep watch for them.
J.   Spanish officer commanding escort.
K.   Hector Balgarnie sen[r]
     F's father.   millionaire, seeking charitable objects.

Z.   Anne Whitefield[,] ward of C.
Y.   Violet Malone, née Robinson. Secretly married to F.
                        Tanner
X.   Mrs Whitefield Tenorio, wife of D, mother to A.
W.   Rhoda Whitefield. Z's little sister. In love with B. Bullied by Z.
V.   Mrs Whitefield, Z's mother, always made by her an excuse for her
     actions. "Mama will not allow me", or "Mama insists.["]
U.   Miss Roebuck Ramsden, C's sister & housekeeper.

I. C & A have been appointed joint trustees & guardians of Z by the
will of her late father, on the ground that A's heterodoxy will correct
C's orthodoxy. (Really the will has been made under the influence of Z
herself, who has privately made up her mind long ago to marry A,
having fancied him from their childhood, in which they have been
playmates).

C is utterly outraged by the appointment of such a co-trustee. A points
out that by the terms of the trust he can decline to act. C retorts that this
will leave Z in A's hands, helpless. A says why not. C indignantly refuses
to abandon a defenceless girl to the care of a libertine. Finally they agree
to leave it to Z whether she will have C or Z [sic] or both.

Z piously says she must obey her late father's wishes. This is one of her
motifs—always pleading a parent's wishes or orders for doing what she
wants.

But B has also a trust—the guardianship of his sister. Y is secretly
married to F, but has promised him faithfully not to reveal the marriage.
She becomes pregnant, but allows her family to believe that she is unmarried. The reason of this is that F's father, an Irish American millionaire,
wishes him to marry an English lady of at least baronial rank & F is afraid
of being disinherited if his marriage with a commoner is discovered.

   Act I

Sc 1. C in his study—full of "The Young Revolutionist." G comes to
read the will & to announce the trust. [*Revision added between "G" and
"comes"*: "or B to talk & then G to" — *apparently* "comes to" *was intended to
be deleted.*] It is an overwhelming surprise, as, though C expected that a

younger man would be named, it was understood that the younger man was to be the exemplary B.

2[.] A, having had a similar communication, comes to confer with C[.] A brings B to introduce him[;] as C knows B & has the highest opinion of him [he] demands of Providence why B was not trustee. B confesses that he loves Z, [*Inserted:* Scene here between the two friends in which he confesses Z's fascination. It is a bond between them. They can always talk of her without boring one another. A remarks that if ever he marries her B will be most welcome to share with him. Horror of C. Also here A's solemn warning to B against the spider-boa pursuit of men by women.] [*Original text continues here*] & that he & she agreed that he should refuse a trust in which he had so strong a personal interest. He is content to take charge of his sister Y.

3[.] Z called in to choose. (She is upstairs talking to C's womenfolk).

4. Announcement of Y's pregnancy. Family council. A heartily approves of her courage. Z again appealed to, will she have this reprobate for her guardian. Must obey her father. Finally, all withdraw in disgust to continue this council in another room without A, because he makes a violent protest that the disgrace, ruin &c is not what she has done to herself but what they propose to do to her. Also he protests against the assumption that the father must be discovered & married to Y. Z pretends to go with them, but slips back at the door to speak to A[.] [*Note in left margin:*] A must invite W somewhere in this scene—See II - 2[.] She replies that she will ask Z's leave.]

5[.] A & Z. In this scene, which is essentially a love scene on Z's part, bringing out her determined pursuit of A, she ingratiates herself by telling him that she has befriended Y, who is at present actually in the house with her. She says B, whose chivalrous delicacy has been beyond praise, knows this. Presently B comes to tell A the result of the family council.

6. A.Z.B. They have resolved to send Y abroad to get over her disgrace; but she refuses to go; and as the reason clearly is that she will not give up her lover or be parted from him, they threaten to decline to have anything more to [do] with her. A is delighted with her resolution. He calls on them to form a counter-council & stand by her. They agree & B goes to fetch Y.

[*NOTE: In Scene 6, "They" are the council (Roebuck Ramsden, Miss Ramsden, &c.), not Z. or B., who join with A. in forming the "counter-council" at the end of the scene.*]

I - 7. A,Z,B&Y. When Y enters, A welcomes her warmly on his hetero-
dox ground of the worship of life & of motherhood. Shocked beyond
measure, she exclaims that she can bear all the conventional reproaches,
but that this insult is too much, and declares that she is married! In a
violent revulsion of feeling A now sees all his theories about the essentially predatory & conventional nature of woman confirmed. Z's charity
to Y is unmasked. The question arises, to whom? The others return to
deliver their ultimatum.

8. Omnes. A sensibly explains Y's secret. C retorts that at least the
disclosure has cleared A himself from a very painful suspicion. Y is
furious, all her dislike of A set boiling by the insinuation. A blandly
explains that it has cleared all of them from the hideous imputation of
moral courage. The act closes with "And yet, who is it?["]

Act II Difference of address.

1. A & E, mostly about the motorcar, to bring out the fact that flight is
possible to the ends of Europe at a moment's notice. B enters & is
introduced to E. General conversation. The new class. E's points of
honor—his h's, his ideas of mésalliance &c. He goes off to look after his
car, telling A & B to go on talking about their ladies: *he* knows.

2. A & B. B pours forth his love for Z. A warns him against the doom
of the drone & the spider, giving a vivid description of the steady purpose of the woman, the impossibility of escape save by absolute flight &
concealment, the death-in-life of capture. Profanation—profanation! B
replies that if only he could believe that Z was pursuing him he should be
the happiest man alive. A's [*sic*] asks what she says to B's suit. B says that
she is too overwhelmed by the death of her father to think of anything
but brother & sister. A then asks whether W is accepting his invitation
(I—4). B replies that Z has forbidden W to hold more than the unavoidable minimum of communication with A. At this E, who is on at the back,
suddenly begins to whistle Pop goes the Weazel, and goes off in music, A
& B stopping to stare at him. A is indignant, this not being the first time
that A [*sic*] has kept women aloof from him by this device. Z & W arrive
dressed for motoring.

3. A challenges Z straight out as to whether she told W to avoid him.
B, unable to bear Z's embarrassment, protests. Z, with simple dignity,
asks B to take W away, which he does.

II—4[.] Z & A. Z alleges that her mother told her to tell W to avoid him.
He explosively protests against this abjection—this eternal filial duty—&
exhorts her to be herself. Her virtue is proof against it all. Passing her he
asks her to signalize her revolt by some bold deed, some American asser-

tion of independence: for instance, will she jump into his motor car &
come to Spain with him. To his horror she says she does not think there
would be any harm in that, since he is her guardian, her father's delegate, and accepts. He backs out, declaring that if there is no harm in the
expedition neither is there any point in it. She tries to hold him to it, and
puts it to him whether, holding so sacred a trust, he could abuse it to
compromise her. He declares that this is the one service he can do her—
the one thing for which she will at the end of her life thank him & in the
same breath with which she curses her natural enemy—her mother. She
says she is sure he cannot mean that. He retorts that the remedy is
simple—dont come. She says 'Oh yes, I will come: since you wish it: you
are my guardian: I think we ought to know one another better; and I
hope my poor influence on you will not be a bad one'. He is dumb-
founded at the consequences of his jibe. B & W return with G Y V & F
[and] interrupt the conversation.

II [—] 5. A Z B W C & F. Introduction of F to A, who has not met him
before. Z announces the trip to Spain as a quite ordinary & proper
excursion, implying that everybody will go, chaperones & all. A consents
for B's sake, to give him a chance with Z. F, who has also a motorcar,
proposes, with C's permission, to take Y. This plunges the company into
gloom. Z says 'Come, dear', maternally-governessily, and takes off W.

II—6. A, B, C, & F. They solemnly explain the state of affairs as
regards Y. The American (F) is chivalrously indignant that the unknown
husband does not come forward. Thinks marriage ought to ennoble a
man, at which A laughs. Wants to know, however, whether according to
the British standard of conduct, her marriage is any valid obstacle to her
motoring with him. A says no. C says yes; but leaves it to B, the brother,
to decide. B says Y can do as she likes—matter for her own feeling: how
little influence he has with her is shewn by her marrying without his
knowledge. Enter Y, who is received very sadly. A B & C withdraw to give
F a chance.

II—7[.] Y & F[.] Discloses the fact that F is the husband. He wants her
to let him own up; defy his father; and work for her; but she absolutely
refuses to face any sort of struggle or work or poverty & pleads all that
she has suffered already by the concealment—does he want to throw all
that away. It strikes him that marriage may be delightful, but that it is not
ennobling. E ends the scene by arriving to tell F that his motor has
arrived & that his motist [sic] wants to see him about the carburettor. F
proposes that Y shall go with him to see the motor. She complies. As they
go, E following, a A [sic] returns & detains E.

II—8. A. E.   A tells E about the trip to Spain & asks him to arrange matters so that B shall see as much of Z as possible. E replies by whistling Pop. A demands an explanation. 'Not a bit o use', says E, '& he may just as well give it up first as last'. 'Why?'. 'Cos she's after someone else'. 'Who?' 'You'. A himself & not B is the bee—the spider. It flashes on A that it is all true. Flight, flight, flight. The motor car is ready: the act ends with his departure for Spain alone (except E, of course).

Act III
In the Spanish mountains—
III—1 & 2 as in old diary to end of the dream.
III 3.   Dawn. All asleep as before. The horn of the motor is heard on the hill. I (the goatherd) rushes in as before & wakes the hero of the magazine rifle, crying Automobile, Automobile! Brigands rush off as before; and shots are heard as before. Brigands rush back. H asks where are the prisoners: the marksman replies that the automobile fired first & that an armoured automobile full of soldiers has appeared at the head of the valley. E whistles Pop goes the Weazel. H reminds A that he shook hands with him last night. What of that? Crows should not pick out crow's een: the robber of the poor must save the robber of the rich. Good, says A. I will if I can. Enter F with a rifle, Y, Z, W, B, C, & J—the whole crew of F's limousine. Z takes poss. of A[.]

End of Act—J asks who the brigands are. A replies "my escort"— Curtain.

8/10/01   [At top right shorthand note (obliterated by Shaw)]
     Act IV.   Granada. Garden of villa overhanging valley. [Above
                "valley" Shaw added "by day"] Alhambra on opposite
                heights.

[First paragraph bracketed at left margin, with the marginal note Tr [Transfer] to Act V—1.]
     1. Z discovered walking in beauty like the night. A arrives, sees her, & mutters "A father! a father for the Superman!" He remonstrates with her for trifling with B. She throws off the mask, lets him see that the will was her own doing & rouses all the devilment & all the poetry in him in spite of himself. When, roused to his danger, he tries to break away, she releases him, sure of him. In the course of the scene she offers her hypocrisy as a thing he can always depend on, knowing that so incalculable a factor as a freedom of thought like his own would terrify him. [The following dialogue is written above the line, in shorthand; the first square bracket insert in it is Shaw's.] "By Heaven I will not marry you." "Oh you will, you

will, you must [Kisses him].["] Finally tells him to send B to her & she will deal frankly with him.

Sc. 1. Afternoon. K & E enter. E has taken a note from Y to F to the hotel on [sic] the motor. Note as follows:—"Dearest   They have all gone to the Alhambra for the afternoon—I have shammed headache & have the place all to myself. Jump into John's motor: his chauffeur will rattle you here in no time. Quick, quick, quick. your loving Violet". [*Altered from 'Ida'*] Addressed to Hector Balgarnie. Hotel? The note is given to K instead of to F. K jumps on the motor; persuades E that it is all right; and is duly landed in the garden. K rouses E's suspicions by pumping him as to Y's surname. Y arrives & E asks her is K the gentleman she expected. No, says K, I am that gentleman's father, I guess. E highly indignant at being had—insists on getting the note back & delivering it—even hints that for two pins he would put K on the motor & take him back to the hotel. Y, alarmed, soothes him & he goes off evidently to give the note to F & warn him.

Sc 2 Y & K. K warns Y that if F marries her he will not have a rap. Y, much offended, defends her social position. K expatiates on the cheapness of the English middle class & explains that if one marries a middle class woman, the American article is better than the English. She says her brother is a poet & author, & this rather impresses him; but he observes that a poet is an object of charity rather than of [sic] an instrument of legitimate family ambition. He regards England as the longlost heritage of the American & will have nothing but the best of it. Motor heard. F arrives.

Sc 3 F K Y. F accuses his dad of dishonorable conduct in opening the letter & makes an affectionate compliment of not cutting & disowning him. Says its vulgar & that if polite English society heard of it there would be an end of his social chances. Distinctly plays for making the letter a guilty secret & blackmailing his parent into consenting to his marriage. Blood gets up: there is a row, in the middle of which the others return from the Alhambra—all except A & Z.

Sc 4 ABC ZVWU & FKY—To them K furiously announces that he forbids F to marry Y—that if he does so he will be a beggar. Hereupon C naïvely lets out the fact that he need not be alarmed, as Y is married already. The murder now comes out. F avows his marriage & declares hotly that Y is married to a beggar anyhow, as never will he accept one farthing from K. K now falls into the extremity of concern for his boy. "Dont be rash, Hector, my boy: Dont be hard upon father. I'm sorry for what I said &c" F is adamant. All entreat him—in vain. Y tries a little in a pouting way; but F takes the highest sentimental ground & makes a heroic exit to seek work. B sympathizes—is deeply moved—Y is furious with B & sympathizes so enormously with K that she quite converts him to her side. She conveys to him that though his son will take nothing from him, his daughter-in-law will take all she can get.

Sc 5 B & Z—the approach of night

Sc 6 last—see opposite—No 1.

ON SHAW'S "MAN WHO STANDS NO NONSENSE" (1904)

One of Shaw's many autobiographical touches in *Man and Superman* appears in Act II just after Jack Tanner has eloquently exhorted Ann to make a Declaration of Independence from her mother. Watching him with quiet curiosity, she responds, "I suppose you will go in seriously for politics some day, Jack." Punctured, he can barely sputter—"Eh? What? Wh—? . . . What has that got to do with what I have been saying?"—to which she replies, "You talk so well" (2: 599).

This incident enriches one of the play's comic motifs: Tanner and Don Juan discover that others often hear their eloquence more than what they say, and at the end of the play when Tanner takes off on yet another torrent of words, Ann's fond pride in his talking, capped by his response—"Talking!"—sparks *"universal laughter."* Joining in, Shaw was laughing at his own famous loquaciousness, and much as Ann imagines a political career for Tanner, his wife imagined one for him. At the same time, Shaw's self-laughter signals his sensitivity to the great gap between words and deeds. What, after all, does either Tanner or Juan *do*?

To fill such a gap personally, Shaw had served for five years on the Vestry and the Borough Council of St. Pancras. Much of *Man and Superman* was written after busy mornings in council chambers. When he at last finished the play in 1903 the issue of greater public service loomed. At first he dodged it: "I am on three committees and two subcommittees of the B.C. [Borough Council]; and I am on two committees of the Fabian Society. And I have a profession which demands the undivided energy of ten men to do it justice. . . . I have other fish to fry."[7] In arguing against Free Trade that September, however, he rhetorically adopted the voice of a Labor member of Parliament, and by December found himself writing Henry John Tozer, a member of the council of the Passmore Edwards Settlement, about a position on the London County Council: "If you can do no better, I am willing to contest the seat" (*Collected Letters 1898–1910*, pp. 370–371, 378).

The upshot tested his mettle: selected by the Progressive Committee in the first week of January 1904, Shaw plunged into the race, only to be brought up short by his inability to corral a running mate. In early

February, after six failures, he at last landed a willing soul, but his man came with a handicap: "My colleague is a baronet . . . He knows nothing of local politics, and I shall have to do everything."[8] That was what he proceeded to do, composing and printing an election address for himself and the baronet, plus a slew of electioneering materials. His postcard appeal to volunteers gives an inkling of his activity: "I am one of the Progressive candidates in South St. Pancras for the London County Council. My colleague is Sir WILLIAM NEVILL GEARY. . . . There will be a stiff fight; and we shall need all the help we can get. There are 14,000 envelopes to be addressed, 7,000 polling cards to be filled in, 7,000 voters to be canvassed. . . . Helpers, carriages and motor cars in unlimited numbers wanted for polling day, the 5th March."[9]

Despite this immense display of energy, Shaw revealed the toll that the campaign took on him in letters to Siegfried Trebitsch—on 5 February, "I am distracted with work, and until after the 5th March I shall have no time for anything. I hope I shall be defeated"—and on 16 February, "I live a dog's life: cursed be all elections for ever and ever! Nothing is worse than giving your whole attention to things that do not really interest you at all. Even the chicanery ceases to be amusing after the first few *coups*."[10]

Under the circumstances, it seems he should have been delighted when he lost, but he sent an opposite signal to Trebitsch on 14 March: "I have been defeated—wiped out—annihilated at the polls, mostly through the stupidity of my own side. Consequently I am perfectly furious. . . . And everybody is delighted—openly and indecently delighted—at my discomfiture."[11]

Michael Holroyd, conjecturing that Shaw campaigned with a jocular lack of tact in order "to make *absolutely certain* of not getting in," believes that his disappointment was pretense.[12] The great effort Shaw devoted to so many details of the campaign, however, suggests a more ambiguous reality: quite possibly he wanted to win and to lose at the same time. In any event, literature may count its blessings that he lost. Starting the next month, Harley Granville Barker produced six matinees of *Candida* at the Royal Court Theatre, launching the many seasons that established Shaw's reputation on the English stage; and in June Shaw began *John Bull's Other Island*, which was followed, a year after his political trouncing, by *Major Barbara*.

In the most wearing days of Shaw's electioneering, a much smaller flash of good luck occurred that, next to his loss, was probably the campaign's most worthy legacy. On 19 February 1904, Shaw wrote George E. Gladstone, Election Committee secretary for the Progressives, about the fanatic, excessively industrious Henry John Tozer, whom he had contacted in the first place about the County Council seat: "The impetuous Tozer has simply taken all the humanity out of my polling instructions. The free & independent voter wont be hustled about like that. It reads like Instructions for Reading the Gas Meter. When Tozer's political bigotry is roused, he has the manners of a policeman who has just been run over at a crossing. On polling day, if I can borrow a 100 h.p. Mors, I shall give it to him to drive: he will scatter death and destruction through the hostile ranks & snatch up and bear away voters of all denominations to the poll. . . . You are his Warden: exhort him; wrestle with his bad angel; and tame him for me. Ask Mrs. Gladstone to play the piano to him for an hour a day until the election: he must be softened at all costs; for his energy makes him indispensable."[13]

To dramatically enforce his request and, perhaps, to give himself a moment of comic relief during that exhausting time, Shaw enclosed the following playlet with his letter. The polling instructions he refers to are probably ones he drafted and Tozer edited, appearing on a card titled "Plain Directions for Voters of All Parties" that reads in part: "Ladies, and those who have never voted before, are sometimes prevented from voting by not knowing how easy it is, and how strictly the privacy of the voter is respected."[14]

Could Henry Tozer be one of those whose stupidity annihilated Shaw at the polls, and thus one to whom the world should be forever grateful?

The Man Who Stands No Nonsense: A Drama (1904)

[PROVENANCE: Typewritten manuscript, one leaf, signed "G. Bernard Shaw" and dated "19th February 1904." Dwight V. Strong Collection, Department of Special Collections, California State University at Fullerton.]

Scene 1. Street outside polling station. Tozer on guard.
ENTER a Voter, looking at Tozer mistrustfully.

TOZER (sternly) The voting is strictly secret.
VOTER (cowed) Yes, govner. No offence, I hope.
TOZER Voting is quite easy and takes only half a minute. When you get inside the polling station give your number and name & a ballot paper will be handed to you. Take the ballot paper to the desk, which looks like a telegraph office—
VOTER Garn! Ow can a desk look like a telegraph office?
TOZER (ignoring the illbred interruption)—and mark the paper carefully.
VOTER (again intimidated) Right, govner (moves slowly to door of station).
TOZER (sarcastically) There is no need to hurry. (VOTER bolts into station.
TOZER follows him up relentlessly, and scene changes to interior of station with officials &c.). You can vote for only two candidates.

VOTER Dont be so cruel ard on a poor uneddicated man, govner. Strike me blind if I ever thought of trying to vote for more.

TOZER (not in the least softened) Put one X against the name of *each* Progressive candidate. (VOTER, not knowing which are the Progressive candidates, marks all four). Do not put any other mark on the paper & do not sign your name.

VOTER Not for the world, govner. Is that all?

TOZER If you spoil a ballot paper, ask for another.

VOTER (doubtfully) Praps the hother govner might regard it as a liberty.

TOZER When you have properly (he emphasizes the word properly so sharply that the VOTER trembles) marked your paper, fold it and hand it to the presiding officer.

VOTER (humbly) I will, govner. All I wish is to do wots right.

A LADY (pitying the poor VOTER) That man is one of your warmest supporters, Mr Tozer.

TOZER (implacably) It is best for everyone, especially (with withering emphasis) ladies, to *vote as early as possible*. Those who wait till the last 10 minutes may not be able to record their votes, owing to the crowd.

THE LADY I am perfectly aware of that, Mr Tozer; and I will not be ordered about by you or anybody. (She flounces out, and leaves TOZER dumb with amazement at the effect of his well meant instructions. The scene again changes to the street outside. The VOTER is sneaking away, almost in tears. Enter to him another voter).

VOTER (trying to look unconcerned) Wot O, Bill.

SECOND VOTER Wot O! Bin votin?

VOTER Just done it.

SECOND VOTER Wots it like?

VOTER No more for me, not never. Treats you like a dorg. Wipes their boots on you. Go in and see.

SECOND VOTER Not me. That ere Shorr an is baronit was larfin at me wen they mide me promise. One's as bad as t'other.

VOTER Blighters the ole bally lot of em. Come an ave a drink.

(Exeunt).

ON SHAW'S "TRINITY V JACKSON" (1912)

In his mid-forties from 1898 to 1904, Shaw's life and career shifted in major ways. Consider, for a start, the cataclysms of the spring of 1898: he broke down physically; gave up theater reviewing, lecturing, Fabian committees, and St. Pancras Vestry work; married; and acquiesced to Charlotte's spiriting him away for an extended honeymoon-convalescence in the countryside. The convalescence—five months in Haslemere, eight months in the nearby town of Hindhead, a month at the seashore, and a six-week Mediterranean cruise—gave him the longest stretch of leisure in his adult life, more than a year for writing and weighing priorities. Aside from injuries in the first weeks, most memorable were the months at Hindhead, in a house he later used as a setting for *Misalliance*: "*The house is in Surrey, on the slope of Hindhead . . . a barren but lovely landscape of hill profile with fir trees, commons of bracken and gorse, and wonderful cloud pictures*" (2: 421).

Among the friendships Shaw made there, the warmest and most enduring was with Frederick Jackson, who gave him a plot for *Captain Brassbound's Conversion,* and became the model for a character in his scenario of *Man and Superman.* Jackson had retired to an estate in Hindhead in 1890. He was twenty-four years older than Shaw, but his Dickensian eccentricities and his interests made him magnetic. He was independent, opinionated, old-fashioned, used to getting his own way, and a touch irascible, but he loved music and had a generous spirit, an open heart, and a keen appetite for friendship. Formerly a solicitor and teacher, he was now a political essayist under the pseudonym "Vox Clamans"—an appellative calling up John the Baptist in John 1:23: "I am the voice of one crying in the wilderness."

In the domesticated wilderness of Surrey, Jackson became a telling crier at a crucial juncture in Shaw's life. Writing Graham Wallas on 24 August 1899, Shaw reflected on his advice: "All this committee work is nothing but being lazy by public machinery. . . . Jackson the Sage said to me the other day when I said something about keeping in contact with life and experience by public work & the like, 'Why, man, youre *bilious* with a surfeit of life & experience. Go and use your imagination whilst it's in its prime.' I pass the admonition on to you" (*Collected Letters 1898–1910,* p. 100). And one year later in notes on *Captain Brassbound's Conversion,* Shaw revealed how much the advice had sunk in by again acknowledging "Mr Frederick Jackson of Hindhead, who, against all his principles, encourages and abets me in my career as a dramatist" (2: 421).

Jackson thus sided with playwriting in Shaw's personal tug-o'-war between creative activities and hands-on public service, a conflict that led him to compose *Man and Superman* and serve on a Borough Council at the same time, then climaxed in his consuming campaign for a County Council seat he did not want to win but disliked losing, and finally subsided when he turned vigorously to playwriting and to supervising his own productions at the Court Theatre. Perhaps his creative impulses would have prevailed naturally in the long run, but Jackson's voice clearly rang in his ears when he most needed to hear it.

The warmth of their friendship comfortably spanned the new century's first decade when Shaw's schedule allowed little time for visits to Hindhead. In September 1910 he played with their relationship in writing Jackson about his voyage to the ancient monastic ruins atop Skellig Michael, a cathedral-like isle off the southwest coast of Ireland: "An incredible, impossible, mad place . . . And you talk of your Hindhead! Skellig Michael, sir, is the Forehead. . . . Hindhead! Pooh! I repeat it in your teeth. POOH!!!" (*Collected Letters 1898–1910*, pp. 941–43).

By the spring of 1912 Jackson found more transcendent matters to chew on, having read Shaw's speech on "Modern Religion," just published as a supplement to the *Christian Commonwealth*. The speech recapitulates the Creative Evolution and Life Force gist of *Man and Superman*, but takes a more specifically religious tack on humanity's potential godliness, and on the nature of God. With relish, Shaw recalls shocking the National Secular Society, the group Charles Bradlaugh had headed, in 1891: "I then said, 'Let us get at simple, scientific facts. Take . . . the Trinity, which is the most obvious common sense.' Now, in the Hall of Science the Trinity was regarded simply as an arithmetical absurdity. 'Do you mean to say,' they said, 'that one person can be three, and three persons can be one?' I replied, 'You are the father of your son and the son of your father. . . . [But, on the other hand, notice] the absurdity of conceiving God as a person with a sex—the male sex. Nowadays we see that it is ridiculous to keep saying, 'Our Father which art in heaven.' What about our Mother who art in heaven?"[15]

Like Roebuck Ramsden throwing *The Revolutionist's Handbook* into a wastebasket, Jackson commented, "I hope to write a criticism on 'Modern Religion' as soon as I have time," then pursued his own bent, promoting an essay that he himself had written about the concept of God, entitled "The Personality of X." Apparently Shaw had given his effort short shrift, prompting him to respond: "I think you make a mistake in treating the subject contemptuously. . . . The infinite greatness of the universe, and the relative smallness of man supply a ready argument for dismissing the idea of the personality of the Deity. . . . Another and even greater difficulty lies in the poverty of our language. 'He', 'she', and 'it' are definite enough, but we have no single word in which to express all these. For that reason I used 'X'. . . . Did I ever show you my scheme for the construction of a scientific language?"[16]

Shaw's schedule gave him little time to reply. Ideas about big and little and the poverty of language were hardly new to him. He was writing *Pygmalion* from March to June and *Overruled* in July. After Charlotte sailed for Italy on 12 April, he took a motor tour of northern England. On 2 May he wrote her from Windermere: "I have a vague notion of going along the Cotswolds to Bath & then east to Hindhead to see Jackson & his new musical settler Rutland Boughton; but I may have to omit this vagabondage. The lumbago is still beyond expression" (*Collected Letters 1911–1925*, pp. 89–90). Lumbago-driven, he arrived in London on

22 May. Otherwise driven, he fell in love with Stella Campbell on 26 June, then took a Continental motor tour from 27 July to 8 September (missing Jackson's eightieth birthday on 15 August) and shortly after his return confronted the serious, prolonged illnesses of his mother, Charlotte, and Stella.

In November, however, a hubbub at Hindhead caught his attention. At Shaw's contrivance early in the spring, Jackson had hired the composer Rutland Boughton as his secretary. Delighted by the young man, Jackson had accommodated him and his family with an open heart, and had savored his musical talents. Now Boughton had revealed that he was not wed to Christina Walshe, whom he had passed off as his wife, and that their three children were actually by a woman from whom he was legally separated but not divorced. The octogenarian was outraged: he had been hoodwinked into witlessly harboring, even abetting, a scandalous impropriety. And aggravating the injury, Shaw took this traumatic moment to josh his old friend and bring up "The Personality of X":

> Do you seriously expect me not to laugh?
>
> Where were your wits? I should have thought that one glance at that dear Chris would have been enough for any man of ten minutes experience. An engaged couple, perhaps. A several-years-married one, impossible.
>
> Why on earth did he not hold his silly tongue? It was not your business to know. I suppose you never asked to see Mrs. Russell's marriage certificate, or Mrs. Bulley's, or Mrs. Anyoneelse's. By blurting the thing out he makes you his accomplice in jactitation— Jackson the Jactitator.
>
> Charlotte says that if THAT enlarged your knowledge of human nature, you never had any knowledge of it. The contempt of women for our sex breaks out on these occasions.
>
> There's nothing to be done. The news must be all over the shop by this time. Your introductions were made in innocence. Technically you are bound to go round and expose the fraud. Humanly you will do nothing so ill natured; and if any mother of a family reproaches you, you can say that if the marriage laws of the country were as decent as those of all the other Protestant countries in Europe, people would not be forced into such frauds, and that, Chris. being a d----d fine girl, you would have done just the same in RB's place.
>
> All the same, I shall give the young rascal a piece of my mind for telling a lie and not sticking to it when he had involved other people in it.
>
> Dont quarrel with him: it's unbecoming at your respective (ap-

parent) ages. You provoked him by writing the words "merciful &
indulgent," as if the girl were a Magdalen. And even Magdalen
was backed up by J.C. But him you regard as a Siamese Twin.

When I have time I will dramatize the inevitable discussion of
The Personality of X on the Day of Judgment. Meanwhile, the
personality of Chris is agreeable to me; and I deny that she needs
the indulgence of the Casanova of Hindhead, *alias* F.J.[17]

Inspired by the moment, Shaw dashed off *The Trinity v Jackson*, a satirical counterpart of the Hell scene in *Man and Superman*, its contrary Don
Juan an adroit caricature of Jackson ("the Casanova of Hindhead") that
highlights Jackson's argumentative side and his domestic spoiling, and its
Archangel Gabriel incidentally sanctifying the word "bloody" that was to
rock His Majesty's Theatre when Mrs. Patrick Campbell, as Eliza Doolittle, uttered it in *Pygmalion*.

In a letter the next day, Boughton expressed appreciation for Shaw's
support, but gently defended "Jackie's" disposition in the matter, feeling
grateful for the family's acquaintance with him.[18] Miffed, not mollified
by Shaw's teasing, Jackson licked his wounds on 19 November by reiterat-
ing his previous generosity to Boughton and defending his moral sensi-
bilities against Shaw's obviously warped ones, adding, "P.S. If I could
trust you, I would send you some confidential letters, which would illu-
mine even your darkness"; and a "P.P.S. It will save my Secretary trouble
of making a copy, if you will be so good as to return the papers on 'The
Personality of X' and 'The Difference between great and small.' F.J."[19]

By the next May, fortunately, all seemed forgiven. After critiquing
Overruled as "only Congreve and water," Jackson advised Shaw that "you
need above all a change of air and scene," then recommended Provence
or the Temple of Neptune at Paestum, and signed off, "Your doting
Early Victorian Governess."[20]

There are no signs, however, of the mortal model for *The Trinity v
Jackson* ever mentioning the play.

The Trinity v Jackson (1912)

*[PROVENANCE: Unsigned holograph manuscript, in pencil on blue paper,
foliated by Shaw: 1–4, dated "Ayot | 17/11/12" at top left of first leaf. T. E.
Hanley Collection, Harry Ransom Humanities Research Center, The University
of Texas at Austin. A typewritten transcription of five unpaginated leaves, made
by Shaw's secretary Ann M. Elder, dated in Shaw's holograph "November 1912"
at foot of final leaf, is in the private collection of Charles A. Berst. Throughout
Shaw's manuscript the abbreviation for "Recording Angel" is written erroneously
as "R.C."]*

Court of Final Appeal. Before the Three Persons—

THE RECORDING ANGEL.[21] Is it any good going on today? There's a lot more.

THE 1ST PERSON. I think we might just take one more. Who's next?

THE R.C. Frederick Jackson.

THE 1ST PERSON. Where is he?

THE R.C. Asking some mountain to hide him, I should imagine, from the nature of his record.

JACKSON. (indignantly stepping into the dock) How dare you make any such observation, sir, about me? I am perfectly ready. I have been waiting for hours.

THE R.C. Short tempered old beggar, you see.

JACKSON. I protest against this. If any observations are to be made as to my character, they should be made after the verdict and before the sentence.

THE 3RD PERSON. Never mind, Mr Jackson. Time, and that sort of thing, dont matter here. For us there is neither before nor after.

THE R.C. Dont start him arguing, or we shall never have done.

JACKSON. I have a paper here on that very subject which I should like to read. (To the Angel Gabriel) Here! Hold my hat, will you?

GABRIEL. (forgetting himself) Hold your hat! you -- - ----- -- -- -- -- -- ---!!!!!!

THE 2ND PERSON. Gabriel, Gabriel, have you forgotten the Sermon on The Mount?

GABRIEL. He asked me to hold his b----- hat.

THE 2ND PERSON. Gabriel: please, PLEASE.

JACKSON. Disgraceful language. Budd would never have used it in my presence. I'm shocked—surprised.

THE R.C. Youll be more surprised before weve done with you.

THE 3RD PERSON. You may swear if you like, Mr Jackson. You can hardly suppose that it matters to us.

JACKSON. It matters to me. I insist on being treated with proper respect.

THE 1ST PERSON. You shall be, Mr Jackson. (To the R.C.) What is this gentleman's record?

THE R.C. Blasphemy, mostly.

JACKSON. Oh! Dont listen to this white feathered liar, my lord. I—

THE 1ST PERSON. One moment, Mr Jackson. You will have an opportunity later.

THE R.C. He built a room and said the proportions of it were God.

GABRIEL. Thats true. I burnt it over his head for it.

JACKSON. A gross fraud on the Insurance Company. My lords, you will understand what I meant when I explain.

THE 3RD PERSON. (with a touch a irony) Indeed, Mr Jackson?

THE R.C. While youre explaining, you may as well explain your subsequent lapse into atheism. You called God X, the unknown quantity. And you said that the Three Persons were a sort of Siamese Triplets.

JACKSON. So they are (uproar). Silence there. I must insist on silence. This is a point of the greatest interest.

MARIAN. Dont excite yourself, uncle. (She fans him with her wings)

JACKSON. Oh, is that Marian? How convenient! Just find that note on The Personality of X for me, will you? And hold my hat. And keep the sun off me with your wings. And get me some soup. And ask for a chair for me, and a cushion. And get me my overcoat: these clouds are damp.

MARIAN. Yes, uncle.

GABRIEL. (taking her by the nape of her neck & removing her to an infinite distance) No you dont, my girl.

JACKSON. How dare you, you ruffian, assault my sainted niece, to whom my life on earth was devoted?

THE R.C. Oh! (He makes an entry).

THE 2ND PERSON. I dont think the Siamese Triplets matter, do they? Really, it may have been an attempt to get at some real belief.

JACKSON. Quite so. You see, IF you had been connected, like the Siamese Twins, not only with one another but with everything else—

THE 3RD PERSON. But we were not, Mr Jackson. How do you get over that?

JACKSON. Oh, well, of course if you wont accept my premisses, you cant expect to profit by my argument. Youre as stupid as Shaw. (Thunder).

THE 1ST PERSON. (hastily) He is going to talk about Shaw.

THE 2ND PERSON. Dissolve the court.

THE 3RD PERSON. He is sentenced to clean his niece's boots continuously for a thousand years.

MARIAN. Oh no. Mercy, mercy.

EDITH.[22] It will do his soul good, Marian.

JACKSON. Ingrate. I shall get heart failure directly the brushes are brought. I never have done anything I didnt like; and I never will. I defy this silly court.

LUCIFER. Hear, hear!

JACKSON. (continuing recklessly) I deny its existence. I can prove its absurdity. Let the court be X— (The bottomless pit opens, and he is falling headlong in when Marian catches him by the boot, which comes off in her hand; but Edith swoops at a single hair which is left on his head and snatches him up into a comfortable seat near the heavenly choir. The 3 Persons, at an imploring glance from Marian, pretend not to notice him. Music and Curtain)

Notes

1. For *The Devil's Disciple* scenario, see "Shorthand Scenario," transliterated by Barbara Smoker, in *The Devil's Disciple: A Facsimile of the Holograph Manuscript* (New York: Garland, 1981): 2–13, from which the last sentence in the shorthand draft for Act II—"The curtain falls on A's exit??"—was inadvertently overlooked by the transcriber. In 1909 Shaw tried to entice G. K. Chesterton to write a play by composing a scenario for him. See Bernard Shaw, *Collected Letters 1898–1910*, ed. Dan H. Laurence (New York: Dodd, Mead, 1972), pp. 874–82. Hereafter this edition and *Collected Letters 1911–1925*, ed. Dan H. Laurence (New York: Viking, 1985), will be cited parenthetically.

2. Hannen Swaffer, *Adventures with Inspiration* (London: Kennerley, 1929), p. 28. Original holograph text of Shaw's reply is in the C. A. Berst collection.

3. Quoted in Michael Holroyd, *Bernard Shaw, Vol. 2: 1898–1918, The Pursuit of Power* (New York: Random House, 1989), p. 71.

4. The Roebuck conjecture and Adams quotation come from Arthur H. Nethercot, *Men and Supermen: The Shavian Portrait Gallery* (Cambridge: Harvard University Press, 1954), p. 298.

5. Bernard Shaw, *Collected Plays with Their Prefaces*, ed. Dan H. Laurence (London: Max Reinhardt, 1971), 2: 533, 539. Hereafter cited parenthetically.

6. For information on the chronology, see (in this order) *Collected Letters 1898–1910*, pp. 174, 5, 275–76, 279, 284, 300. Laurence reports notes for *Don Juan in Hell* in a notebook, and others for that scene and *The Revolutionist's Handbook*, dated 31/5/01, in the British Library, Add. Mss. 50735, 50727. As possible sources for the play besides Shaw's autobiographical short story, "Don Giovanni Explains" (1887), Laurence records the six-week Mediterranean cruise the Shaws took on 21 September 1899, from which they made "an expedition up country to Granada" and the Sierra Nevada (*Collected Letters 1898–1910*, p. 104). At sea, Shaw read Wilfrid Scawen Blunt's *Satan Absolved* (see *Collected Letters 1898–1910*, pp. 111–14). Furthermore, on 27 February 1900 at the Prince of Wales's Theatre, John Martin-Harvey presented and starred in *Don Juan's Last Wager*, translated from José Zorrilla's 1844 play, *Don Juan Tenorio*.

7. TLS to F.H. Cripps-Day, 7 July 1903, in Berst collection.

8. In *Bernard Shaw's Letters to Siegfried Trebitsch*, ed. Samuel A. Weiss (Stanford: Stanford University Press, 1986), pp. 66–67.

9. See Dan H. Laurence, *Bernard Shaw: A Bibliography* (Oxford: Clarendon Press, 1983), 1:58–62. Volunteers card in Berst collection.

10. *Letters to Trebitsch*, p. 67.

11. Ibid, p. 68.

12. Holroyd, *Bernard Shaw, vol. 2: The Pursuit of Power*, pp. 46–47.

13. ALS, in Dwight V. Strong Collection, Library of California State University, Fullerton. The racing cars of Émile Mors, a French electrical engineer, first manufactured in Paris in 1895, were 4-cylinder open two-seaters, designed by Henri Blasier, with a slow-revving 9.2 liter engine, capable of speeds up to 77 m.p.h. They won several major distance races between 1899 and 1905.

14. *Shaw Bibliography*, 1:60.

15. In *The Religious Speeches of Bernard Shaw*, ed. Warren S. Smith (University Park: Penn State University Press, 1963), pp. 40–42.

16. ALS (dictated), 11 April 1912. British Library Add. Mss. 50539, fols. 10–12.

17. ALS, 17 November 1912, in Berst collection.

18. ALS, 18 November 1912. British Library Add. Mss. 50529, fols. 69–72.

19. ALS (dictated), 19 November 1912. British Library Add. Mss. 50539, fols. 19–20.

20. ALS, 3 May 1913. British Library Add. Mss. 50539, fols. 21–22. In the 1916 preface to *Overruled* Shaw made a veiled allusion to Jackson's comments on the play, identifying him only as "an earnest and distinguished British moralist."

21. Speakers' names are written in capitals and lower case in the holograph manuscript, and in uniform capitals in the typescript copy. The capitals are used here for readability as well as for uniformity with Shaw's use of capitals in "The Man Who Stands No Nonsense."

22. Relationship undetermined.

REVIEWS

REVIEWS

Guided Tour Through *Heartbreak House*

A. M. Gibbs. *Heartbreak House: Preludes of Apocalypse.* New York: Twayne Publishers, 1994, 151 pp. + xvii. Illus. Index. $22.95 (cloth), $12.95 (paper).

Among the several bonuses provided by this, the latest contribution to Shaw criticism by the Australian scholar, A. M. Gibbs, and the second of Twayne's Masterwork Studies devoted to a Shaw play—an annotated select bibliography, a chronology of Shaw's career in relation to *Heartbreak House,* an appendix listing major productions and casts—the best bonus is the selection of illustrations. There is a flamboyant Punch drawing of Leon Quartermaine and Edith Evans as Hector and Ariadne (from the 1932 London revival) and its style makes the play seem very much part of the Noël Coward world. But the photo-reproduction of (not-then-Sir) Cedric Hardwicke as Captain Shotover with a mad white mane and burning eyes shows that already in 1932 the character was being thought of as Shaw's Lear. There is also an atmospheric picture of Henry Travers as Billy Dunn (in the 1920 New York premiere), where the conception of the part is clearly that of an over-the-hill hooligan, very much the drinking Dunn. (Unfortunately, the photo of the interesting set for that same production is reproduced in so reduced a state that one can only just make it out.)

But these bonuses merely decorate a substantial and innovative discussion of Shaw's most elusive and ambiguous (still) play. It is a tribute to Professor Gibbs's skills as a scholar and critic that his exposition of the matrices from which the play came—biographical, historical, social, and literary—and his analyses of the play's symbolism, dramaturgy, ideas, and characters do much to reduce the mystery of *Heartbreak House.*

Gibbs begins by providing the literary, theatrical, and historical context in which the play was written, as well as a survey of the critical responses to the play since its premiere. He notes that the origin of the play in Shaw's mind most likely came from Lena Ashwell's account of the retirement of her father, Commander Charles Ashwell Pocock, R.N., after a life of exotic travels, to a ship converted into a house. He also demonstrates how the play at first generated fairly exasperated responses but thereafter gradually garnered more admiring reviews until it reached its current high position with audiences and actors, and with theater and academic critics. The meat of the monograph, however, lies in the much longer section called "A Reading," which is divided into four chapters: "A Chamber of Echoes" (a shorter version of which was published in *SHAW* 13), "Discontinuities," "Symbolism and the Supernatural," and "Preludes of Apocalypse."

Gibbs reads the central theme of the play thus: "Heartbreak is ultimately seen not as a negative state but as a release from the bondage of desire—a painful stage on the path to tranquility. . . . The escape from desire and hope that lies beyond heartbreak, the removal of the goals of happiness and security that come about when 'your boats are burned,' is seen by Ellie as creating for her new and unlimited powers of achievement." That is essentially Shavian, converting the moment of greatest sorrow into the moment of greatest power: the misfortunes of life are as nothing to heartbreak. Perhaps that paradox of heartbreak making strength accounts for the difficulty of reconciling the play's apparent wish for destruction with its enthusiastic ending.

While *Heartbreak House* may present the greatest challenge to would-be interpreters of its mysteries, it is surrounded by evidence of its cousins and connections among Shaw's letters, his experiences, and his reading, even among fairy tales. And of these relationships Gibbs makes the most. For the biographical connections, Gibbs relies mainly on the letters, and shows elaborately how Mrs. Patrick Campbell and Shaw's fiery feelings toward her nourished the portrayal, on the one hand, of Ariadne and Hector's assessment of her amorous ethics, and on the other, Hesione's capacity to reduce grown men to the level of babies. Gibbs (following Margot Peters's lead) views Shaw's troubled relationship with the young Erica Cotterill as the source of Ellie's attachment to Captain Shotover.

Although this biographical background is interesting and valuable, more valuable still is Gibbs's investigation of *Heartbreak House's* connections with Shaw's reading in the novels of the Victorians and in the drama of his contemporaries. Most fascinatingly, Gibbs links the Shotover shiphouse to precedents in Dickens, Austen, and Peacock, showing that Shaw travesties Dan Peggotty's clean and tidy 'arc-like' house in *David Copperfield* and Captain Harville's hospitable house, which looks out to sea in *Persuasion,* but mimics the mad country houses of *Nightmare Abbey* and *Crotchet Castle.*

Besides detailing the links between *Heartbreak House* and both *The Cherry Orchard* and *The Father,* Gibbs reviews the influence of *King Lear* and *Othello* on the play. Several of the Shakespeare connections have already been made by Weintraub and Meisel among others, but Gibbs always adds to what he recapitulates as when he compares the scene where Mangan is bound to a chair by hypnotism and cruelly discussed by Ellie and Hesione to the scene in *King Lear* where Gloucester is bound to a chair and his eyes gouged out by Cornwall at Regan's urging (with, Gibbs says, the attendance and assistance of Goneril—he has forgotten that Goneril is not present at the binding and gouging).

Gibbs has much to offer about the play's use of archetypal material. For example, Gibbs details the way Ellie resembles Goldilocks (one of Hesione's nicknames for Ellie, of course), not merely in her physical appearance, but also in her ambiguous nature, naive and innocent sleeper to begin with but interloper and usurper later. Given this duality in her nature, I think Gibbs too readily agrees with Peter Ure that the play as Ellie's dream hardly works out; we have not yet had a critic try to see if it works out.

In the next to last chapter, Gibbs illuminates the apocalyptic motif in the play by drawing on Lawrence's novels from the same period, *Kangaroo* and *Women in Love,* and noting their sense that because of World War I both individual character and social unity had disintegrated. Gibbs sees this disintegration reflected in Shaw's experiments with fluidity of characterization and structure in *Heartbreak House.*

Prior to the appearance of Gibbs's reader's companion to *Heartbreak House,* the best guides to the play were J. L. Wisenthal's and Margery Morgan's chapters on the play in *The Marriage of Contraries* and *The Shavian Playground,* respectively, but Gibbs's monograph is a worthy extension of their work and the most convenient compendium of sources, contexts, and interpretations of this, Shaw's most impenetrable play. Let us hope Twayne will continue this series with more guides as good as this one to Shaw's other major plays.

John A. Bertolini

Benn Levy and Shaw

Susan Rusinko. *The Plays of Benn Levy: Between Shaw and Coward.* Ruther-ford: Farleigh Dickinson University Press, 1994. 220 pp. Illus. Index. $36.50.

Early in 1960 the English playwright Benn Wolfe Levy had a play, *The Tumbler,* reworking in modern terms the Agamemnon legend, running at the Helen Hayes Theatre on Broadway. That March he turned up at a concert reading at the Grolier Club constituting the first American per-formance of Shaw's "A Glimpse of the Domesticity of Franklyn Barna-bas." The thinly veiled G. K. Chesterton spoof had been excised from *Back to Methuselah* but published later, with Shaw's short fiction, in his collected edition.

The Chesterton role of the pompous Immenso Champernoon was played brilliantly from his usual wheelchair by comedian Michael Flan-ders, weaned on Shaw himself and on a night off from his long-running *At the Drop of a Hat.* He alone would have drawn a crowd, but he was also backed by such volunteers as Celeste Holm, Viveca Lindfors, and Kevin McCarthy.

I counted my blessings at a bit of standing room, but my wife Rodelle recalls sharing a bench intending to seat two—the audience packed the place—with Charlton Heston (who had the lead in *The Tumbler,* with Rosemary Harris) and someone else she thought had introduced himself as the playwright Ben Hecht. She had not yet heard of Benn Levy, although his first American success was *Art and Mrs. Bottle* (1931; first London production in 1929). His comedy, *Clutterbuck,* had become a staple of summer theaters and Edward Everett Horton had already made a career of *Springtime for Henry,* first produced in 1931.

That was always Benn Levy's ill-luck. Playgoers remembered the hits of this stylish and many-faceted contemporary of Rattigan and Coward, but seldom his name.

Susan Rusinko's lucid and lively *The Plays of Benn Levy* will now correct that. Levy had learned from Shaw and continued the process of liberat-ing the theater from what Shaw had labeled "Sardoodledom." In *Art and Mrs. Bottle,* as Rusinko writes, "in a manner evocative of Shaw's *Major Barbara,* . . . a father returns to reacquaint himself with his family. Like Undershaft, who is unsure whether Stephen or Adolphus Cusins (Dolly) is his son, Celia is uncertain about which of the two women, Judy and Sonia, is her daughter."

Levy's range was eclectic. After World War I flying service, Oxford, and the beginnings of a publishing career, he had his first stage success with *This Woman Business,* about five self-described misogynists who retire to a country house to escape female company. Rusinko sees the play's dialogue and its reliance upon paradoxes as a "Shavian style." The duels of sex, the reversals, the character (a woman this time) who, like John Tarleton in *Misalliance,* is quick to quote authorities, all suggest Shaw— and like G.B.S., Levy was attacked for "lack of movement."

Noël Coward, almost Levy's exact contemporary, also began with a play so much like Shaw—it was *The Young Idea*—that G.B.S. returned the script to Coward, suggesting that he find his own voice. But Levy spoke in many voices—problem plays, plays of ideas, modernizations of myth, Feydeau farces, verse dramas, comedies of manners, musical libretti, television melodramas. His fate, however, was not to put his stamp on any one of them so memorably as to be—in the manner of Coward's witty, geometrically designed comedies—identified with a manner or a mode of his own. And when the post-Rattigan generation of angry and absurd young men came along, Levy's plays went into eclipse. By the season of the myth-based play that brought him to New York, and his seat on the bench at the Grolier, his career had given way to the Osbornes and Pinters. And *The Tumbler,* despite its stellar cast, had withered at the box office. There would still be the Broadway production of *The Rape of the Belt* later that year—in London a high comedy of 1957—but only one more new play (*Public and Confidential,* 1966) would follow.

Levy died in 1973, four years after a Bristol production of his 1937 play *The Poet's Heart,* in which Tim Piggott-Smith and Jeremy Irons had their first big roles. Although Levy had already put his Shavian heart on his sleeve in a number of plays, *The Poet's Heart: A Life of Don Juan* even borrowed its title from the last line of *Candida* and the dream interlude of *Man and Superman,* from which its mixture of the realistic and the abstract was derived. Even the characters recall Shaw's, and the aging hero, a John Tanner figure grown old, confesses, "Seekers after love are seekers after happiness. I want more than happiness." The play weaves in and out of the *Don Giovanni* characters and plot adapted by Shaw, complete to a statue of a general, and in its prose-poetry and fantasy it is a morality play that can stand respectably with Shaw. Yet when one wants G.B.S., why go for a facsimile? It was Levy's problem throughout his life.

Despite its derivative quality, *This Woman Business* (1925) had shown remarkable maturity for a new playwright of twenty-five. Yet he had actually written it at eighteen! After it, among the adaptations, farces, and problem plays, came high comedies of ideas in the manner of Shaw and Giraudoux, which made contemporary and relevant the stuff of myth. The first was the fey Barriesque *Mrs. Moonlight* (1928), which also has a Shavian theme in dealing with the arrest of aging; the last would be *The Rape of the Belt* and *The Tumbler,* in 1957 and 1960, *Rape* evolving from the ninth labor of Hercules and *Tumbler* from the Agamemnon story. In *Rape,* the retelling of the seizure of the belt of Antiope the Amazon, Rusinko observes, Levy has reversed the setting of his first play, as *Rape* takes place "on matriarchal territory." But when the Amazons do battle on male terms Antiope sees self-betrayal and refuses to accept the return of the belt, saying, "Even if I took it, it would no longer be ours. We have betrayed it." And they part "in Shavian style," Antiope telling Heracles, "You—are a man. . . . You carry the heavy past on your back, so yours is a world of fear. . . . "

"You are a true woman," Heracles answers. "You carry the future under your heart, so yours is a world of hope. . . . "

The playful philosophic debate in the tradition of mythological burlesque sometimes falls into the prosaic, but it largely works. Rusinko feels that the comedy stands up well to Jean Giraudoux's *Amphitryon 38* (1929), which is high praise. And it did run more than a year, with one of its leads Constance Cummings, Levy's wife, who acted in his plays from 1936 onward and may have inspired some of Levy's strong yet attractive female roles. (Without her generosity in making documentation available, Rusinko acknowledges, her book could not have been written.)

Elected to the first postwar Parliament in 1945, Levy served in the Commons for a full term, until 1950, returning then to playwriting but remaining outspoken on public issues. Fortunately for his work in the theater, he did not feel that he had to pack all his polemics into his plays, which retain their grace, and often, too, the inconclusive endings he saw as more like life than audience-pleasing formulas.

Rusinko, the author of books on Pinter, Stoppard, and Rattigan, and of a book on modern English theater, does not narrate Levy's life, as her study focuses upon the plays, but the life reveals itself nevertheless in the development of his work for the stage, in the chronology, and even in the illustrations. Levy in the Royal Navy in World War II, with his wife and children on the beach, in a bust by Jacob Epstein, furnish a different aspect of the man than do stills from the theater. Yet the book is by no means a hagiographical handling of the plays. Rusinko looks hard at Levy's excesses of subplots and prolongations of jokes, his tendency to let characters "inhabit the ideas, rather than vice versa," his use of Briticisms that fail to cross the Atlantic intelligibly. Benn Levy emerges whole, and Rusinko may, indirectly, spur reassessments and revivals of plays that make him an English equivalent of S. N. Behrman, Robert Sherwood, or Philip Barry, all who also owed something to Shavian comedies of manners and ideas. Coward never left the stage and Rattigan is back. Levy's return may come.

Stanley Weintraub

Bernard Shaw: Socialist and Dramatist

Tracy C. Davis. *George Bernard Shaw and the Socialist Theatre*. Westport, Conn., and London: Greenwood Press/Praeger, 1994. 184 pp. + xxii. Illus. Index. $59.95 (cloth), $16.95 (paper).

Davis's book purports to be an analysis of Shaw as a political dramatist, supplemented by some incidental discussion of his views on women and on imperialism as they relate to his plays. Such a study could explore new territory, especially as it would analyze the tensions in Shaw between the socialist and the artist. The book is too diffuse, however, to be definitive, and it does not dislodge such books as Erich Strauss's *Shaw and Socialism* (1942 and 1949) and Paul A. Hummert's *Shaw's Marxist Romance* (1973). The book also tends to be overly attentive to biographical matters that often have only a tangential relevance to Davis's alleged main concerns. Shaw's late-nineteenth-century political views are cogently analyzed in her presentation of the ideas of Sidney Trefusis, the loosely autobiographical protagonist of *An Unsocial Socialist*. She too often loses sight, however, of relating these ideas to Shaw's later work in drama, and she skirts too briefly Shaw's modifications of Marxism (under the influence of Stanley Jevons) and his later subsuming of his socialism into his philosophy of Creative Evolution. Neither does she dwell on the generally recognized tensions in Shaw's twentieth-century dramatic and nondramatic works between the evolutionary (or Fabian) and the revolutionary (partly Marxian) impulses as he became progressively disillusioned with liberal democracy. One often has the feeling that Davis's book, after all, is not greatly concerned with Shaw as a political dramatist.

The strengths of Davis's book lie in some of its incidental aspects and insights rather than in its overall conceptions and execution. Her discussion of the Stage Society and its relation to the Independent Theatre Society and the Vedrenne-Barker seasons at the Royal Court Theatre is illuminating, as is her review of the forces and personalities involved in the foundation of a national theater in Britain. Her presentation of Shaw's views on women is interesting, and her analysis of *Captain Brassbound's Conversion* from both a feminist perspective and from an imperialistic and postcolonial one has cogency. Occasional judgments in passing are challenging, when, for example, she sees Ann Whitefield not so much as a disruptive agent in Tanner's life as one who is absorbed finally into his system (and society's), which defines the ultimate role of a woman as domestic—as being the caretaker of her husband's family. Then, too, Davis's aligning of the spirited but finally defeated Joan of Arc with the energetic, the visionary, and the defeated suffragettes in the early twentieth century is refreshing. Her use of unpublished materials and of out-of-the-way sources is often much to the point, and her bibliographical essays indicate the breadth and scope of her research and are valuable both to the beginning scholar and to the advanced Shavian.

With so much going for her and her book, one regrets that it is not a better one. The style is often awkward and opaque; one is sometimes puzzled by the exact meaning of a given sentence. More damaging is her lack of enthusiasm for her subject and her begrudging attitude toward Shaw and his work. All too often she adopts the same attitudes toward Shaw as did his earlier critics and uses their outdated judgments of his works (and personality) to support her own views. Her remark that only a handful of his plays is now read is hardly true, and her assertion at the end of her book that Shaw lived too long is a bit ungracious. And how about the tone of this statement in a discussion of *Widowers' Houses:* "it lacks the raisonneur who made some of his later plays as tedious as their message was unmistakable." The statement is not only belittling but scarcely accurate since Shaw's plays are most often a debate among several individuals, with the truth not being lodged in a single "raisonneur" but emerging from a synthesis of contrasting ideas and values expressed by the different characters. A true Shavian would not say that Shaw began writing *Widowers' Houses* in 1888 nor that he died at ninety-six. Nor would such a scholar misspell the name of Lord Summerhays (a delicious name to indicate the vacuousness of this character in *Misalliance*) as Lord Summerhay. In supporting Beatrice Webb's judgment that *Misalliance* is an erotic farce unredeemed by the "intellectual brilliancy" of the dialogue, Davis reveals not only a distrust of the broadly comic but her own lack of knowledge of theater history. Since World War II this play has been saved from the blindness of academic critics by its success in performance, and it is now established as a classic play in the modern repertoire. An insensitivity to Shaw's comic inventiveness and his geniality in the theater also prompts her to support Kate Terry Gielgud's 1899 appraisal of *You Never Can Tell* as a failure because it mixes the comic with the tragic. Most modern critics would regard this fusion of genres as one of Shaw's great strengths. And finally J. L. Wisenthal in his introductory remarks to *Shaw and Ibsen* disproves her assertion that Shaw ceased to be an active proselytizer for Ibsen after *The Quintessence of Ibsenism* (1891), at least until he began as drama critic for the *Saturday Review* in early 1895.

Davis's misguided remarks on *Major Barbara* reveal most crucially her failure to understand Shaw, and anyone ignorant of this great play would scarcely be tempted to read it after consulting Davis's account. She seems to have mistaken propaganda for art in her extolling of Galsworthy's *Justice* over *Major Barbara*. Galsworthy's play, she says, led to actual prison reforms whereas Shaw's play did not do so, at least directly, nor did it "inspire Balfour or any other politician to improve social amenities in the East End." Instead of Galsworthy's use of careful arguments, she maintains, Shaw "preferred to lavish verbal wit on circumstances teetering on the frontiers of the farcical." Davis also cites Winston Churchill's high opinion of *Justice* and its influence upon his prisons report, but she neglects to mention Churchill's glowing remarks on *Major Barbara* when he saw it again after twenty years: "there was not a character requiring to be redrawn, nor a sentence nor a suggestion that was out of date. My children were astounded to learn that this play, the very acme of modernity, was written more than five years before they were born." Elsewhere Davis asserts that in *Major Barbara* Shaw, unlike Galsworthy and Granville-Barker in their dramatic works, failed to perfect the naturalistic technique, but revealed instead a penchant for allegory. Davis does not realize fully that just this faculty in Shaw for creating living characters that are also embodiments of timeless archetypes gives to them a universal aspect and causes his plays to resonate in the mind. In short, she does not respond to the mythic dimensions of Shaw's characters in this play—and elsewhere. To his credit as artist Shaw also fully dramatized social milieu and let it speak for itself, and he was often concerned with moral and metaphysical issues at the expense of the purely political.

It is rather late in the day, I think, to patronize in a concluding discourse the second greatest dramatist in English by describing his plays in this manner: "Most of his major dramatic works are hybrids or montages of stump speech, journalistic op-ed, and thesis play peppered with jokes and lengthy diatribes." In her concluding remarks Davis also opines that Shaw, unlike Brecht, was unable to fuse "editorial " with "plot" to create a fully viable work of art. At least Brecht did not think so and paid Shaw the compliment of drawing upon *Major Barbara* and *Saint Joan* for his *Saint Joan of the Stockyards*. It is as if Davis had never considered the work of the distinguished modern critics of Shaw such as Eric Bentley, Louis Crompton, Bernard F. Dukore, Charles A. Berst, Maurice Valency, Alfred Turco, Jr., and J. L. Wisenthal, all of whom have collectively established Shaw as a preeminent dramatic artist. If she had done so, she might have approached her subject at once more lightly and more seriously, and thus used to better effect the abundant materials at her disposal.

Frederick P. W. McDowell

John R. Pfeiffer*

A CONTINUING CHECKLIST OF SHAVIANA

I. WORKS BY SHAW

Shaw, Bernard. *Arms and the Man,* in *Literature: Reading Fiction, Poetry, Drama, and the Essay.* Edited by Robert DiYanni. Third edition. New York: McGraw-Hill, 1994. Also includes an extract from a G.B.S. piece titled "Interpreter of Life." Not seen.

———. *Bernard Shaw and H. G. Wells.* Edited by J. Percy Smith. Toronto: University of Toronto Press, 1995. Letters, both published and unpublished, between G.B.S. and H. G. Wells, during forty years. To be reviewed in *SHAW* 17.

———. *Bernard Shaw: Theatrics.* Edited by Dan H. Laurence. Toronto: University of Toronto Press, 1995. Letters by G.B.S. To be reviewed in *SHAW* 17.

———. *The Complete Prefaces, Volume 2: 1914 to 1929.* Edited by Dan H. Laurence and Daniel J. Leary. London: Allen Lane, 1995. The second of three volumes. To be reviewed in *SHAW* 17.

———. Eight hitherto unknown letters to Edith Œnone Somerville. Described in Otto Rauchbauer, *The Edith Œnone Somerville Archive in Drishane: A Catalogue and an Evaluative Essay.* Dublin: Irish Manuscripts Commission, 1995. Prints extracts and full texts of the letters. Not seen.

———. Entry in Kelly's Hotel guest book. *The Book of Kelly's.* Compiled by Bill and Vonnie Kelly with Ronan Foster. Dublin: Zeus, 1995; p. 37. Facsimile of Shaw's holograph: "7th–19th August 1922—Important to Artists and Men of Letters—Rosslare Strand is one of the best in Ireland to draw or write on with a walking stick. G. Bernard Shaw 19/8/22." See Kelly, Bill, in Books and Pamphlets, below.

———. Excerpts from the Preface to *Major Barbara,* the Preface to *The Irrational Knot,* and *Pygmalion,* in *The Oxford Book of Money.* Edited by Kevin Jackson. Oxford & New York: Oxford University Press, 1995. On the subject of money: "Money is the most important thing in the world."

———. "Hedda Gabler 1890," an excerpt from *The Quintessence of Ibsenism,* in *Literature: An Introduction to Critical Reading.* Edited by Lee A. Jacobus. Upper Saddle River, N.J.: Prentice Hall, 1996. Not seen.

*Thanks to Richard E. Winslow III for discovering and supplying page copies for a number of entries in this list. Professor Pfeiffer, *SHAW* Bibliographer, welcomes information about new or forthcoming Shaviana: books, articles, pamphlets, monographs, dissertations, films, videos, reprints, and the like, citations of which may be sent to him at the Department of English, Central Michigan University, Mount Pleasant, MI 48859.

———. "Interpreter of Life." See *Arms,* above.

———. *John Bull's Other Island,* in *Modern Irish Drama.* Edited by John P. Harrington. New York & London: Norton, 1991; pp. 119–203. Included is an extract from the play's "Preface for Politicians." See also Harrington, John P., in Books and Pamphlets, below.

———. Letters to and from. *Theatrical Letters: 400 Years of Correspondence between Celebrated Actors, Actresses, Playwrights, Their Familiars, Friends, Lovers, Admirers, Enemies, Producers, Managers, and Others.* Edited by Bill Homewood. London: Marginalia Press, 1995. Includes eleven letters (listed in the following order): 1896, Ellen Terry letter to G.B.S.; 28 February 1897, Ellen Terry letter to G.B.S., answered by G.B.S. letter of 1 March 1897; 26 November 1904, G.B.S. letter to John Vedrenne, manager of the Royal Court Theatre; 29 July 1912, Mrs. Patrick Campbell letter to G.B.S., answered by G.B.S. letter of 9 August 1912; 9 November 1913, G.B.S. letter to Ellen Terry; 7 January 1918, G.B.S. letter to Mrs. Patrick Campbell; 10 June 1949, G.B.S. postcard to Arnold Wesker (young actor); and 15 March 1948, William Turner Levy letter to G.B.S.—G.B.S. wrote his answer on Levy's letter on 18 March 1948.

———. Letters to Katie Samuel. In Dan H. Laurence, "Katie Samuel: Shaw's Flameless 'Old Flame.' " *SHAW; The Annual of Bernard Shaw Studies.* Volume Fifteen. University Park: Penn State University Press, 1995. Shaw's previously unpublished correspondence to Samuel includes two hitherto unknown sets of verses addressed to her.

———. "Preface for Politicians." See *John Bull,* above.

———. *Pygmalion.* New York: Dover, 1994. Republishes the Constable (London) edition of 1916. Includes the Preface and "Sequel."

———. *Pygmalion,* in *Literature.* Fourth edition. Edited by James H. Pickering and Jeffrey D. Hoeper. New York: Macmillan, 1994. Republishes the 1941 revised edition.

———. *Pygmalion,* in *Lives Through Literature: A Thematic Anthology.* Second edition. Edited by Helane Levine Keating and Walter Levy. Englewood Cliffs, N.J.: Prentice Hall, 1995. Includes writing and discussion topics. Other plays included are by Sophocles, Shakespeare, Ibsen, Wilde, Susan Glaspell, Wile, Miller, Alice Childress, and Sam Shepard.

———. *Pygmalion,* in *The McGraw-Hill Book of Drama.* Edited by James Howe and William A. Stephany. New York: McGraw-Hill, 1995. Not seen.

———. *The Quintessence of Ibsenism.* New York: Dover, 1994. Republishes the Brentano's (New York) edition of 1904.

———. *Shaw on Music.* Edited by Eric Bentley. New York: Applause, 1995. A paperback reissue of the collection issued by Anchor Books in 1955.

———. Ten letters or extracts in *The Oxford Book of Letters.* Edited by Frank Kermode and Anita Kermode. Oxford & New York: Oxford University Press, 1995. The introduction declares that G.B.S., with Lady Mary Wortley Montagu and Horace Walpole, must be in any short list of the best letter writers in the language. Reprinted from Dan H. Laurence's four-volume *Collected Letters,* the letters included are to Gilbert Murray (14 March 1911), Mrs. Patrick Campbell (22 February 1913), Lillah McCarthy (30 July 1916), Mrs. Patrick Campbell (7 January 1918), St. John Ervine (22 May 1918), Ada Tyrrell (28 January 1928), Helen Harris (26 August 1931), Esmé Percy (20 April 1932), Edward Elgar (30 May 1933), and H. G. Wells (12 September 1943).

———. "This Is the True Joy in Life:" *All the News That's Fit!* 15 (August 1995): 7. Text (slightly altered from the "Epistle Dedicatory" to *Man and Superman*) provided without source information in this monthly health periodical. "Being used for a purpose recognized by yourself as a mighty one. Being thoroughly worn out before you are thrown on the scrap heap, and being a *force* of nature instead of a feverish, selfish little clod of ailments and grievances—complaining that the world will not devote itself to making you happy."

———. "Toast to Albert Einstein." Edited by Fred D. Crawford. *SHAW: The Annual of Bernard Shaw Studies.* Volume Fifteen. University Park: Penn State University Press, 1995.

II. BOOKS AND PAMPHLETS

Barfoot, C. C., and Rias van den Doel, editors. *Ritual Remembering: History, Myth and Politics in Anglo-Irish Drama. The Literature of Politics, The Politics of Literature: Proceedings of the Leiden IASAIL Conference.* Volume 2. Amsterdam and Atlanta: Editions Rodopi V.V., 1995. Publishes three papers on Shaw. The first, by C. C. Barfoot, "By Way of an Introduction: The Case of *Saint Joan,*" uses Shaw's treatment of the Joan story to ask and answer, "In *Saint Joan* was Shaw as interested in the conflict between the French and English as he naturally was in the centuries' old struggle between the English and the Irish, with himself as a secular Protestant Anglo-Irishman very much in the middle? Young Joan the saint to be, as one who might be seen as stirring the individual con-science against the power of the Church and even eventually against the tyranny of the State, is also regarded by the dramatist as the harbinger of those Nationalist sentiments which would trouble and confuse Europe as a whole for the next five hundred years, and in particular have marked the history of Ireland with the blood of martyrs." Barfoot appears unaware of the considerable literature on this theme. The second paper, by Stanley Weintraub, "Jesting and Governing: Shaw and Churchill," reports at length the remarkable relationship of Shaw and Churchill, retrospective for Churchill to 1897. The third paper, by Rodelle Weintraub, "Votes for Women: Bernard Shaw and the Women's Suffrage Movement," explains, "If one examines the usual source books about Shaw: The *Shaw Diaries* and *Autobiography;* the various biographies; the published *Letters,* one would come away wondering why Shaw, the Irish subversive who was so active in radical politics otherwise, had seemingly so little to do with and for the Women's Suf-frage movement. . . . As a supporter of suffrage, he is nearly absent from the Pankhurst biographies and from most books about the suffrage movement in Great Britain. But if one goes to the primary sources, writings, speeches, and plays by Shaw, one comes away with a portrait of an early, consistent advocate of full equality for women, including the right to vote."

Berst, Charles A. *Pygmalion: Shaw's Spin on Myth and Cinderella.* New York: Twayne, 1995. Not seen. From the publisher's advertisement: "Analysis of Eliza Doolittle's contribution to her own transformation. . . . Berst suggests that Shaw meant us to recognize Eliza's change as a 'mystical evolution' to womanly maturity."

Billips, Connie, and Arthur Pierce. *Lux Presents Hollywood: A Show-by-Show History of the* Lux Radio Theatre *and the* Lux Video Theatre, *1934–1957.* Jefferson, N.C., & London: McFarland, 1995. Names the cast for the 27 November 1939 production of *Pygmalion* as well as the cast for the commercials during intermissions.

Black, Martha Fodaski. *Shaw and Joyce: "The Last Word in Stolentelling."* Gainesville: Univer-sity Press of Florida, 1995. From the publisher's advertisement: "Black's detailed demon-stration of Shaw's presence in Joyce's work is so overwhelming that one can only wonder at the determination of Joyceans to ignore it all these years."—R. F. Dietrich. To be reviewed in *SHAW* 17.

Bryden, Ronald. See *You Never Can Tell,* below.

Buckalew, Flora C. "Bernard Shaw's 'Unavoidable Subject.' " *SHAW: The Annual of Bernard Shaw Studies.* Volume Fifteen. University Park: Penn State University Press, 1995.

Conlon, John J. "The Complete Prefaces, Volume I, 1889–1913" (review of *The Complete Prefaces,* edited by Dan H. Laurence and Daniel J. Leary). *Magill's Literary Annual, 1995.* Edited by Frank N. Magill. Pasadena: Salem Press, 1995; pp. 145–47.

Coogan, Tim Pat. *Eamon De Valera, The Man Who Was Ireland.* New York: HarperCollins, 1993. One Shaw reference, to an interview reproduced in the *Irish Press* (14 December 1940): "If I were in Churchill's place I should put it more philosophically. Instead of saying I will reoccupy your ports and leave you to do your damnedest, I should say—

'My dear Mr. de Valera, your policy is magnificent but is not modern statesmanship. . . . You need not consent to the Treaty; and you will share all the advantages of our victory. All you have to do is sit tight and say: "I protest! England will do the rest. So here goes." ' " De Valera was furious and denounced Shaw in an interview with the Associated Press.

Craft, Robert. *Stravinsky: Chronicle of a Friendship*. Revised and expanded. Nashville: Vanderbilt University Press, 1994. Shaw is mentioned at least eight times in Craft's entries between 1950 and 1971.

Dardis, Tom. *Firebrand: The Life of Horace Liveright*. New York: Random House, 1995. Liveright knew Shaw and read "hundreds of plays, mostly modern ones by G. B. Shaw, Arthur Pinero, and Oscar Wilde."

Dietrich, R. F. "The Newtonian Universe" (review of *George Bernard Shaw and Christopher Newton: Explorations of Shavian Theatre* by Keith Garebian). *SHAW: The Annual of Bernard Shaw Studies*. Volume Fifteen. University Park: Penn State University Press, 1995.

———. "Shaw and Yeats: Two Irishmen Divided by a Common Language." *SHAW: The Annual of Bernard Shaw Studies*. Volume Fifteen. University Park: Penn State University Press, 1995.

Dukore, Bernard F. *Barnestorm: The Plays of Peter Barnes*. New York & London: Garland, 1995. "Although Barnes is familiar with Swift and Shaw, in whose tradition of satiric comedy he belongs, he is unconscious of their direct influence on his work." In eleven additional references Shaw is more or less a touchstone for Dukore's discussion.

———. "Shaw and the Eiress" (review of *Shaw, Lady Gregory and the Abbey: A Correspondence and a Record*, edited by Dan H. Laurence and Nicholas Grene). *SHAW: The Annual of Bernard Shaw Studies*. Volume Fifteen. University Park: Penn State University Press, 1995.

———. "Trusting the Author." *SHAW: The Annual of Bernard Shaw Studies*. Volume Fifteen. University Park: Penn State University Press, 1995.

Einsohn, Howard Ira. "Ideology, Utopia, and Faith: Shaw, Ricoeur, and the Passion for the Possible." *SHAW: The Annual of Bernard Shaw Studies*. Volume Fifteen. University Park: Penn State University Press, 1995.

Esslin, Martin. "Modern Theatre, 1890–1920," in *The Oxford Illustrated History of Theatre*. Edited by John Russell Brown. Oxford & New York: Oxford University Press, 1955; pp. 341–79. Shaw's role is not elaborately represented. Esslin mentions *Arms, Caesar, Heartbreak, Man of Destiny, Superman, Misalliance, Pygmalion, Joan,* and *Widowers' Houses*.

Evans, T. F. "Shaw, Chesterton, and *Magic*." *SHAW: The Annual of Bernard Shaw Studies*. Volume Fifteen. University Park: Penn State University Press, 1995.

Fisher, James. "Edy Craig and the Pioneer Players' Production of *Mrs Warren's Profession*." *SHAW: The Annual of Bernard Shaw Studies*. Volume Fifteen. University Park: Penn State University Press, 1995.

Fishgall, Gary. *Against Type: The Biography of Burt Lancaster*. New York: Scribner's, 1995. Includes a substantial account of the film production of *Devil's Disciple*, starring Kirk Douglas as Dick Dudgeon and Lancaster as Anthony Anderson. The film opened in 1959 to bad reviews, but ranked number forty-eight among hit films of the year—a good showing. Lancaster in 1950 told columnist Sidney Skolsky that Shaw was his favorite author.

Foster, Ronan. See Kelly, Bill, below.

Friedgen, Juliette. "*Caesar and Cleopatra*." *Magill's Survey of Cinema*. Volume One. Edited by Frank N. Magill. Englewood Cliffs, N.J.: Salem Press, 1981; pp. 383–85. The film is not a classic, but has its merits, "particularly the casting of Claude Rains as Caesar and the counter-casting of Vivien Leigh as the young, feisty, spoiled Cleopatra, who provides an interesting contrast to the mature leader of the Roman Empire."

Gahan, Peter. "Ruskin and Form in *Fanny's First Play*." *SHAW: The Annual of Bernard Shaw Studies*. Volume Fifteen. University Park: Penn State University Press, 1995.

Garlan, Patsy, and Nicholas Scarim. *Wings of Fire, A Musical Play Adapted from Bernard Shaw's Saint Joan*. Not seen. Produced by the College of Marin Drama Department, Kentfield, California, 3–19 March 1995.

Gilbert, Julie. *Opposite Attraction: The Lives of Erich Maria Remarque and Paulette Goddard*. New York: Pantheon Books, 1995. In 1950 Goddard agreed to play in *Caesar* for four weeks touring Massachusetts. The last entry in Remarque's diary, 7 March 1965, reads, "Movie version of *Zorba the Greek* is one of those false myths that proport that only irresponsible adventurers know how to live. One should examine all such truths (like B. Shaw did)."

Gilbert, Martin. *In Search of Churchill: A Historian's Journey*. New York: John Wiley & Sons, 1994. Churchill's collection of books included many sent by G.B.S.

Greene, Douglas C. *John Dickson Carr, The Man Who Explained Miracles*. New York: Otto Penzler, 1995. Toward the end of the 1930s Carr listed five types of books he read, including detective stories; ghost stories; the works of Chesterton, Shaw, and J. B. Priestley; books of criminology; and the literature of the late seventeenth century.

Greer, Mary. *Women of the Golden Dawn: Rebels and Priestesses*. Rochester, Vermont: Park Street Press, 1995. Not seen. One of Greer's four featured women is Florence Farr, who was especially significant in the life and work of G.B.S. From a review in *Choice* (June 1995).

Griffiths, Trevor. "Drama," in *The Year's Work in English Studies*. Volume 73 (1992). Oxford: Blackwell Publishers, 1995. Includes remarks on only two Shaw references, with a statement that he has not seen *SHAW* this year.

Hager, Thomas. *Force of Nature: The Life of Linus Pauling*. New York: Simon & Schuster, 1995. Pauling discovered Shaw and read all his plays, including the prefaces and introductions.

Hall, Parnell. *Actor*. New York: Mysterious Press, 1993. The Actor of the title is a private investigator with fond memories of his participation in college theatrical productions who is invited to step into the role of Bluntschli in *Arms and the Man* for a summer stock company. The plot of *Arms and the Man* is well reported, and there is a great deal of the dialogue included as an integral part of the story. One interesting theme is the determination of who should have top billing, the almost-recognizable "name" from a canceled television sit-com who has the role of Sergius or the complete unknown who has the role of Bluntschli. Also amusing are the narrator's speculations regarding G.B.S.'s reactions to modifications to the dialogue and to an unexpected (and unwritten by G.B.S.) final scene. There is, of course, a mystery for the narrator to solve between performances. Annotation supplied by Carol Riddle, Central Michigan University.

Hare, Marion J. See *Six of Calais*, below.

Harrington, John P., ed. *Modern Irish Drama*. New York: Norton, 1991. Includes extracts of reprinted writings on Shaw by M. J. Sidnell, "Hic and Ille: Shaw and Yeats" (1971); Norma Jenckes, "The Rejection of Shaw's Irish Play: *John Bull's Other Island*" (1973); and David Krause, "*John Bull's Other Island*" (1983).

Hayman, Ronald. *Thomas Mann: A Biography*. New York: Scribner's, 1995. In *Felix Krull* Mann may have been thinking of a male equivalent of Eliza Doolittle. In September 1951 Mann writes that he has read Shaw in order to write about Krull.

Heston, Charlton. *In the Arena: An Autobiography*. New York: Simon & Schuster, 1995. Seven references to Shaw. Heston knows and respects Shaw's works. He played the lead in *Cashel Byron* in 1949 in the CBS *Studio One* production. In a predictive mood for the U.S. he quotes Shaw: "A government which robs Peter to pay Paul can always depend on the gratitude [*sic*] of Paul."

Himmelfarb, Gertrude. *The De-Moralization of Society: From Victorian Virtue to Modern Values*. New York: Knopf, 1995. Three references to Shaw include one mildly significant one:

"Late-Victorian England produced not only the writers associated with the *fin de siècle* but a host of others who were not:" James, Meredith, Stevenson, Bridges, Kipling, Conrad, Shaw, Doyle, Housman, Galsworthy, Bennett, Buchan, Belloc, and Chesterton.

Holroyd, Michael. *Lytton Strachey: The New Biography*. New York: Farrar, Straus & Giroux, 1994. At least fourteen references to Shaw, in the context of the G.B.S./Strachey relationship.

Hugo, Leon. "In Search of Shaw: An Interview with Dan Laurence." *SHAW: The Annual of Bernard Shaw Studies*. Volume Fifteen. University Park: Penn State University Press, 1995.

Jenckes, Norma. See Harrington, John P., above.

Johnson, Timothy W. *"Pygmalion, "* in *Magill's Survey of Cinema*. Volume Three. Edited by Frank N. Magill. Englewood Cliffs, N.J.: Salem Press, 1980; pp. 1399–1403. "A masterpiece."

Jones, A. R. "Michael Holroyd (1935–)." *Dictionary of Literary Biography, Volume 155: Twentieth-Century British Literary Biographers*. Edited by Steven Serafin. Detroit: Gale Research, 1995; pp. 167–79. The prefatory bibliography lists eighteen books and articles with "Shaw" in the titles. About three pages describe Holroyd's work on his biography of Shaw and the positive reception of the biography by reviewers, dismissing the controversy about Holroyd's documentation of sources.

Kaplan, Joel H., and Sheila Stowell. *Theatre and Fashion: Oscar Wilde to the Suffragettes*. Cambridge: Cambridge University Press, 1995. Not seen. Reviewed in *TLS* (27 January 1995), p. 19. An analysis of the Shavian milieu.

Kelly, Bill, and Vonnie Kelly, with Ronan Foster. *The Book of Kelly's*. Dublin: Zeus, 1995. In the chapter titled "Famous Names at Kelly's," pride of place is given to G.B.S. with a full-page photo and a facsimile of Shaw's holograph entry in the guest book. A selection of Kelly's notable recipes for vegetarian dishes and desserts suggests why the establishment was attractive to Shaw. See Entry in Kelly's Hotel guest book in "Works by Shaw," above.

Kennedy, Dennis. "The Waste, The Waste," in *Waste: Shaw Festival 1995* (Shaw Festival production program, 1995). Kennedy's essay on Granville Barker's *Waste* is threaded with his knowledge of the Shaw/Barker relationship.

King, James. *Virginia Woolf*. New York & London: W. W. Norton, 1994. A Woolf diary entry of 13 June 1932 is the basis for King's account: "When she [Woolf] dined with Shaw, she was impressed with how vigorous the seventy-four-year-old [*sic*] man of letters was and wanted to be infused with similar creative juices. And at Rodmell that June the air was alive with the buzzing of bees: 'like arrows of desire: fierce, sexual . . . the whole air full of vibration: of beauty, of this burning arrowy desire.' "

Koritz, Amy. *Gendering Bodies/Performing Art: Dance and Literature in Early Twentieth-Century British Culture*. Ann Arbor: University of Michigan Press, 1995. Writers discussed include Wilde, Yeats, and Shaw. Not seen.

Krause, David. See Harrington, John P., above.

Laurence, Dan H. See "Letters to Katie Samuel" in Works by Shaw, above.

Li, Kay. "Hong Kong in *Buoyant Billions*: The Exotic in Bernard Shaw." *SHAW: The Annual of Bernard Shaw Studies*. Volume Fifteen. University Park: Penn State University Press, 1995.

MacCarthy, Fiona. *William Morris: A Life for Our Time*. New York: Knopf, 1995. Displays an impressive knowledge of Shaw's relations with the Morris Family. Mentions also *Heartbreak, Philanderer, Pygmalion, Unsocial Socialist,* and *Widowers' Houses*.

Macrae, Alasdair D. F. *W. B. Yeats: A Literary Life*. New York: St. Martin's Press, 1995. Has more than ten references to Shaw, including the reminder that Yeats had a "grudging respect" for G.B.S.; the "grudge far outweighed the respect." Macrae himself appears to respect, but not to admire, Shaw.

Mencken, H. L. *A Second Mencken Chrestomathy. Selected, Revised, and Annotated by the Author.* Edited by Terry Teachout. New York: Knopf, 1995. Reprints "George Bernard Shaw" from the August 1916 number of *Smart Set.*

Mezon, Jim. See *The Philanderer,* below.

Newton, Christopher. See *You Never Can Tell,* below.

Ochakovskaya, Marina. "Three Dialogues with Russian Culture" (review of *Bernard Shaw and Russian Culture at the Turn of the Century* by Anna Obraztsova). *SHAW: The Annual of Bernard Shaw Studies.* Volume Fifteen. University Park: Penn State University Press, 1995.

Oiye, David. See *The Six of Calais,* below.

Parini, Jay. *John Steinbeck: A Biography.* New York: Henry Holt, 1995. Prints part of an unpublished Steinbeck letter of 14 April 1928 with reference to Shaw. Extracts:

> Shaw occupies a peculiar place in the minds of reading people. I have no doubt that a few generations will show him up as a charlatan. He is an artist but he is never able to be all artist and no charlatan. . . . Rather than the greatest writer of the day, I should say he is the greatest press agent. . . . Please don't think I derogate his work. His work is fine, but it is not as fine as is generally considered. It appeals to the very young mind, such as my own when I was seventeen. His wit is so dazzling that we never stop to consider that he has never said anything very important. And you must admit, often his wit is obvious and vulgar. He and Anatole France will be buried together and will be forgotten together.

Paris, Barry. *Garbo: A Biography.* New York: Knopf, 1995. Irving Thalberg tried unsuccessfully to persuade Shaw to sell the rights to *Saint Joan* for Garbo.

Perry, Anne. *Highgate Rise.* New York: Ballantine, 1991. G.B.S. makes a cameo appearance in this mystery yarn that has a family of Shaws as victims/suspects and a detective with a wife named Charlotte.

Peters, Margot. "Bernard F. Burgunder: Collector of Genius." *SHAW: The Annual of Bernard Shaw Studies.* Volume Fifteen. University Park: Penn State University Press, 1995.

Peters, Sally. *The Ascent of the Superman.* New Haven & London: Yale University Press, 1996. In this critical biography, Peters explores Shaw's background and beliefs, interests and obsessions, relations with men and women, prose writings, and dramatic art. In deciphering Shaw's enigmatic personality, Peters uncovers a convoluted and extravagant inner life as she shows Shaw to be a man who championed will even while believing that his erotic inclinations were the secret mark of the born artist. To be reviewed in *SHAW* 17.

The Philanderer: Shaw Festival 1995 (Shaw Festival production program, 1995). Includes "Director's Notes" by Jim Mezon and "The Dramatist's Dilemma" by Brian Tyson noting that *Philanderer* is a good example of Shaw's occasional difficulty in completing a play. The play satirizes the pseudo-Ibsenites, the medical profession, and the divorce laws, yet it collapses into conformity with a substitute Act III until recent productions in London (1991) and this 1995 Shaw Festival offering appended the original Act III as Act IV.

Pierce, Arthur. See Billips, above.

Plunka, Gene A. *Antonin Artaud and the Modern Theater.* Rutherford, N.J.: Fairleigh Dickinson University Press, 1994. One reference: Artaud played Retiarius in *Androcles.*

Prater, Donald. *Thomas Mann: A Life.* Oxford & New York: Oxford University Press, 1995. At least seven references to Shaw, including a description of Mann's warming to Shaw when Mann accepted the invitation to give the half-hour memorial talk on G.B.S. for the BBC Third Programme in January 1951. He gained respect and interest when he read *Heartbreak, Apple Cart, Saint Joan,* and the Preface to *Androcles.* In the *Listener* publication of Mann's talk, G.B.S. was "Mankind's Friend" and "the laughing prophet of a humanity emancipated from the gloom of tragedy" who had done his best with the gleaming weapons of word and wit to raise humanity to a "new level of social maturity."

Rae, Lisbie. "Making Sense of Shaw: Newton at the Shaw Festival 1980–1993." *SHAW: The Annual of Bernard Shaw Studies.* Volume Fifteen. University Park: Penn State University Press, 1995.

Richardson, Dorothy. *Windows on Modernism: Selected Letters of Dorothy Richardson.* Edited by Gloria G. Fromm. Athens & London: University of Georgia Press, 1995. Richardson knew Shaw and mentions him at least seventeen times in these letters. Included is one to Shaw of 27 August 1950 in which she addresses with her own wit their mutual interest in spelling and levels of language usage. Extract:

> Taking, too, from the labour of learning to spell & to read, the fascination of inconsistencies—the joy, for example, of discovering that Chol-mon-de-ley is pronounced Marchbanks (as Twain discovered first).
>
> Grammar, agreed, don't truly matter. Yet rivalries are there. A Cornish Council school teacher asked to judge, by two disputant evacuees, between " 'Didn't ought to 'ave" and " 'Adn't ought to 'ave" was assisted by a local lad, who declared that the Londoners mean "shouldn't of."

Sauer, David K. " 'Only a Woman' in *Arms and the Man.*" *SHAW: The Annual of Bernard Shaw Studies.* Volume Fifteen. University Park: Penn State University Press, 1995.

Savage, Roger. "The Staging of Opera," in *The Oxford Illustrated History of Opera.* Edited by Roger Parker. Oxford & New York: Oxford University Press, 1994; pp. 350–420. Several references to Shaw, including the notation that Shaw was recognized as a perceptive turn-of-the-century critic of music and drama.

Scarim, Nicholas. See Garlan, Patsy, above.

Sidnell, M. J. See Harrington, John P., above.

The Six of Calais: Shaw Festival 1995 (Shaw Festival production program, 1995). Includes "Director's Notes" by David Oiye and "Rodin, Shaw and the Six of Calais" by Marion J. Hare, which explains the source of Shaw's inspiration for the play as a combination of Rodin's earlier making of a bust of Shaw, eventuating in a life friendship, and Shaw's knowledge of Rodin's plaster and bronze of *The Burghers of Calais.*

Stevenson, Robert Louis. *The Letters of Robert Louis Stevenson, July 1884–August 1887.* Volume Five. *The Letters of Robert Louis Stevenson, August 1887–September 1890.* Volume Six. Edited by Bradford A. Booth and Ernest Mehew. New Haven & London: Yale University Press, 1995. Stevenson was one of the earliest famous admirers of Shaw. The several references to Shaw in these volumes reflect Stevenson's approval of Shaw's novels *Cashel Byron's Profession* and *The Irrational Knot,* to which Stevenson had been introduced by his friend William Archer. Stevenson's letter to Archer of 9 March 1886 is devoted entirely to his appreciation of Shaw the novelist: "A talent that few will have the wit to understand, a talent of strength, spirit, capacity, sufficient vision, and a sufficient self-sacrifice, which last is the chief point in a narrator."

Stowell, Sheila. See Kaplan, Joel H., above.

Taylor, A. J. P. *From the Boer War to the Cold War: Essays on Twentieth-Century Europe.* Edited by Chris Wrigley. London: Allen Lane, 1995. Not seen. According to the advertisement, the collection includes "A blunt reappraisal of George Bernard Shaw as writer, sage and philosopher."

Tyson, Brian. See *The Philanderer,* above.

Tytell, John. *The Living Theatre: Art, Exile and Outrage.* New York: Grove Press, 1995. The Living Theatre, led by Julian Beck, Judith Malina, and Hanon Reznikov, challenged the moral complacencies of a conservative world from the 1950s to the 1970s. Shaw is referenced in the account of the creation of *The Yellow Methuselah,* a spectacle fusing elements of Shaw's *Back to Methuselah* and the cosmically surreal *The Yellow Sound* by painter Wassily Kandinsky. The play was written and directed by Reznikov. The set was designed by Beck, featuring a 150-foot painting that scrolled by means of cranking.

Beck also designed 140 costumes. Rehearsing in Rome, Beck played Shaw, interviewed members of the audience, and used their taped responses. Malina played the serpent in Eden and, later, Lilith.

van den Doel, Rias. See Barfoot, above.

Vidal, Gore. *Palimpsest*. New York: Random House, 1995. In one interesting Shaw reference, Vidal describes Nancy Astor's account of G.B.S., with Shaw listening: "Marshall [*sic*] Stalin and me! But there we were together in his office. Bernard Shaw and I had made the trip to the Soviet, and there was Shaw on the train, busy reading a book, never once looking out the window because he knew, of course, everything in the world and so never looked at anything. Anyway, Marshall Stalin, after listening to Shaw for awhile, gets up and goes to a map and points to England and then to all of that pink which was one empire back then and says, 'How did this little island manage to take over so much of the world?' Shaw answered because we gave them the King James translation of the Bible." Later Astor asked, "Marshall Stalin, when are you going to stop killing people?" Answer by Stalin: "Lady Astor, the undesirable classes do not liquidate themselves."

Walker, Alexander. *Audrey: Her Real Story*. New York: St. Martin's Press, 1994. A single remark: Otto Preminger wanted Audrey Hepburn to play Shaw's Saint Joan, calculating that her flat-chested, androgynous figure would be perfect for the Maid in man's armor. Jean Seberg was cast instead.

Washington, Peter. *Madame Blavatsky's Baboon: A History of Mystics, Mediums, and Misfits who Brought Spiritualism to America*. New York: Schocken, 1995 (c. 1993). A number of references to Shaw, most substantively in connection with evolution as represented in *Methuselah*, and Shaw's connection with theosophy and Blavatsky through his friendship with Annie Besant, for whom Blavatsky, among others, was a mentor.

Weintraub, Rodelle. See Barfoot, above.

Weintraub, Stanley. "Shaw's Diary Fragments: Some Additions." *SHAW: The Annual of Bernard Shaw Studies*. Volume Fifteen. University Park: Penn State University Press, 1995.

————. *Shaw's People: Victoria to Churchill*. University Park & London: Penn State University Press, 1996. This collection of biographical essays explores a variety of relationships important to Shaw's life and work from his early days in London to the end of his life. Separate chapters focus on Shaw's associations with Victoria, Oscar Wilde, "General" William Booth of the Salvation Army, H. L. Mencken, Edith Adams, W. B. Yeats, James Joyce, Frank Harris, T. E. Lawrence, Sean O'Casey, Siegfried Trebitsch, and Winston Churchill. To be reviewed in *SHAW* 17.

————. See Barfoot, above.

Whitmore, Jon. *William Saroyan: A Research and Production Sourcebook*. Westport, Conn.: Greenwood, 1994. Saroyan once stated that Shaw had the greatest influence on him. Two references to Shaw appear in the annotations of primary works by Saroyan, a third in a secondary work. Additional references are indicated in the index.

Wilson, Marilynn. "*Major Barbara*," in *Magill's Survey of Cinema*. Volume Four. Second Series. Edited by Frank N. Magill. Englewood Cliffs, N.J.: Salem Press, 1981; pp. 1495–97. The overall reception from both critics and audiences was only moderately enthusiastic.

You Never Can Tell: Shaw Festival 1995 (Shaw Festival production program, 1995). Includes "Director's Notes" by Christopher Newton and "Shaw's Heavenly Twins" by Ronald Bryden, which describes the complicated negotiations by Shaw with the several popular actors who might have filled the role of Valentine but did not and the inspiration for the play in Sarah Grand's novel *The Heavenly Twins*.

Young, Louisa. *A Great Task of Happiness: The Life of Kathleen Scott*. London: Macmillan, 1995. Not seen. A review in *TLS* (11 August 1995, p. 24) suggests that Shaw is mentioned in this biography of Shaw's sculptress friend, widow of the Antarctic explorer Captain Robert Falcon Scott.

III. PERIODICALS

Adams, Elsie B. "Shaw & the Socialist Theatre" [review of *George Bernard Shaw and the Socialist Theatre* by Tracy C. Davis]. *ELT* 38, no. 4 (1995): 539–42.

Aschiem, Skip. "*Profession* No Longer Scandalous" (review of the 1995 Lyric Stage production of *Mrs Warren*). *Boston Globe* (29 September 1995), p. 46.

Begley, Marita. "The Shavian Sell." *Condé Nast Traveler* (June 1995), p. 86. A chatty two-hundred-word puff of the Shaw Festival in Niagara-on-the-Lake. It "lures hundreds of thousands of visitors every year."

Bemrose, John. "Bring on the *Cavalcade:* The Shaw Festival Revives a Pageant" (review of the production of Noël Coward's *Cavalcade*, much of which relates to G.B.S.). *Maclean's* (10 July 1995), p. 49.

————. "Romance and Ruin: The Shaw Opens with Sweetness—and Murder" (review that discusses the Shaw Festival production of *You Never Can Tell*). *Maclean's* (12 June 1995), p. 57.

Brozan, Nadine. "Chronicle: In England, No Raves for Raquel Welch. . . ." *New York Times* (14 April 1995, Metro), p. B7. Touring regional theaters in England, *The Millionairess* starring Welch did so poorly that its opening in the Albery Theater in mid-May was put on hold.

"Christopher Newton." *Current Biography* (February 1995), pp. 26–31. A useful summary of Newton's achievements, especially as Shaw Festival artistic director.

Einsohn, H. I. Review of *Bernard Shaw and H. G. Wells*, edited by J. Percy Smith. *Choice* (November 1995), p. 467.

Hampton, Wilborn. "Shaw's Mrs. Warren Again, Now Shorn of Wickedness" (review of the Pearl Theater production of *Mrs Warren's Profession*). *New York Times* (10 April 1995), p. C12.

Hendrickson, Ken. Review of *Henry Irving's Waterloo: Theatrical Engagements with Arthur Conan Doyle, George Bernard Shaw, . . . Assorted Ghosts . . . War, and History* by W. D. King. *Journal of Military History* 59, no. 1 (January 1995): 160.

Jackson, Russell. "Shaw's Reviews of Daly's Shakespeare: The Wooing of Ada Rehan." *Theatre Research International* 19, no. 3 (1994): 203–13. "Daly's productions do indeed seem—in the light of the collateral evidence of scripts, photographs and other reviews—to have had many of the faults Shaw derided. It is important, however, to remember that the notices which have represented them most vividly for posterity happen to have been motivated by Shaw's habitual combination of artistic and sexual desire, his longing to have Rehan's art at the service of his own."

Kemp, Peter. "Wells Without Wildness," (review half-devoted to *Bernard Shaw and H. G. Wells*, edited by J. Percy Smith). *TLS* (23 October 1995), pp. 4–5.

Leithauser, Brad. "On With the Shaw" (review of several of the 1995 season's Shaw Festival productions, including *You Never Can Tell* and *The Philanderer*). *Time* (24 July 1995). p. 66.

Londraville, Janis. "*Lady Griselda's Dream:* May Morris's *Man and Superman*." *Independent Shavian* 33, no. 1 (1995): 6–14. In *Lady Griselda's Dream* May Morris found a way to comment upon her relationship with Shaw by portraying the artist as a kind of bloodsucker. Griselda Fairweather, the play's tragic heroine, has some understanding that loving the artist is a trap. He is interested in her only in terms of how she will further his art. He will use her energy, he will drain her, and then he will leave her. Shaw explored this same idea five years later in *Man and Superman:* "the artist will vitiate the female power, or 'Life Force.' " However, in *Lady Griselda's Dream*, Griselda decides to be true to her artist, even if it means denying herself marriage and family.

Maurer, A.E. Wallace. Review of *SHAW* 12. *Modern Drama* 37, no. 4 (Winter 1994): 683–85.

McDowell, Frederick P. W. "Heartbreak House Critique" [review of *Heartbreak House: Preludes of Apocalypse* by A. M. Gibbs]. *ELT* 38, no. 4 (1995): 536–39.

Moseley, Phil. "Portland Stages Shine With Shaw: What *Mrs. Warren's Profession* Loses in Time is Gained in Performance" (review of the Portland Stage Company production). *Portsmouth (N.H.) Herald* (7 May 1995), p. E2.

Nightingale, Benedict. "Shakespeare and Shaw Center Stage in London." *New York Times* (12 March 1995), pp. 12, 32. A notice anticipating the London production of *The Millionairess* starring Raquel Welch.

O., J. "Editor's Choice: He's No Gump." *American Theatre* (October 1995), pp. 50, 56. No fewer than nineteen major productions of Shaw's plays are slated in the 1995–96 season in the U.S. Eight of these will be of *Arms and the Man*, fourth to *All in the Timing* by David Ives (first), *Three Tall Women* by Edward Albee (second), and *The Sisters Rosensweig* by Wendy Wasserstein (third).

Peters, Catherine. "I Wrote the Play to Have My Liza" (review of Birmingham Repertory Theatre production of *Pygmalion*). *TLS* (12 May 1995), p. 18.

Rae, Lisbie. "Christopher Newton: Unsure but Incredibly True." *Canadian Theatre Review* 79/80 (Summer/Fall 1994): 116–19.

> The rebel of thirty years ago who skipped across the Niagara River to escape the dullness of Shaw and Canada has mellowed in Newton into a sense of amazement: "I'm amazed at the richness of the repertoire available. . . . I want people to see why I am excited by these plays." . . . With a stable ensemble of experienced Shavian actors, with a playbill that stretches their skills in an adventurous range of Shaw's contemporaries, with an approach to Shaw unequalled in the world for exploring the passions beneath the surface, Christopher Newton has made surprising sense of the Shaw Festival in Niagara-on-the-Lake. While he has not yet closed the book on Shaw, he certainly knows the subject from "A" to "Z."

"Sci-Fi for Your D: Drive: Bradbury Commits a Classic to CD-ROM." *Newsweek* 126 (13 November 1995): 89. Includes Bradbury on the writers he likes: "I [read] all the great poets. Emily Dickinson, Yeats, Frost. I go back to Shaw most often. He's a superb, gigantic pomegranate that explodes all over the place; I love him so much I put him into a science-fiction story called 'GBS Mark V.' I learn from all of these people and bring it over into science fiction."

"Shaw," in "Victorian Bibliography for 1993." *Victorian Studies* 37, no. 4 (Summer 1994): 759–60. Lists twenty-five items, retrospective to 1990, a few of which have not appeared in this Checklist.

"Shaw, Bernard." *ACAD*. (1992–August 1995). Lists fifteen entries, a few of which have not appeared in this Checklist.

"Shaw, Bernard." *FirstSearch* (January 1981–September 1995). Lists about 250 items from fifty-three databases, a number of which have not appeared in this Checklist.

"Shaw, George Bernard," in "IASAIL Bibliographic Bulletin for 1993." *Irish University Review* 24, no. 2 (Autumn/Winter 1994): 315–16. Forty-one items, a few of which have not appeared in this Checklist.

"Shaw, George Bernard," in "Modern Drama Studies: An Annual Bibliography," compiled by Irene M. Dutton and Nancy Crozier. *Modern Drama* 38, no. 2 (Summer 1995): 196–98. Lists thirty-eight items, a few of which have not appeared in this Checklist.

Stowell, Sheila. " 'Dame Joan, Saint Christabel'." *Modern Drama* 37, no. 3 (Fall 1994): 421–36. In *Joan* Shaw refused to allow "the pastness of the past"; he wanted his audiences to feel more than that they too as members of the court that tried her might have burned Joan; he wanted them to realize they are probably burning her still. . . . It is, as I have tried to show, a point that Edwardian suffragettes had been at pains to argue, both on stage and off. Yet if Shaw's initial thoughts of a militant Joan were first stirred by such examples, his introduction of a tragicomic epilogue, in which his heroine is rehabilitated by the orthodoxy that had tried and condemned her, argues a peculiar prescience. In an instance of life imitating art (imitating life), suffrage champion Christabel Pankhurst—criminal and stained-glass Saint of the *Bystander*'s 1912 cartoon—was in 1936 made Dame of the British Empire.

Wellens, Oskar. "*Candida* in French (1907)." *Shavian* 7, no. 7 (Spring 1995): 6–11. Provides a description of the reception of the play in its first French performances, including an account of Shaw's French translator, Augustin Hamon, whose role in the mounting of *Candida* included providing introductory comments on Shaw's life, on his works, and on *Candida*. The critics were divided, and so was the audience.

———. "Early Hitherto Unnoticed Flemish Performances of *Mrs. Warren's Profession* (1894)." *Notes and Queries* 42, no. 2 (June 1995): 205–6. Reports the dates of five performances in October and November 1909, with reviews indicating that the play was an immediate success. These performances deserve to figure prominently in the stage history of the play.

Wiley, Catherine. Review of *Shaw's Daughters* by J. Ellen Gainor. *Modern Drams* 37, no. 4 (Winter 1994): 683–83.

Wisenthal, J. L. Review of *Bernard Shaw, The Drama Observed*, edited by Bernard F. Dukore. *Nineteenth Century Prose* 22, no. 1 (Spring 1995): 80–83.

———. Review of *The Playwrighting Self of Bernard Shaw* by John A. Bertolini. *Modern Drama* 37, no. 4 (Winter 1994): 685–86.

Independent Shavian 33, no. 1 (1995). Journal of the Bernard Shaw Society. An Index to Volume 32 (1994) is supplied as an insert. Includes "G.B.S. Confesses" by Shaw, "Lady Griselda's Dream: May Morris's *Man and Superman*" by Janis Londraville, "Holroyd Lecture Highlights the Shaw Collection Formed by Sidney P. Albert, " "Corrigenda," "Letter from England" by T. F. Evans, "A Shavian Pen Pal" by Mansfield Frazier, "Is Gingrich a Shavian?", "The Black Girl in Search of God: In East Oakland," "Society Activities," "News About Our Members," "A Texan Bashville," "Obituaries," "The Young Stephen Spender Reads Shaw," "Joseph Conrad: Shocked by Shaw," "A Chesterton-Shaw Debate Enacted," "Ayot Productions," and "Our Cover." See also Londraville, Janis, above.

Shavian 7, no. 7 (Spring 1995). The Journal of the Shaw Society. Includes "Editorial, " "Obituary," "How to Become a Critic" by Shaw, "*Candida* in French" by Oskar Wellens, "Bernard Shaw—The Patient" by John Cole, "Our Theatres in the Nineteen Nineties" by Adolphus Bastable, "Scoring a Century" (review of *SHAW* 14) by Leon Hugo, "A Valuable Study" (review of *Heartbreak House: Preludes of Apocalypse* by A. M. Gibbs) by T. F. Evans, "Shorter Notices," "Literary Survey," "Scraps and Shavings," and "Notes of Meetings." See also Wellens, Oskar, above.

IV. DISSERTATIONS

Hay, Jeffrey T. "The Colloquial Musical Metaphysics of Francis Hueffer and George Bernard Shaw." University of California, San Diego, 1994. *DAI* 55 (February 1995), 3532–A. It "places the musical thinking of these two critics within its historical and intellectual context . . . working in Great Britain . . . from 1870 to 1900." They derived their musical ideas from Schopenhauer. "Shaw was familiar with the thinking of Wagner and Hueffer and by 1891 had grown familiar with the bases of Schopenhauer's thought." Shaw "argued the works of great composers indicated that such a force as the world will was active." Also, social and cultural progress were encouraged by dissemination of works of great composers. The last chapter examines Hueffer's and Shaw's rethinking of the classical music canon.

V. RECORDINGS

Androclyes [sic] *and the Lion*. See *My Fair Lady* (Critic's Choice Video), below.

Caesar and Cleopatra (1945 color film starring Vivien Leigh, Claude Rains, and Stewart Granger, 123 minutes), #43421. $39.95. Filmic Archives, The Cinema Center, Botsford, CT 06404. Phone: 1–800–366–1920. 1995 catalogue. Lists also *Major Barbara* (1941 film starring Wendy Hiller and Rex Harrison, 131 minutes), #64361, $39.95; and *My Fair Lady* (1964 film starring Rex Harrison and Audrey Hepburn, fully restored), #50091, $29.95.

Major Barbara. See *Caesar and Cleopatra*, above.

My Fair Lady (1964 film starring Rex Harrison and Audrey Hepburn, "fully restored version," 170 minutes [sic]), #56358, $19.95. Time Warner Viewer's Edge, P. O. Box 85098, Richmond, VA 23285–5098. Phone: 1–800–262-6868. 1995 catalogue. Lists also *Pygmalion* (1938 film starring Leslie Howard and Wendy Hiller, 95 minutes), #30064, $6.95. This is not the Janus Films British release but a public domain print in the U.S. of MGM's 1938 release, issued in the slower LP mode to save tape. MGM replaced Arthur Honegger's soundtrack score, for economic reasons, with one by its own employee, Dr. William Axt, who is credited for "additional composition" with Honegger. Besides major changes in the score, the MGM 1938 release has revised credits and several re-edited scenes, notably the "at home" sequence at Mrs. Higgins's.

My Fair Lady Gift Set (includes a letterbox format of the enhanced 1964 film, starring Rex Harrison and Audrey Hepburn, and the 60–minute documentary "My Fair Lady: More Lovelier [sic] Than Ever," six 70 mm. frames struck from the original negative, a portfolio of costume drawings by Cecil Beaton, "and more"), #38804, $24.95. The Video Catalog, P.O. Box 64267, St. Paul, MN 55164–0267. Phone: 1–800–733–2232. 1995 catalogue.

My Fair Lady: Gift Set (includes restored, letterbox format 1964 film starring Rex Harrison and Audrey Hepburn, outtakes from the original film, a 60–minute documentary (1994), a portfolio of costume designs by Cecil Beaton; 190 minutes), #HYFOX008167, $79.98. Critic's Choice Video, P.O. Box 749, Itasca, IL 60143–0749. Phone: 1–800–367–7765. 1995 catalogue. Lists also *My Fair Lady: 30th Anniversary Edition* (1964 film starring Harrison and Hepburn, 190 minutes), #HYFOX008166, $18.77; and *Androclyes* [sic] *and the Lion* (1952 film starring Victor Mature; 100 minutes), #HYHVC80422, $29.95.

My Fair Lady. See *Caesar and Cleopatra*, above.

Pygmalion. See *My Fair Lady*, above.

Writers and Poets (a three-CD set of "Historic Recordings" by Shaw, Joyce, Eliot, Doyle, Priestley, Tolstoy, Yeats, C. Day Lewis, Milne, Sackville-West, Spender, and Woolf. Issued by EMI (1994), in England. Contains Shaw's "Spoken English and Broken English" originally issued by Linguaphone Institute in 1927 (item G3 in Shaw Bibliography). CD 1 (8) "Now is the winter of our Discontent" (Shaw's reading of the Shakespeare soliloquy from *Richard III*, recorded on 19 and 27 October 1926 "for posterity" but not issued [G2 in Shaw Bibliography, misdated as recorded on 3 November 1926]).

CONTRIBUTORS

Stuart E. Baker, Professor of Theatre at Florida State University, Tallahassee, has just completed a book on Shaw's philosophical convictions entitled *On Becoming God: Bernard Shaw's Terrible Religion of Realism and Responsibility.*

Jacques Barzun, critic and cultural historian, is University Professor Emeritus of Columbia University and member of the American Academy of Arts and Letters and of the American Philosophical Society. His many publications include *Berlioz and the Romantic Century* (1950; 3rd edition, 1965).

Charles A. Berst, Professor of English at UCLA and member of the *SHAW* editorial board, is author of *Bernard Shaw and the Art of Drama* and editor of *SHAW 1: Shaw and Religion.* His newest book is *Pygmalion: Shaw's Spin on Myth and Cinderella.*

John A. Bertolini, Professor of English and Film at Middlebury College, Vermont, and member of the *SHAW* editorial board, is author of *The Playwrighting Self of Bernard Shaw* and editor of *SHAW 13: Shaw and Other Playwrights.*

Fred D. Crawford, general editor of *SHAW*, has written several books and articles on modern British literature. He has completed a study of the Richard Aldington-Lawrence of Arabia controversy and is researching a biography tentatively entitled *Lowell Thomas: His Own Man.*

Norma Jenckes, editor of the scholarly journal *American Drama*, teaches playwriting and dramatic literature at the University of Cincinnati. She edited the Garland facsimile edition of *Arms and the Man.*

Dan H. Laurence, author of *Bernard Shaw: A Bibliography* and editor of Shaw's *Collected Letters* and *Shaw's Music*, was Literary and Dramatic Advisor to the Shaw Estate from 1973 to 1990 and is an Associate Director of the Shaw Festival, Ontario. His latest publications are *Theatrics* and, with Daniel J. Leary, the second volume of Shaw's *Complete Prefaces.*

Frederick P. W. McDowell is Professor Emeritus of English at the University of Iowa and member of the *SHAW* editorial board. He has written many articles, essay-reviews, and reviews on Shaw and his works. He has also written two books on E. M. Forster.

Richard Nickson is President of the Bernard Shaw Society and editor of its journal *The Independent Shavian.* Of the seventy poems in his *Staves: A Book of Songs*, more than half have been set to music by a variety of composers.

Margot Peters, member of the *SHAW* editorial board, is author of *Bernard Shaw and the Actresses* and *Mrs. Pat: The Life of Mrs. Patrick Campbell.* She edited the facsimile edition of *Mrs Warren's Profession* and has written numerous articles on Shaw and Shavian theater.

Sally Peters, a member of the *SHAW* editorial board, teaches literature at Wesleyan University. She has published widely on Shaw, modern drama, and dance and is author of *Bernard Shaw: The Ascent of the Superman.*

John R. Pfeiffer, Professor of English at Central Michigan University, is bibliographer of *SHAW*. His recent articles are on Günter Grass, John Stuart Mill, Richard Francis Burton, and nineteenth-century science fiction.

Alfred Turco, Jr., Professor of English at Wesleyan University and member of the *SHAW* editorial board, is author of *Shaw's Moral Vision* and editor of *SHAW 7: Shaw: The Neglected Plays*.

Brian Tyson, English Professor Emeritus at the University of Lethbridge, Alberta, is author of *The Story of Shaw's "Saint Joan"* and editor of *Bernard Shaw's Book Reviews in the "Pall Mall Gazette"* and of a forthcoming second volume of book reviews.

Stanley Weintraub, Evan Pugh Professor of Arts and Humanities at Penn State, edited the *Shaw Review* and *SHAW* from 1956 through 1990. He has written or edited more than forty books on Shaw and his times, the most recent of which is *Shaw's People: Victoria to Churchill*.

J. L. Wisenthal, member of the *SHAW* editorial board, teaches English literature at the University of British Columbia. His work on Shaw includes *The Marriage of Contraries: Bernard Shaw's Middle Plays; Shaw and Ibsen;* and *Shaw's Sense of History*.